Praise
Six Weeks for Boat Mail

Listen to a Benny Goodman soundtrack while reading *Six Weeks for Boat Mail*, and fully immerse yourself into a personal history of 1940s family life in WWII America. Bonnie Park's second book is an entertaining, wartime adventure across disparate continents. The intimate peek into her family's relationships reveal the War's societal limitations and beliefs that shape their lives. Inspired by the discovery of her mother's handwritten letters, the author's untold narrative expertly melds history in tandem with the fates and fortunes of her patriotic family. Women readers today will be gently reminded how some things change yet stubbornly remain the same.
    - Leslie Miller, Editor, *Reimagining A Place for the Wild*

This well-researched and insightful history digs deep into the personal lives of the Bedford family during World War II. The use of primary source letters and the author's anecdotal comments puts wind in the sails of this delightful narrative!
    - Shawna Anderson, Family Historian, and retired educator

The author's use of letters mailed between continents authenticates the unique personal sacrifices of WWII. As one who is set up to use my sewing machine every day, a several month hunt for a sewing machine "shuttle," and the notion of having that essential part re-cast is unimaginable. Historic evidence takes this entertaining and intimate narrative down to the detailed level of a tiny sewing machine needle!
    - Cindy Knowles, Cindy SewSew

I'm in awe! It takes great skill for an author to combine a lifetime of family letters and personal information into an engrossing story. This historic, family-focused novel explores the period shortly before the U.S. entry into WW2 and into the war years through letters between her newly-married parents, other family members and a huge amount of other research relating to that period in our history. Having read many tales focusing on the United States or the Pacific and European theaters during the War, I also found it refreshing that this book goes beyond to explore Central and South America at the time, including travel and dangers. Highly recommended!

- Nancy Porter, author of *Skeletons in the Closet: Adventures of a Gold Rush Family* and Owner/Travel Specialist, gts2go.com

Love was in the air, but war loomed on the horizon. Robin Skinner and Buster Bedford threw caution to the wind and married in June 1941, preceding the December 7 Japanese attack on Pearl Harbor. While Buster fights in the historically significant New England and Carolina field maneuvers, Robin sails to her childhood home, which happened to be a copper mining camp in the Chilean Andes. Without the immediacy of phone calls or emails, their only means of communication were letters, often lost or delayed. *Six Weeks for Boat Mail* tells the story of trains, planes, automobiles and waiting for censored mail. Author Bonnie Park weaves a tale of mystery and romance from the letters her parents left behind.

- Michele Morris, author of The Cowboy Life

Six Weeks for Boat Mail

*George!
The sequel to Brides of 1941!
Enjoy*

Bruce B. Dale

Six Weeks for Boat Mail

Bonnie Bedford Park

Copyright ©2022 Bonnie Bedford Park
All rights reserved.
No part of this publication may be reproduced, stored in a retrieval system, or transmitted in any form or by any means, electronic, mechanical, photocopying, recording, or otherwise, without written permission of the publisher: bonnie@spikypigpress.com

Published in the United States by
Spiky Pig Press
Park City, Utah
spikypigpress.com

ISBN: 978-1-7326140-2-4
Library of Congress Control Number: 2022919119

Book cover art by: Michelle Rayner, Cosmic Design
Interior design by: Katie Mullaly, Surrogate Press®

All spelling, capitalization and punctuation in the original letters have been preserved to honor the authenticity of the written correspondence.

It is my great honor to dedicate this book to my late brother,
Dr. Robert F. "Bob" Bedford
October 6, 1942 – September 2, 2022

His kindness and commitment to service,
like our parents, had no bounds.
A family historian in his own right, mother insisted,
"My side of the family is much more interesting."
Somewhere in the afterlife, you can admit to her she was right.

"Bobby" with Robin Bedford, waiting for
Buster's return from the Pacific Theater.

*"One of my great regrets
is that I have missed so many of his growing moments…"*
Buster Bedford, letter from the Philippines - May 15, 1945

With gratitude to Robin and Buster, for their playful and loving presence
in our lives, who taught us resilience and to "think for ourselves."

Table of Contents

Prologue 1
Chapter 1: Aims in Life 4
Chapter 2: Traveling Rhythms 15
Chapter 3: The Grasshopper and Other Bugs 36
Chapter 4: Settled and Happy 47
Chapter 5: Surprise Correspondent 63
Chapter 6: Desperado 73
Chapter 7: Christ the Redeemer 81
Chapter 8: In the Nude 94
Chapter 9: Double Ocean Trouble 108
Chapter 10: KGEI Radio 125
Chapter 11: Hornet's Nest 134
Chapter 12: One to Grow On 143
Chapter 13: Paper Anniversary 153
Chapter 14: Othello 166
Chapter 15: Accelerated Training 177
Chapter 16: Flip the Calendar 190
Chapter 17: Circuits of Victory 199
Chapter 18: Tally-Ho 216
Chapter 19: Blue Notes 229
Chapter 20: Light My Fire 241
Acknowledgements 247
About the Author 249

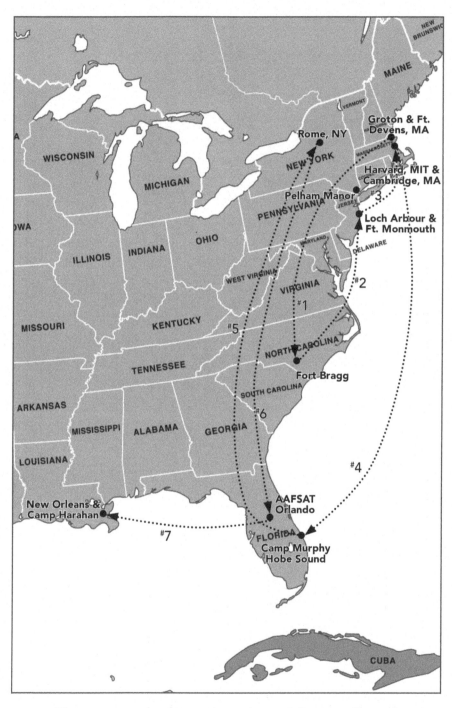

"You move around so frequently - we just can't keep up with you."
Dorothy Skinner McLeod in a letter to her sister, Robin, June 1942

Prologue

In January 1941, Buster Bedford made a weighty decision to postpone his post-graduate education. Distracted by a sense of duty, social responsibility, and patriotism in anticipation of imminent U.S. military involvement in Europe, he left Columbia Law midway through his second year.

His trajectory into the nation's service began six months prior when, on July 30, he enlisted in the National Guard of the State of New York and was assigned to the Cavalry Division of the 21st Reconnaissance Squadron. From the Columbia campus it was a flat, two-mile walk through Central Park to the Squadron A Armory where, one night a week, he drilled for four hours. The Armory, born of a group of gentlemen horseback riders in the 1880s, still sniffed of good breeding. The magnificent brick fortress occupied an entire city block at a fashionable address: Madison Avenue and 94th Street. Nancy Randolph, a light-hearted society columnist at the *Daily News*, referred to this bunch as "the fashionable Squadron A."

Then came a turning point. With increasing seriousness of the international situation, military leaders recognized the time had come to put the Guard on active service footing. They needed to up the training game and turn out soldiers capable of winning a war. A headline in the society column of January 17, 1941, read: "Squadron A Laddies are Bound for Army."

Troop A, 21st Reconnaissance Squadron was "federalized" ten days later on January 27. Squadron A moved immediately to Fort Devens, Ayer,

Massachusetts, where Colonel Gilbert Ackerman led the VI Corps, U.S. First Army. Buster fell in as a U.S. Army Private under Major Walter Lee, commander of the 2nd Squadron of the 101st Cavalry Regiment. Day in and day out, sandwiched between reveille and taps, military training and physical conditioning ran the laddies ragged. Rigorous calisthenics, straight-ahead marching, double-quick drills, obstacle courses, bayonet fixing, grenade throwing, and more were packaged with one end goal: Stronger bodies built stronger confidence and stronger morale.

Off the bat, Buster qualified to drive an Army scout car in the mechanized unit. Then as a "motorcyclist" he trained to read terrain, speedily hand off messages to scout cars on the move, "flop" his cycle, take cover, and fire. The marksmanship badge pinned to the flap of his left breast pocket announced his sharpshooter status. As a free-range Florida kid, he learned early on about guns and ammunition hunting in the Everglades. At age thirteen Buster claimed bragging rights as a certified NRA Junior Rifle Corps "Marksman—First Class." Later, on the Princeton University skeet team, muscle memory served. He winged little clay pigeons out of the sky with speed and accuracy. But Buster's bailiwick of interests went beyond guns. He pointed his compass with intention toward tactics and techniques of radio communications in the Signal Corps.

Robin, his bride of ten weeks, departed New York Harbor's Pier 57 on Friday, August 29, bound for the port of Valparaiso, Chile. She'd eagerly anticipated the post-college graduation promise kept by her parents, Lelia and T. Wayne Skinner, to visit the El Teniente mining camp near Rancagua, Chile. They resided in Sewell, at 7,000 feet above sea level, where Kennecott Copper's Chilean subsidiary, Braden Copper, operated the mine.

T. Wayne accepted a job with Braden as a mining engineer in 1911. Lelia joined him as a new bride in 1916. There they put down roots in "Campamento Americano," the residential section of the Chilean mining camp reserved for foreign personnel.

Until age five, Robin lived pitched on a hillside in the "Ciudad de Escaleras" (city of stairs). It's where her younger siblings, Dorothy and Russell, were born and her earliest childhood memories were cemented.

Prologue

The distinct personalities of the Skinner children were uniquely shaped by the circumstances of their parent's employment. Hand-written letters filled chasms of time and place between them.

When the ear-deafening steam whistle blast of the S.S. *Santa Elena* signaled departure, Robin stood on deck, a lump in her throat. Two-hundred miles north near the crisp Massachusetts/New Hampshire border, Buster hunkered with the 101st Cavalry on a one-week maneuver. Tobacco smoke, gun powder, and pheromones of young men in combat displaced the otherwise pastoral fragrances of piney forest. Recall the words of John Muir: "Between every two pines is a doorway to a new world." This situation was something like that, but far from the tranquil way Muir intended.

Buster's regiment operated as a force among the 15,000 men of the Blue Army in the New England Maneuvers. Thousands of rounds of ammunition and a wide spectrum of weaponry found their way into action: .30-caliber machine guns, 37-mm anti-tank cannons, grenades, land mines. Men in the trenches white knuckled 10-gauge shotguns.

Army officers took measures to ensure live ammunition did not reach the maneuver area. It wasn't a sure thing. Some commanders bent the rules.

The "Blues" cautiously screened movements from reconnaissance of the hostile Red Army. The "Reds" possessed numerical superiority of 25,000 troops. Through realistic sham wars like this, the military posture of the *new* U.S. Army improved. Strategically they grew bigger and stronger. It wasn't Buster's first rodeo. He'd launched into a phony conflict days after he'd enlisted as a member of the National Guard the previous year. In August 1940, he put it like this in a note to his parents, Nat and Ethel Bedford: "We arrived here (God and the Major only know where it is) after driving all Sunday and Monday. Somewhere in the Adirondack foothills near Canton, this is about the most God-forsaken town I have ever seen."

Aims in Life
Chapter One

As the *Santa Elena* made wake out of New York Harbor and churned past Ellis Island and the Statue of Liberty, the toing and froing over Robin's decision to sail was put to rest. She gazed at the horizon and bid the city goodbye. Buster had taught her to recognize the icons of Manhattan's "race for the sky." The Chrysler Building, identified by its famous steel spire; the Empire State Building, tallest in the world; the RCA building and all of Rockefeller Center, hub of art, style, and entertainment.

For now, Robin had only the ship's rail to lean on. For fifteen cents, Buster posted an airmail letter that flew from Winchester, Massachusetts, to the port of Cristobal, Panama, on the Atlantic side of the Canal Zone. Postmark stamps reveal a swift, thirty-four-hour delivery. It arrived two days before the S.S. *Elena* docked on September 4 amidst a bustling waterfront.

Here, the U.S. Government managed fortifications in the area five miles on either side of the canal. An Associated Press article, written under a Panama dateline the previous year, reported on a U.S. War Department plan shaped by the Army and Navy. Live mines, sown by a U.S. mine-laying fleet, were laid at both ends of the Panama Canal. It explains why, when the Grace liner approached Cristobal, an experienced harbor pilot boarded the *Elena* and guided her safely to port. In fact, special contingents of pilots were assigned to meet every incoming ship at a considerable distance.

Aims in Life

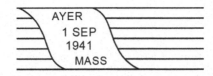

PVT N.F. Bedford, 2nd SQ. HQ. 101 Cav., Fort Devens, Ayer, Mass. – Monday, September 1, 1941 (airmail)

Mrs. N. Forrest Bedford Aboard S.S. Santa Elena
c/o Grace Lines
Panama, Canal Zone
Sunday, August 31

My Beloved,

After a good night's sleep and a bit of philosophizing on your departure, I feel a good deal better this morning, but I doubt if that empty feeling in my heart will ever be gone until you have come back to me. There is no thing or no person other than yourself who can drive it away…

He seized this one-sided circumstance and rose to the bait Robin set a month ago when she asked for "a list of everything you want out of life, and everything you want Junior to have, or to strive for, or to be."

To occupy his mind, Buster honorably laid it out:

All I can do is to express to you some principles of guidance and try to point out some of the opportunities for service which are open for a man in the fields in which I am versed. That word <u>service</u> is the important word. If a man on his death bed can feel that he had added something to the lives of others on this earth which he is leaving, then he should be able to die happy.

In the way elderly individuals reflect and repeat themselves at the end of the line, Buster often remarked, "B-bug (his pet name for me), I've led a good life." It was true. He didn't leave a financial legacy, yet he went richly rewarded for random acts of kindness (before they were labeled as such) and, so far as I know, a clear social conscience.

I suppose that's worth millions in the twenty-first century when an "old white guy" contemplates afterlife possibilities.

For Robin's benefit, he elaborated further.

...lacking the desire to help others, man is but a poor, lost creature indeed, for eventually his selfishness will bring down upon him the dislike and even the hatred of both men of good-will and other selfish men. Even now Stalin reaps the fruits of his treachery in making an accord with Hitler instead of standing tight in his alliance with France and England...when this war is over, no matter who wins, Stalin will have no friend left in this world...

Buster staged himself in the grand scheme, deep in thought, puffing on his pipe.

We might as well be practical about this business of serving others...High-sounding dreams of the future are seldom brought to life unless a basis is built up solidly over a long period of time...any great effort on my part is blocked in the short run by my present lowly position in the Army...in the long run by the very fact that the world is at war.

He was not downhearted over the long-run outlook, provided he was able to devote all his energy to overcoming the short-run problems.

Wars are fought by soldiers, but the peace is made by lawyers.

Cynics will hoot over that view of the law profession, date-stamped 1941, but he sincerely believed it. Inspired by Abraham Lincoln, Buster espoused the ideals of liberty, hard work, justice, and equality.

Do I not, then, have an advantage that is possessed by only a few hundreds of other men?

The percentage of lawyers in the general population at the time? A lot less than nowadays. He concluded, as if auditioning for a lead role on the world stage.

With the idealism of youth, the training of the lawyer, and the experiences of the soldier as a firm foundation, who is in a better position to render great services in the long run than I? ...at the risk of boring you, I am going to try first to formulate ideas for the betterment of the Army, a subject which I know you must hate, but which I hope you will hear with the ears of my best critic that you are.

To be continued, Buster signed off that Sunday afternoon. He was due for lunch in Boston with family friend Ed "Iceberg" Smith. Ed was like an uncle to Buster. One who was hard to find at home with his wife and three boys due to the amphibious nature of his profession. Presently he served as commanding officer of the U.S. Coast Guard Cutter *Northland* and Commander of the Greenland Patrol, the force that protected that island by countering German attempts to make use of its territory or coastal waters.

When sudden uncertainty as to his own whereabouts knocked Buster upside the head, he added this:

P.S. Better send future letters to Pelham to be forwarded.

Pelham Manor, a village of Westchester County, New York, was the home of Buster's parents, Nat and Ethel. They were entrusted to redirect precious contents of the mail carrier's satchel.

Tracking Robin's voyage beyond the wasp waist of the Panama Canal, Buster's next letter flew airmail c/o the S.S. *Santa Elena*, Callao, Peru. For an extravagant thirty-one cents, it began with a satisfied palate. Over Sunday's dinner, which Buster described as "a very pleasant meal of fried chicken and deliciously spiced ham," he spilled ideas across the table with another guest.

I talked with Mr. Byrd, head of the war industries board of the Boston area, about the Army, in which he is very much interested.

The "war industries board" was Great War nomenclature for an agency decommissioned on January 1, 1919, post WWI. Despite that, Mr. Byrd assumed the title, all ears, because he owned the same daunting task: to determine the serious mass production industrial demands this mechanized war would place on America.

We were so engrossed in our discussion of morale, production and use of armaments, and training of the troops that I am afraid I completely neglected Mr. Byrd's very charming daughter...It sometimes amazes me how completely married to you I have become in the past three months...

Fortified by the conversation with Mr. Byrd, Buster drilled further into the subject of service, elaborating on ways to improve the armed forces. His dream? To be decorated with the bars and badges of an Army officer. He typed two single-spaced, feather-weight onion skin pages using the narrowest of margins.

...for unless this war is in the end definitely won by the democracies, then any plans that we may have for the future will definitely be destroyed...

The lecture served to help Buster formulate ideas. For Robin? Odds are she regretted asking about his dreams.

My next discussion on my aims in life will be sent down to Rancagua...I am looking forward with great interest to receiving your letters about your trip and the people whom you have met.

Gee, I hope that your Mother appreciates how much of my life I have given up in letting you go at all...

A one liner that revealed how the contract of marriage worked in the 1940s. By virtue of the Tiffany ring on her finger, he owned her every move.

Or so he believed.

Buster returned to the New Hampshire woods for the next round of Army maneuvers, fighting more phony battles from his field radio cubby hole. He wrote Robin c/o the S.S. *Santa Elena*, Antofagasta, Chile. The cost to communicate up-ticked: forty cents postage. As Robin sailed toward blue skies, sunshine, and spring skiing atop feet of snow in the Andes, Buster layered for fall.

The weather has turned cool now, so during the long night watch I have to bundle up in sheepskin, vest, windbreaker, overcoat and balaklava to keep warm... the sun has just gone down. The sky is still pale with your favorite little silver and gold feather clouds. I know the sunset here can't compare with the tropic brilliance of the one you are seeing tonight over the Caribbean, but your little clouds do remind me of you...

While he felt terribly lonesome, Robin's time was more fully occupied swanning about the *Elena*. Enthusiastic and extroverted, she played ambassador extraordinaire for FDR's "Good Neighbor Policy," first introduced in 1933. Not in an official capacity, of course, but her knack for making friends was one advantage of never having a real home or family life. When it came to skiing, she'd made it her business to become a sporting fan of the good-will exchanges brought about by the Pan American Games, as much as the Winter Olympics. Six months before, while at Smith, the First Lady stirred the student body as to the responsibility of youth to the future. Forthwith, Robin took to reading Eleanor Roosevelt's nationally syndicated column, "My Day." Coincidentally, in the days just prior to boarding the *Elena*, it was the First Lady's emboldened pen that fortified Robin port to port for five-thousand nautical miles: "People grow through experiences, if they meet life honestly and courageously. This is how character is built..."

Such little memories cause great waves of nostalgia to well up within me... Tonight, for instance, I hate the little feather clouds. All I can think of is my desire to be sharing new beauties with you—that Caribbean sunset, the first sight of the Southern Cross as the quick darkness of the tropic night descends upon you. Somehow I feel that I have lost something that should be mine—my privilege to build new memories that will be ours and ours alone...so that no other thoughts could exist but of each other when those scenes are again brought to mind.

I'm sorry dear. Maybe I'm just spoiled or selfish or something...I am glad that you can take such a wonderful trip and that you will be able to see your parents again...

Whatever the explanation, his love for her left him feeling less certain about everything. It distilled to this:

I hate the thought...after a hard week in the field...not finding you there to take care of me.

Where did Robin stand on that point? She put it in her own words just a few weeks before their wedding: "I guess I never stopped to realize or let myself think about having a legal residence or home, dear...Honey, I'm going to do everything on earth, to make you the happiest man alive..." So, it follows, as a new bride, she prepared meals to his liking and kept the laundry whites bright.

Beyond domestics, he found her playful spirit provocative. Nearly his equal on horseback, and at the business end of a tennis racquet, she could outswim most men and look like a fit fashion model doing it. On their honeymoon he taught her to drive. From that point forward, they agreed she was better behind the wheel of their 1939 Lincoln *Zephyr*. And faster. Which came in handy because Buster, by nature, was impossible to rush. She chauffeured him from their post-honeymoon love nest at the Groton Inn to the gate at Fort Devens where *her* punctuality carried weight with *his* superiors when he stepped in line to form ranks on time.

It was so wonderful to have you with me this summer—you were so wonderful to marry me in spite of the fact that I was in the Army—that I really should not complain…When your letters start to arrive, when you tell me of the things you have seen…I will feel the force of your love more fully…

As a biology major, Robin trained to observe and document events empirically in a lab notebook. Her window into that analytical world was hardly poetic. Buster wanted and expected much more in the form of descriptive detail.

Ah, if you only knew how I look forward to those letters as one of the first hard tests of your love…Night has fallen now, my darling, the cold Northern moon— the same one we shared at Plymouth the Spring I fell in love with you—is full and bright in a cloudless sky…

Eleven weeks after first meeting over Christmas break in Florida, 1939, they rendezvoused at a snow train destination in Plymouth, New Hampshire. There, in the White Mountains, he fell hard in more ways than one. It's where her athletic prowess first struck him. As a novice skier, it was tough to keep up on the fall line she picked down Cannon Mountain's Ravine Trail.

That night, Tuesday, September 2, under a nostalgic New England moon, Buster twirled lines over in his mind and fiddled with a pencil and eraser while on radio watch. He enclosed this poem before sealing the envelope.

<u>*Lines on Love and Beauty*</u>
The scent of the pine grove at evening
Fresh and clean
The grace of a palm frond a-waving
Smooth and lean
A feather of cloud in the heavens
Fleecy and white

Aims in Life

The sight of the stars in the midnight
Clear and bright
In each one alone there is beauty,
Yet you know
That sharing it all with your sweetheart
Makes it grow
Such memories are food for all lovers
Which if stored
Can brighten their lives till the ending
With their hoard
NFB

Their hoard? Raised as an only child, this was Buster's reference to the most precious treasure imaginable: progeny.

Seven days into the voyage, a message pulsed from Fitchburg, Massachusetts, to Guayaquil, Ecuador, 152 miles south of the equator. The gesture marked one year since Buster proposed in a canoe on Princeton University's Lake Carnegie, beneath a waxing crescent moon. An invisible hand slipped the "Telegrama" under cabin door 128. Robin opened the sealed envelope evenly, without a rip, as if it were meant to be its own gift. She fished out the folded postal telegraph and read his note without stops.

"WISH I COULD BE WITH YOU ON ANNIVERSARY OF OUR ENGAGEMENT GET YOURSELF FLOWERS AND THINK OF ME."

The gesture was kind, but instructions to "get yourself flowers" might have deflated her.

History tells us floriography, a complex means of coded communication, dated back to the Victorian era. Flower type and bloom colors were used to express feelings that strictures of the time did not permit.

Later, in 1918, the adage "say it with flowers" was adopted by the Floral Telegraph Delivery Service, FTD. Smart marketing branded "swift, dependable delivery" with the image of Greek god, Hermes, that little man with winged feet, messenger to Zeus.

By 1941, affiliated florists accepted orders for dispatch to any part of the world. But, as Buster discovered, not in this port city of Ecuador. He would later ask, "What kind of a town is Guayaquil that it didn't have a florist where I could wire you flowers?" After which he elaborated on a prohibitive price tag of sixteen dollars. Nearly three-hundred dollars when adjusted for inflation today.

Otherwise occupied, it was just as well Robin ignored the idea. The blooming petals would fly from cabin wall to window when the boat ran aground.

Though I have no evidence that Buster read the shocking news, the story appeared in *The New York Times* on 9 September.

> "GUAYAQUIL, Ecuador, Sept. 8 (AP) - The 9,135-ton Grace liner Santa Elena ran aground today at Rio Guayas, fifteen miles from this port. Tugs and barges were dispatched at once to unload her cargo. High tide tonight is expected to lift her from the sand."

Surely there were experts among the cruise-party who, while stuck, would pore over nautical charts. Of interest to Robin was the proximity of Darwin's fabled Galapagos Islands. That magical sanctuary of evolution lay six-hundred miles west, over the rim of the horizon. At the time it was a closely guarded secret that Secretary of State, Cordell Hull, a strong supporter of FDR's "Good Neighbor Policy," worked to garner consent of Ecuadorian political leaders to use of the strategically located archipelago. They came around to understand that arming the Galapagos would protect Ecuador as much as the United States. Within the year, headlines revealed "Air Bases Established on Galapagos Islands." From the main base on Baltra, the U.S. Army Airforce was well positioned to protect the Pacific side of the Panama Canal, in the same way Caribbean bases protected the Atlantic side.

At his parents' home in Pelham, Buster's irritation festered.

Aims in Life

Six Weeks for Boat Mail

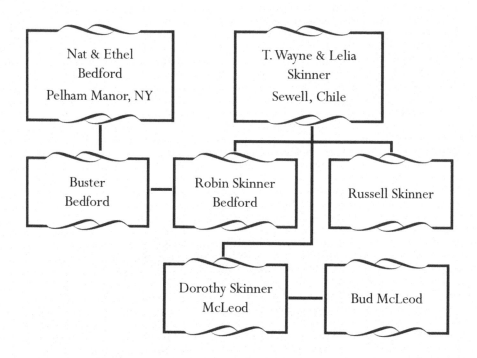

Traveling Rhythms
Chapter Two

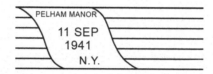

N.F. Bedford 1283 Manor Circle, Pelham Manor, N.Y. – Thursday, September 11, 1941 (airmail special delivery)

Mrs. N. Forrest Bedford
Aboard S.S. Santa Elena
C/o Grace S.S. Lines
Valparaiso, Chile
South America

Tuesday, Sept. 9
My Beloved,

    Your first two letters mailed from Panama arrived Saturday. Although they were short, they were very sweet and I appreciated them. However, when I return from the present manoeuver I hope to find letters of interest to my <u>mind</u> <u>as well as</u> to my <u>heart</u>, for the one without the other makes me wish that I had never allowed you to leave me...

    While she met with new and exciting scenes, finding beauty and adventure to occupy her mind, Buster drifted in space.

Six Weeks for Boat Mail

...How am I to drink the cool wine of the air, to cheer for Princeton's Tiger, to be warmed by a log fire at Pelham without feeling so keenly that the pleasure is incomplete without you?

A needle riding on vinyl filled the Pelham Manor parlor with New York "best set" piano bar society sound: the fluttering melodies of Eddy Duchin. Buster paced and pined. RKO Pictures® 1939 comedy-drama, *Love Affair*, proved shipboard romances happened then, as they do today. Except a more innocent Hollywood (governed by the Motion Picture Production Code—the Hays Code) left scenes of lustful kissing up to the imagination. He dared go no further than fantasize Robin whirling on the dance floor, until thoughts of her blue eyes bubbling over glasses of pink champagne crept in.

Feeling lonely and isolated, he fell back on his reasoning as to why he permitted her trip.

I hope that you will come back from your visit with your parents with a deeper and wiser knowledge of family life.

Doubtful. Robin wrote only *once* in her five-year diary about "life with whole family." It was the summer of '39. They lived in hotels for weeks!

And now enough of my lecturing, for I know you dislike it intensely...

As the youngest of four kids growing up under Buster's roof, I intensely disliked it, too.

Then, as if the celluloid snapped, Buster took a different tack.

...If you want to know my dreams of the future, you have only to read Walter Davenport's editorial on "Victory."

In a *"magnificent"* article in September's issue of *Fortune Magazine* he was completely carried away by the scope and organization of Davenport's thought. The columnist, long on anecdotes, conversationally corroborated Buster's personal aims, such that...*a group of willing, intelligent, and forceful young men* (like him) *might yet produce that <u>World</u> government for future peace and continued prosperity for all.*

Traveling Rhythms

Intoxicated with optimism, Buster dropped ten dollars on a *Fortune Magazine* subscription to be delivered to a father-in-law he was yet to meet.

My best to my new Father, a big kiss for my new Mother, and for yourself read Elizabeth Barrett Browning's sonnet on How Do I Love Thee and think of me, whose heart belongs to you alone forever and ever...

The following night, Buster neatly tapped out both sides of a sheet of stationery, font size ten, single-spaced. He tucked two letters for the price of one in an envelope that posted for sixty cents, airmail special delivery.

Home is the soldier, home from the wars, but the husband has no place to go. Which is just another way of saying that corps manoeuvers are over after a grueling three weeks of sleepless nights and endless days.

Back at Devens, the men slept off exhaustion. Overnight problems, by design, deprived them of sleep. Now most boys at the fort looked for an answer to this question: Would they get furlough before an imminent move South? The Carolina Maneuvers loomed. Like integers in a multiplication table, troops to be fed, sheltered, clothed, and armed would converge in the Carolinas.

History tells us leaders would emerge in the maneuvers of 1941 to bolster the mechanized warp and woof of the *new* U.S. Army. Meanwhile, Buster wondered if his application to Signal Corps School at Fort Monmouth had been, or would be, accepted.

...Will my transfer <u>ever</u> come through, or will I go South with the rest of them? I guess it really doesn't make a great deal of difference.

Last night on radio watch I got the poetry bug again after reading through most of our little Pocket Book of famous poetry, and, thinking of the innumerable times you have asked how much I love you, jotted down the following bit of verse... Any failure in the scanning you can attribute to the late hour at which the lines were composed.

<blockquote>
"How do I love thee?" What should I cry?
"Deep as the ocean, high as the sky?"
'Tis a thought too oft used.
To describe my love—refused.
</blockquote>

Six Weeks for Boat Mail

"Shall I compare thee to a summer's day?"
"A steal from Shakespeare," they'd say.
"My love is like a red, red rose?"
Burns' sweet music—everyone knows.
"She walks in beauty, like the night?"
George Gordon, Lord Byron, copyright.
"A loaf of bread, a jug of wine and thou?"
Fitzgerald's Omar Khayyam, I vow.
"With thee conversing, I forget all time?"
Milton's smooth line which needs no rhyme.

Each timeless line gives a truth
About your beauty, charm and youth.
But how express a thought by me
With some originality?
Who knows? Here goes:

The Brownings I adore,
He with his One Word More,
She with her sonnets which please,
Sonnets from the Portuguese.
Their love was different, complete:
He worshipped at her feet

Desiring only to share
Life's joys and sorrows there.
She, true, loving, virtuous wife:
"I love thee with the breath, smiles, tears, of all my life."

This is better, more expressive.
Tender, loving, and possessive.
But, on the other hand,
Can't I make some demand?
Why not? God wot.

My love is like a flower
"Tended by the hour"
Eternally it grows
But if neglected it lies,
Perhaps too soon it dies.
Poor rose:

Like a flower it's true,
Faithful always to you
Forever and ever
Cultivated with care
Pleasures for you 'twill bear
Fair weather:

This such joys will bring
Heaven and earth will sing
Songs of gladness.
And with each spring rain
My love will grow again
Sweet madness:

So there ne'er will be
Two so happy as we
On land or ocean.
Thus my love is shown
Dependent on your own
Devotion.

Heigh ho, there you have it in a nutshell. Even if it doesn't prove anything else, it shows that I have sat up many a night thinking about you...

And if optimism is a form of faith, he believed she was thinking about him, too.

Mother and Dad are due here tomorrow night...How about some snapshots of your family?

Did he know what his new in-laws looked like?

Six Weeks for Boat Mail

With that thought, Buster rolled another piece of flimsy airmail stationery around the platen. He crammed a narrow-margined page with words meant to score points with Robin's mother, Lelia. She would think highly of his ability to type. She'd nagged her two daughters, Robin and Dorothy, for years about typing as always being "something to work on."

Likewise, in the 1970s, Buster insisted accurate touch-typing was a respectable secretarial skill a girl like me could always fall back on. When keyboarding erupted into the workforce a decade later, my proficiency played well. Women in management knew how to type, while old dogs were forced to learn new tricks.

```
PELHAM MANOR
  11 SEP
   1941
   N.Y.
```

N.F. Bedford 1283 Manor Circle, Pelham Manor, N.Y. – Thursday, September 11, 1941 (airmail)

Dear ~~Mrs. Skinner~~, Mother,

Will you accept the above appellation from me? I do hope so, for I want you to feel that you have gained a son rather than lost a daughter. At any rate, your letters to me and to my other Mother have been so full of kindness and understanding that I am going to risk calling you "Mother," even though I have never had the pleasure of seeing your face... You have given me a good start toward becoming a real son.

Lelia had written Ethel Bedford, Buster's mother, "to start a friendship" when news of their youngsters' engagement was about to break. She kindly wrote Buster, too.

Now it was Buster's turn to befriend his mother-in-law.

By the time this letter reaches you our Robin (my nickname for Roberta) will be with you again. How happy you must be. And how I envy you her presence. Just a little over a year ago when I asked Robin to marry me, I had fond hopes that I might be able to take her to Chile on our honeymoon, thus to enjoy the double pleasure of the voyage and of meeting you and Mr. Skinner. When the war and the Army killed that hope, there was still the thought that you might come up here for the wedding this Summer so that I could keep her with me. It could not be, for which I was very sorry.

Lelia's conundrum: an invitation to Bud McLeod, the Montana-born and raised beau of Robin's younger sister, Dorothy, led to Lelia's decision to stay put in Chile. Hence, she missed Robin's graduation and wedding. A letter Lelia wrote in July pinpointed dates: "We have had a very rushing time ever since Bud arrived at the Santiago Airport June 16…It was a very happy four weeks (lacking three days). Every minute so precious! They were married with a civil ceremony—here, June 22, at home with some of our most intimate friends."

Buster kept typing.

Even now, when she has been gone from me for over two weeks, I find it hard to become used to her absence…I am slowly reconciling myself to the situation, and, although nothing but the U.S. Army could ever part her from me again, I feel that in the present situation my present sacrifice might be worth the gain of the whole…

What did he ask?

Impart to her some of your own understanding and domestic wisdom…

Reflecting on the past two months of married life he innocently recounted his feelings.

…she will make as fine a wife as ever lived on this earth. Not that she is perfect, any more than I am a perfect husband, but she has the ultimate stuff of which near perfection—or at any rate enduring love—is made…

In a 1939 marriage forum on the Smith College campus, Robin learned there was no such thing as a "perfect" partner. They often ribbed each other about the fallacy of perfection.

She is usually considerate, any inconsiderateness probably stemming from the fact that she has, for a number of years, been accountable to no one but herself in her personal affairs.

Lelia might have sniffed at his judgement. Buster tempered:

She is undeniably loving and kind. Most important of all she is open-minded and willing to do more than her share to make our marriage a successful compromise of temperaments. If anything at all is lacking, it is only such incidentals as can be quickly adjusted by exposure to the routine of her own home...

One upshot of Robin's peripatetic youth? For twenty-two years she'd eluded domestic drudgery. For example, Bon Ami, a branded cleaning powder for polishing sinks and tubs since 1886, held no meaning beyond its literal French translation, "good friend." Of which she'd made many.

Buster placed responsibility for this learning curve squarely on his mother-in-law's shoulders:

...a basic knowledge of home economics, a desire and energy to be a good housekeeper, the knack of making a real home—aptitudes which she has, as yet, had little or no opportunity to exercise.

After assuring Lelia the two of them were intellectually and recreationally nearly perfectly matched, he asked for one last thing.

"...that you return her to me by early December at the latest."

When Robin's letter dated September 10 arrived, Buster unfolded the official Grace Lines airmail stationery with anticipation. It was thin as spring-roll pastry, watermarked by the ghostly image of "Esleeck Clearcopy Onion Skin."

```
S.S. Santa Elena
   10 SEP
    1941
  Grace Lines
```

Onboard S.S. Santa Elena – Grace Lines September 10, 1941

My dearest one –

And aren't you the wonderful husband to remember our anniversary—I was just thrilled to death when I saw the radiogram under my door—and I really missed you an awful lot that day...

Hopefully she missed him an awful lot on other days, too.

Traveling Rhythms

Just about half the passengers left on the boat are getting off today. Eight of the younger group are going—leaving about four—one bound for Orica and three for Santiago…We had a big farewell party last night…even my roommate is leaving me.

Her passage was booked with a fifty-percent students' reduction on steamship fare; double occupancy was standard. For the next seven days she'd live a little larger.

I 'spose you are definitely in radio school by now—or else they aren't sending you…

On the day Robin sailed out of New York harbor, Buster awaited news of his transfer to Fort Monmouth, eager to attend Signal Corps Officers Candidate School (OCS). She was yet to receive his special delivery letters from New England, which waited for her a bit further south in Callao, Lima's chief port to the world.

Yesterday afternoon we anchored in Salaverry, Peru for four hours—and eight of us decided we'd go ashore—partly for the fun we'd have getting off the "Elena" into a little boat alongside in the roughest sea you ever saw.

A "little boat" technically known as a "ship's tender." Something bigger than a dinghy. Unstable, nonetheless.

Everybody did it 'cept one Peruvian lad who didn't jump quick enough and tumbled into some awful cold water and had to be fished out.

She held back. Never mind the slums of Colombia's seaport, Buenaventura, or *Elena's* tugs and barges rescue near Guayaquil. She cheated his heart and mind and left it with an abrupt sign-off.

No more space, dearest—Take care of yourself—We'll probably be in Valpo the 17th.

Your loving Robin

When Robin noted the date *Elena* would dock, it stuck with Buster. Then came her biggest marital mistake to date.

She neglected to cable c/o Pelham Manor to confirm her arrival.

Six Weeks for Boat Mail

Buster was desperate to know she was safe. Despite the expensive (and unreliable) radio relay system used for transoceanic phone service to Chile in 1941, he placed a call.

They would not speak again for months. Except, of course, through letters. The first one began with an apology for his volcanic outburst. Until her return, Buster would direct correspondence to "his" Mrs., in keeping with patriarchal rules of 1940s envelope etiquette:

Mrs. N. Forrest Bedford
C/o Mrs. T.W. Skinner
Braden Copper Co.
Rancagua (Sewell)
Chile, South America

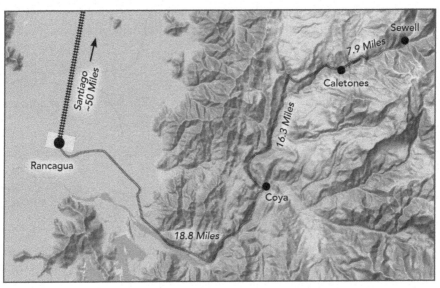

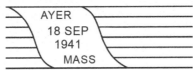

**PVT N.F. Bedford 2nd SQ. HQ. 101 Cav., Fort Devens, Ayer, Mass –
Thursday, Sept. 18, 1941**

My Beloved,

Please forgive me for that telephone call. If my voice sounded too harsh, if I made you unhappy, I am truly sorry… I, at least, had the satisfaction of knowing that you had arrived safely…

He formulated carefully chosen words on the train ride back to Devens.

When I know that you have no pressing business to attend to on the boat, that you are meeting interesting people and seeing fascinating sights every day…I resent the lack of contact between us…I get the feeling that you do not think enough of me to spend those few minutes a day which would keep me happy.

He enlightened her.

I like to feel that you are willing to do those thoughtful little <u>extra</u> things that make love live and grow stronger through the years—things that you don't feel you <u>have</u> to do, but you <u>like</u> to do because you know that it will make the person you love happier.

As simple as a freshly poured cup of coffee delivered bedside in the morning.

Bluntly, he added: *Without such things love becomes mere sexual gratification or intellectual association.*

Well, I've said as much as I am going to say on the above subject. My three day leave from Monday through Wednesday was a pretty grim affair of just sitting and waiting for letters from you.

Grim as he felt, his social activities were not as limited as he led Robin to believe.

Monday night he escorted Joyce Thompson to the Rainbow Grille, midtown Manhattan. "Joycie" was one of Robin's Haven House housemates at Smith and a bridesmaid in their wedding who now taught at New York's first progressive school, The Little Red School House on Bleeker Street.

I spent a pleasant Tuesday evening with Dizzy and Gina…playing bridge.

In Washington, D.C., no less.

I was unable to get down for the announcement party Sunday…Gina was quite tickled with her cable from you.

Robin considered Dizzy her larger-than-life bon vivant "pet," whom she'd known for ten years. They'd shared odd beginnings, she from Chile and he as a nine-year-old immigrant from Chambéry, Savoie, France. Her matchmaker heart sang with news that Dizzy and her own maid of honor, Gina, would tie the knot in January.

Moreover, Dizzy captivated Buster with his stories. Hitler was out to destroy the French national spirit and make France a subject province of the Hitler empire permanently. That September night, while dealing cards one at a time clockwise around the table, Dizzy divulged wartime intel. His dad (a WWI French Flying Ace) presently served in D.C., as personal representative to Charles De Gaulle. It pleased Buster to hear firsthand about the underground nerve center of resistance to Nazi control. Particularly the fact that the German force of occupation was worried.

Ouah! The "Free France" movement would stop at nothing.

Buster relayed news of other members of the "gang" he knew would interest Robin. Johnny, a Princeton man, and Scottie, his girl from Smith, expected to be married as soon as she graduated. At present, Johnny served as a field artillery radio man at Fort Bragg, N.C. Buster hoped to see him on maneuvers in Carolina.

Now, let me get on to the thing which has inspired me to sit up until late at night writing you this letter, the thing which was so beautiful that I felt I must share it with you no matter how angry I might have been...

The wonder of the Northern Lights.

It was breathtaking: pale greens, cold whites, deep purples, brilliant lavenders shot down in streamers of light like the ribbons on a May Pole. Now it was dark and the stars shown with a crystal brilliance; then there was a great burst of white light as though the day of reckoning had come...

Scores of citizens inquired with Massachusetts officials as to the cause of the disturbance in the sky. Was it due to *war*? War games? An invasion from Mars? As if writing a guided meditation for the Ascension, Buster's description ranked among the best news reporters.

All of a sudden the fringes of the white light gave way along the horizon edges to a constantly shifting tint of color and the white columns from the arch of Heaven began to revolve like the spokes of a wheel...

He'd mustered all the descriptive power within him to illustrate the type of letter he expected of her.

I must go to bed now. Tomorrow I will look for your letter from Callao which Mother mailed from Pelham today. I will save a little space in which to comment...

The next morning, he awoke in the barracks bright and cheery. Not for long. Reading her post from Callao, she gave him the inspiration of a jellyfish. He spanked her with this:

...Until your letters vastly improve in quality and quantity, I shall feel that you have been a very poor wife for the past month and shall not bother writing you again...

To an Absent Wife

*What is love? Who knows.
A sunset shared at evening, a rose
Pinned in the hair of a loved one can make
Two hearts beat together, the earth shake.*

*What is love? Well, now,
I cannot say for sure. A vow
Taken before an altar is not enough alone
To last forever, if 'twere known.*

*What is love? It's more
Than passion merely, It's lore
Lies in the knowing how and where and when
Of sweet consideration for your friend.*

*What is love? I'll say
This much about it: every day
It brighter burns if fuel it is fed. A note,
A cheerful thought, a future hope
Expressed therein for later sharing,
That will keep your lover caring!*

NFB 9/20/41

He waited nearly a week. When it came time to break the silence, he did it with his tail between his legs.

Bad news today, my sweet. Just talked to Dad over the telephone last night about my transfer to Ft. Monmouth and he told me that everything had gone through O.K. as far as Col. Ackerman of the 101st.

The Colonel objected to his leaving the regiment.

So, on Sunday we leave for Ft. Bragg, N.C. My new address until Oct. 28 will be 2nd Sq. Hq. 101 Cav. Army P.O. 306, Ft. Bragg, N.C. I'm awfully sorry, dear...

It was a blow to ego and aspiration. But the news wasn't all bad.

Meanwhile I have taken over Frank Bangs' job as 2nd Squadron Radio Sergeant...

A door swung open for Buster when Bangs was accepted to West Point.

Although I will not be drawing a Staff Sergeant's $72.00 a month, I believe I will be given the rank of Acting Staff Sergeant, the stripes that go with it, and the opportunity and authority which the job offers.

It represented a jump of four grades to nearly the top of the enlisted man's possible achievements.

With his leap from the bottom of the heap came a new sense of security and empowerment. Despite the fact Robin was just ten days into the visit with her parents, Lelia and T. Wayne, he was ready to bargain over the length of her stay. FDR's address to the nation on Labor Day delivered a solemn warning that the "task of defeating Hitler may be long and arduous." The "Fireside Chat" that followed on September 11 stunned him.

I have started looking up boat and air schedules...I am not very anxious to have you come up the Atlantic coast by boat...

Roosevelt told of an incident involving the Wickes-class destroyer USS *Greer*. A German submarine, U-652, skulking in North Atlantic waters, deliberately but unsuccessfully attempted to torpedo the *Greer*. Tit-for-tat, the U-boat was subjected to a retaliatory depth charge attack. Bottom line, the Germans fired first without warning. Buster knew it was the very area where family friend "Iceberg" Smith patrolled southeast of Greenland. The incident constituted the first known act of aggression between Germany and the United States. FDR laid it out this way: "These Nazi submarines and raiders are the rattlesnakes of the Atlantic. They are a menace to the free pathways of the high seas. They are a challenge to our own sovereignty.

Traveling Rhythms

They hammer at our most precious rights when they attack ships of the American flag—symbols of our independence, our freedom, our very life."

History tells us passenger traffic on Pan American Airways was on the uptick. Air travel was perceived to be far less dangerous than other modes of transportation.

The Clipper trip will be more enjoyable, too, if your parents feel it is possible.

The Pan American "Clipper" was the "jumbo" airplane of the day, with seventy-four seats, dressing rooms, and a fine dining salon. Preparation for landing had nothing to do with tray-table and seatback announcements. The ticket on the Boeing 314 came with a high price, plus a surcharge for one-way travel tacked on. Buster anticipated that the senior Skinners might balk at the extravagance, but it was for safety's sake.

We can get your main baggage when the boat arrives in New York.

The luggage weight allowance aboard the Clipper was based on the price of the passenger's plane ticket. Sixty-six pounds (or thereabouts) was the magic number. Robin would travel with her suitcase. Her oversized Hartmann "cushion top" wardrobe, could be shipped Valpo to New York.

In retrospect, it makes sense that as modes of transportation evolved in the first half of the twentieth century, luggage did, too. Suitcases more appropriately sized to fit in train car compartments, aboard aircraft, and in automobile trunks replaced the early twentieth century steamer trunk. At Saks Fifth-Avenue, celebrities paid top dollar for the evolving Hartmann line, where their jewelry displays breathed a pagan tropic tempo, beckoning travel to Latin America—good neighbor style.

For breadwinners employed with Braden Copper, the Hartmann Agency on Fifth Avenue offered discounted "export prices." That's how Robin came into possession of the top-drawer label.

Tomorrow we start on our long trek south, so I am not sure how often I will be able to write this next week…P.S. Am I forgiven my trespasses? Please say "yes."

"A very poor wife," indeed. *He'd* threatened to ghost *her*. Tit-for-tat, she might not write him at all. The timing could not have been worse. U.S.

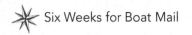 Six Weeks for Boat Mail

Army troops all along the eastern seaboard—400,000 of them—moved like a khaki shadow from their home stations toward the Carolina maneuver area. Nothing made a serviceman's face fall faster than when a batch of mail failed to turn up a letter addressed in his sweetheart's familiar script.

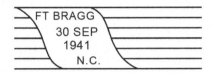

Pvt. N.F. Bedford, 2nd SQ. HQ. 101 Cav., A.P.O. 306, Fort Bragg, N.C. USA – September 30, 1941 (airmail)

Sunday, Sept. 28
My Beloved,

Tonight I am sitting in my scout car on Sheridan Range, a dust blown field only three miles south of camp.

The troops staged at a transition camp the way a tour group might overnight at an airport hotel before an early morning flight.

This is the start of the Great Southern Adventure. Although it is only a little after 9:00 P.M., I am the only one still awake, for we must arise at 4:15 tomorrow to start on the fast leg of our journey.

Even though the wind is rising outside blowing dirt everywhere, though there is a ring around the moon in an overcast sky predicting the storm blowing this way from New York, though I am tired and dirty, I still have to tell you about something beautiful I saw this afternoon.

They made camp at about two-thirty, expecting to rest. An announcement soon followed. Church services would be held at four o'clock. Buster described what amounted to a pop-up chapel at the core of a gathering.

On the hour we marched over to a small clump of trees on the edge of the range. There we found the band playing as the troops assembled, an altar set up on the back of one of the cargo trucks, and the Colonel's command car drawn up alongside flying the American and 101st Cavalry flags…

He described the service as short and simple, consisting of a psalm, a couple of hymns, and two prayers.

...But as we knelt to pray in the grassy spot with the wind whipping the flags and the altar candles flickering I felt closer to God than I have in a long time. Somehow, for the first time, there was a real 101st Cavalry group spirit, and above that there seemed to hover another spirit, less obvious but no less real, which promised to look after the boys as they set out upon this long, hard, and somewhat dangerous adventure.

Buster's personal spirituality was evidenced by the King James Version of *The Holy Bible* in his duffle. A gift from his mother, Ethel, on his twenty-first birthday. Her poignant inscription inside the cover concluded, "And may it be thy faithful chart, And ever point thy onward road." The men, coalesced around refreshed interdenominational strength, would take that onward road south in the morning.

Just one more thing before I go to bed: I would like to describe our regimental flag which I saw for the first time today. Next to the American flag I believe it is the most beautiful thing I have ever seen. The field is a bright cavalry yellow fringed with the same material. In the center is the great American Eagle. Above the eagle's head sails the ship of state and on its breast is the shield of the 101st Cavalry. It is reported to have cost the fabulous sum of $700.00.

With your little kodachrome picture hanging here before me in the scout car, I send you a good-night kiss with all the love I bear for you warming my heart as I go to bed.

The regiment launched pre-dawn. Bumping along at a snail's pace, Buster crafted words in his head to describe sweeps of rolling landscape without landing his scout car in a ditch. He put them on paper for Robin that night.

Tonight, after travelling 211 miles, we are in Goshen, N.Y. Although the weather has been chilly all day—uncomfortably so in these open cars—the scenery has been unsurpassable as we rolled over the Litchfield Hills, across the Connecticut River, and down the Hudson River Valley. All day long I have thrilled to the beauty of the

Six Weeks for Boat Mail

Connecticut woods, now half-changed into their fall colors, more lovely than ever because the deep green furnishes such a soft background for the brilliant red of the sumac and the bright yellows, brown and oranges of the maple, oaks, and birches. Truly, this is the loveliest season of the year, when peace and plenty should reign o'er the earth...

A time of year when, as far as he was concerned, all the sounds of battle should come from the football field.

The harvest is there, all right, great orange pumpkins too large to lift, squashes as big as a man's chest, pears and peaches and shiny red apples which seem to cry out to be eaten or pressed lovingly into cider, but instead of peace and you beside the living room fire with chestnuts toasting on the hearth, here I am on my way to battle, mimic battle though it is. May God see fit that such sacrifice will be sufficient to preserve the way of life I love.

The way of life he loved was the America grounded in the U.S. Constitution. At the time he signed on as a National Guardsman (over a year ago) he was a law student at Columbia. Maneuvers of 1940 heightened his perspective on national defense. Since then, every life choice filtered through a personal arsenal of democratic principles to preserve America's freedoms.

Mother suggests that while travelling in Europe she always used to number her letters to Dad so he would know if any were lost... Don't you think that is a good idea? I will start with this one.

Buster's mother, Ethel, hailed from Macedonia. She'd arrived in America as a twelve-year-old immigrant from the Ottoman Empire in 1898. In 1926, she embarked on a "Grand Tour" of Europe, in part to visit her homeland, but mostly to celebrate her fortieth birthday in Roaring Twenties style. Nat remained stateside; Ethel sent letters flooded with stories of music, theatre, and food. Treasured accounts in <u>numbered</u> envelopes ensured every nugget found its way home. Aboard S.S. *Leviathan* she timed her return to orchestrate Buster's eighth birthday party.

Mother and Dad have just arrived to take me out to dinner and say good-bye...

Three days later, Buster posted what constituted a three-letter featurette.

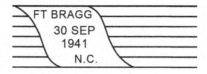

Pvt. N.F. Bedford, 2nd SQ. HQ. 101 Cav., A.P.O. 306, Fort Bragg, N.C. USA – September 30, 1941
Marked ②

Tuesday, Sept. 30
My Beloved,

Last night, at Goshen, N.Y., we had our last taste of luxury for some time to come. Mother and Dad arrived soon after the regiment and took a room at the Goshen Inn. A good hot bath soon took the numbness out of my bones and an Old Fashioned finished warming me up.

Two other boys escaped the mess tent at Buster's invitation. The party of five dined on a savory supper.

...cantaloupe, hot soup, lamb chops, huckleberry pie, topped off with good coffee and brandy—then sat for a while in front of a big log fire.

The lay of the land changed overnight.

We arose at 4:30 this morning to continue our journey. Dawn revealed fields around us covered with frost and the cold was biting. The first hour of driving took us up hill and down dale through valleys where the morning mists were so thick that we could not see thirty feet in front of the car...

By noon, after crossing the Delaware River and passing Lafayette College at Easton, we had reached Allentown, Pa. where we had lunch at the fairgrounds. Mother's fried chicken, brought to us yesterday, made lunch pleasant.

A fried chicken picnic was a five-star motherly touch for a man on maneuvers. Ethel hacked whole fryers. Cleaved parts dipped in egg, dredged in flour, turned by tong in splattering oil. Crispy brown skin and moist meat on every wing, crunchy drumstick, second joint (thigh) and

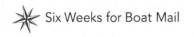

breast. Southern comfort food that, in my opinion, Colonel Sanders never got right.

This afternoon we have progressed steadily through the rolling farmlands of the Pennsylvania Dutch—probably the most picturesque and certainly one of the richest farming regions in the U.S.

Doubtful Buster knew anything of Robin's Pennsylvania farming heritage.

The weather is warmer down here; the fields are still green and the leaves of the trees are more subdued in their coloring...Our comfort won't last long though, for in an hour we will be in Harrisburg and by tonight we will be at Boonsboro, Md., up in the mountains...

Thinking of you constantly as our car starts to roll again...

He picked up the travelogue early, Wednesday, October 1.

I start this letter just as the morning sun pokes its head over one of the Blue Mountains of Western Maryland. Today the weather is warm again, brought on the wings of a Southern breeze...after the cold of the last two nights, it is well appreciated...

The troops moved in the direction of vexed nuisances. Buster drove the open scout car through southern rains. Gassing the vehicle involved a funnel and a five-gallon can. He fixed a trouble light, the rudimentary bulb that plugged into a receptacle on the left side of the dash, by which he wrote. He was hot, tired, dirty, and expected they would drive all night to keep to their schedule.

Just as Paul Simon would one day write lyrics describing the countryside in his traveling rhythm *Graceland*, Buster detailed a similar scene.

We proceeded down the trail of the armies of the War Between the States. Yesterday we passed Gettysburg, today Antietam and Sharpsburg. The Maryland countryside was parched and dry—no rain since July. Red clay along the road looked as though it had been stained that color by the blood of former soldiers...

From the foot of a mountain ridge, the long pull uphill was slow and tedious. Heavy trucks ground along amidst a motorized dirt-churning column. The smell of exhaust extended for miles. Horses of the 1st Squadron, hauled in tractor-trailers, stood with their feed and tack, accompanied by their eight-man squad. With a too-fast stop on the sudden downhill, those cavalrymen risked being squished by their equine counterparts.

...we rounded a bend and found ourselves looking down 2,000 feet on the richness of the Shenandoah Valley of Virginia.

The stunning views of the Skyline Drive, a depression-era project that began in 1931, offered recurring panoramas to the east and west. For obvious reasons, the CCC erected stone "guard walls" and miles of chestnut log guardrails, when they constructed the now historic Scenic Byway.

The troops seemingly rode the sky. Large, dark, electrically charged cumulonimbus clouds took on the appearance of shape-shifting mythical creatures. They provided escort along the ridge with a highpoint elevation of 3,680 feet.

Not the ideal time to be seated in an open scout car.

My favorite part of the Shenandoah National Park, through which the Skyline Drive runs, is its mountain meadows. Nowhere else have I seen such lovely, enormous meadows on the very tops of the mountains...

Perennial wildflowers put on a flashy show well into the fall: black-eyed Susans, goldenrod, and tall spikes of scarlet-red cardinal flower.

At sunset, the convoy dropped out of the mountains and rolled through the night under a brilliant, three-quarters moon. As they awaited inspection at the maneuver area, Buster snuck in a wash and shave—the first since his bath at the Goshen Inn. His three-day travelogue caught the next airmail run out of Miami. His post-script confessed this:

P.S. Note ② on the outside of envelope. I forgot to number first one I sent...

The Grasshopper and Other Bugs
Chapter Three

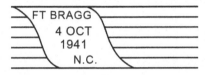

Pvt. N.F. Bedford, 2nd SQ. HQ. 101 Cav., A.P.O. 306, Fort Bragg, N.C. USA – airmail 10/4/41

Friday, October 3,
My Beloved,

Your sweet letter of Sept. 24th reached me today, my first day in camp. It was so nice and so loving that it made me feel very ashamed of all the cruel things I said about you when I was so angry...

Rightly so, he regretted the tantrum.

Tonight I am sitting in my scout car (only source of light here) beneath that famous Carolina moon—now in the full brilliance of the harvest season. As it shines down on me through the scud of windblown clouds I can't help feeling better knowing that the same moon must be shining on you and you must be thinking of me— for it's our moon, you know, and no one can share it but us together...

A harvest moon, the kind Canadian singer-songwriter Neil Young made famous. Buster chafed, imagining the moonlight shining in her eye, then surrendered to his surroundings.

The Grasshopper and Other Bugs

We are situated in what used to be a big crop field on top of a gently rolling hill. All around us are peach orchards. At first blush it all sounds quite picturesque, but it isn't. The weather is hot and sticky, the peach orchards are the home of little black gnats which don't bite but do get in your eyes, ears, nose, mouth, and food.

Robin related to fruit flies as ideal lab subjects used extensively in genetic research. Drosophila multiply inexhaustibly wherever they live; ripening peaches were consummate in more than one sense of the word.

We sleep on the ground under big pyramidal tents with only a bed-tick full of straw for comfort.

"Tick" is not to be confused with the pathogen transmitting parasite. "Ticking," a tightly woven fabric, was intended to prevent contents, in this case straw, from poking through.

All privates and corporals sleep six to a tent. Fortunately, as a Staff Sergeant, I have only two tent-mates. Our paraphernalia takes up the rest of the room... The openness of the field protects us from snakes and spiders.

Lucky Buster. The poor bastards of the *"Old Seventh Regiment"* were hunkered down in a swamp. Right off the bat, a Black Widow sunk its fangs into a Sergeant in the 101st Artillery Unit.

On a dime, he shifted gears from camp to cars.

From the Massachusetts Bureau of Motor Vehicles I understand you have been a bad girl again.

Again?

When you came back from Gina's on Aug. 10 you went through Templeton, Mass. too fast, (tsk, tsk! And after you had promised me to obey all speed laws, too!)

Was she pulled over?

No.

Which explains why—while not innocent—she was entirely unaware of the transgression.

The car, registered with New York plates, traced her from the Commonwealth to the address on Manor Circle. That's where Buster

Six Weeks for Boat Mail

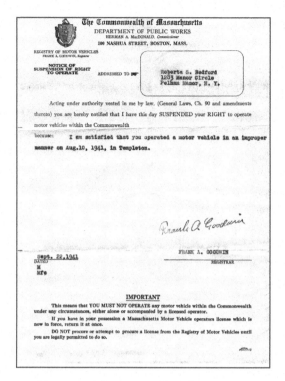

It's impossible to surrender a license one has never possessed.

pulled the citation from his parents' mail pile. The "Notice of Suspension" lacked specifics. He investigated to learn more.

...your permission to drive a car in Mass. has been suspended and the New York Bureau of Motor Vehicles notified.

She was in trouble in two states, and with her hubby, too.

He'd personally taught Robin about the art and excitement of driving. Eager to learn, she obediently gripped the wheel of their *Zephyr* "ten and two." But when the co-pilot seat was empty? She pushed the limits like young drivers often do.

Ten days before the offense, one of her "bosom buddies" teased, "It is good to know that so far no ardent M.P.'s have captured you and dragged you away because you are driving without a license." Then she confided (as besties always do) that she, too, had been doing the same all summer.

On the tenth of August, Robin sped solo, but not unnoticed, turning wheels of the *Zephyr* gracefully through historic Templeton Massachusetts.

The bad timing was coincidental. Four days before, Frank A. Goodwin, Registrar of Motor Vehicles, took a stance…"unless we save gasoline there is bound to be rationing." To that end, he announced reduced speed limits across the Commonwealth. Motorists driving faster than 40 mph in the open country and 25 mph in thickly settled areas would lose their licenses.

The Grasshopper and Other Bugs

Robin was counted among the 2,667 drivers who received a suspension notice from Goodwin's office that September. Buster omitted any mention of the need to surrender her operator's license. Presumably because he knew she didn't have one.

Well, you can square yourself when you get back by signing an affidavit <u>never</u> to drive over the speed limit again—subject to 5 days in jail if you are arrested again in Mass. <u>or N.Y.</u>....

The penalty for driving without a license? A ten-dollar fine; <u>no</u> prison time.

Now that he had her attention, Buster changed the subject. The latest rumor running around camp was another useful ruse to suggest Robin abbreviate her trip: A water shortage would force shortening of maneuvers.

Make your reservations on early boat (Nov. 17) <u>now</u> and I will let you know how things develop.

Under pressures of senior year at Smith, Robin set her intention months before: "I think I'd rather have the summer to play in." True to her word and in keeping with the Fable by Aesop, she aspired to be the grasshopper, not the ant.

It makes me very happy to know that your golf game is improving...

As he sat under the broiling North Carolina sun, her skiing expedition sounded attractive, too. Springtime in the Andes permitted both.

By happenstance, her letters revealed an almost forgotten aspect in the history of U.S. foreign relations. It centered on the sport she loved most. The boom in skiing fostered exchange-of-persons programs between the Americas, organized by the U.S. Department of State's "Division of Cultural Relations." In the Massachusetts' winter leading up to her June graduation from Smith, Robin tracked up the Northeast's finest terrain. Coincidentally, the Chilean ski team did, too.

It started when five teammates, and the president of the National Ski Association of Chile, debarked the *Santa Elena* in New York Harbor, on January 27, 1941. As <u>the first</u> athletes in winter sports history to travel north from the Southern Hemisphere, the team was elevated to celebrity status, especially among the college crowd. For twenty-three days they were guests of the Harvard and Yale ski clubs with whom they tuned up all over the hills of New England.

Feeling a certain ski-fever kinship, Robin kept an eye on the Chilean's well-publicized cross-country progress. They'd visited several western cities and nine winter resorts: Winter Park, Aspen, Alta, Sugar Bowl (Tahoe's oldest resort), Yosemite, and Mt. Rainier among them. Highlight of the swing west was Sun Valley, where the third Pan American Ski Championships were held in mid-March, after which, on March 28, they embarked from the port of New York and returned to Valpo.

In a turnabout move, Robin formulated her own John Muir-like quest, to wit: "The mountains are calling and I must go." Below the equator, the snow field at Farellones beckoned. This, the host site of the Pan American Ski Championships of 1937 and 1938, is where Ski Club Chile controlled a marvelous skiing district with thirty or more square miles of open slopes, none of it "lift-served." The Club's lodges and many private huts, nestled in a fairyland of white at 7,200 feet, anchored the base area. From Santiago, the thirty-mile motor trip east to the mountain village took an hour and a half. She'd secured a room at the Club's newest lodge, one that opened in June 1936, eleven months before the *first* Pan American Ski Championships. It had since gained a reputation for good food, modern conveniences, and attentive service. Sleeping quarters accommodated up to one hundred guests.

It wasn't until she reached Santiago, on her return route to Campamento Americano, that Robin spilled vivid details of her skiing expedition. She wrote from a social hotspot at the busiest intersection in the capital city. The Hotel Crillón, a thirty-bed luxury hotel on Augustinas Street, was well known to celebrities, intellectuals, diplomats, and executives of Braden Copper. At Fort Bragg, Buster would share tidbits of the airmail letter bearing the Crillón's regal crest. From their crusty digs, tea and cookies served daily at five o'clock sounded divine.

Yet something in her words forced him into this highbrow moment.

The Grasshopper and Other Bugs

Have you read any of the other books I gave you besides the Reader's Digest condensations? Those condensations are good and some of them are well worth re-reading and thinking about...

He recalled an article about cigarettes.

When I asked you to give up smoking I had what I thought to be good reasons for it and I wanted you to know them. It would disappoint me terribly if I thought that you had just given up because I had asked you to do so, or else had merely given up smoking when I was around...

Who today doesn't know of a sneaky someone like that?

The double-standard of the day blew through Buster's circling smoke rings. He puffed his pipe like a pacifier and outlived every doctor that ever told him to quit.

How?

The relaxing habit relieved stress and anxiety.

A corn cob pipe, the iconic accessory of General Douglas McArthur, would thematically suit Buster. For now, under the command of Lieutenant General Hugh A. Drum, he opted for the security of his Irish-made Peterson's pipe. Drum, the Commanding General of the 400,000 soldiers of the "First Army," would oversee rumbling troops as they crisscrossed nearly 1.5 million acres of wasteland, woodland, and some cultivated areas in an all-out sham war, over sixteen counties in North and South Carolina.

As General Drum said, these maneuvers are going to be made as much like real war as is possible...

Drum didn't miss a beat, evidenced by Buster's letter of Monday, October 6. The troops were up pre-dawn, 3:30 a.m., and off on their first maneuver.

Let me tell you, the Carolina dawn is dank and chill.

While some sarcastic wise-ass might have whistled "Carolina in the Morning," Buster cued off the famous poet Carl Sandburg, rephrasing words to one verse of Sandburg's best-known works, *Fog*.

Six Weeks for Boat Mail

The fog comes on little cat feet, spreading like an octopus over cornfield and woodland, chilling to the bone...

By 7:00 o'clock, the sun was up, and the temperature warming.

From our hilltop base camp we have proceeded out along the red clay roads... we are now in the midst of the pine woods parked beside a Negro's cabin. Just where we go from here, I have no idea.

Raised in the south, Buster comfortably reminisced scenes of his youth. He did not toe the racist line. No doubt, many others in the regiment did.

Time out, we are being strafed by an airplane.

Gunners practiced strafing tactics from a fighter plane. Bombers dropped small paper bags filled with flour.

...My job requires a great deal of running around fixing things, getting information that someone up above forgot to send out, and in general making a nuisance of myself at all hours of the day and night...

Unlike Aesop's ant colony, where order prevailed, a demoralized Buster explained the military caste system that lacked.

...I cannot find anywhere a clear delineation of duties of different officers and non-commissioned officers.

In the eyes of history, Buster was remarkably insightful. The maneuvers of 1941 were conceived as a pre-war mobilizing event to reveal flaws of organization and standardization.

The greatest deficiency exposed?

The shortage of young, adequately trained officers.

Well, I have a job to do here, so I had better close this letter. I only started it because I didn't want you to think I was too blue...<u>learn a lot</u> to help make us a happy home and write as often as you can...

On the outside of the envelope, he wrote ④, then recorded a gladsome football score from the Tiger's season opener: *P.S Princeton - 20; Williams - 7.*

One night, five days later, the Harvest Moon fell out of the sky.

The Grasshopper and Other Bugs

Well, it might as well have, as Buster had no use for it. He wanted his "grasshopper" to share in this miserable sham. As the hot Carolina sun set through the branches of the pine wood in which he was camped, he had this to say:

Over the landscape lies a pall of dust kicked up by the churning wheels of our mechanized units…the woods are parched…floored with pine needles dry as excelsior…stars offer no comfort…the moon is but a floodlight to show the way to enemy airplanes…

Un-damped by rain since July, the roads of red clay were ground to fine powder.

…Our khaki clothing has long since turned a salmon pink, every pore of the wool clogged with dust. My own shirt, where perspiration and clay have met, is stiff as a board…Our motorcyclists look just like (American) Indians, their faces and hands are so thoroughly covered. Eyes become bloodshot, skin parched, and hair stiff and tangled.

Added to the discomfort was scarcity of water for drinking, let alone water for bathing. What about food?

A lot of solders stuff themselves with soda-pop and candy…

They were just kids, after all. His unit was more imaginative.

Frequently we move so fast and far that our supply trains and field kitchens are unable to keep up with us, and even when they do they only leave us sandwiches for lunch…

Buster swore the most compact and nutritious food was bouillon; condensed cubes of beef concentrate stirred into boiling water.

We take it straight in the morning in place of coffee or mix two cubes with a can of vegetable soup at night, add water, and get a real meal out of a canteen cup… Small cans of Vienna sausage are good anytime of the day. They can be jammed between the carburetor and exhaust manifold and thus heated even though the scout car is on the road…Sardines and saltines make a good light lunch for hot days…

Six Weeks for Boat Mail

Occasionally we really have a feast on canned chicken and once I produced a can of anchovy fillets for hors d'oeuvres.

Many national armies provided salt tablets to their troops in WWII. Buster never mentioned them. He wisely replaced sodium lost through exertion and perspiration with dietary sources. Talk of electrolytes at the time pertained to motor vehicle battery maintenance. Today, those ionic compounds are found in premium beverages like Hoist®, military grade hydration powder sticks and pouches used for military field feeding and endurance athletes, alike.

When the troops returned from five days in the field, he was *"tickled to death"* to find three letters.

They were grand dear... Your letter of September 28th about the mine was a fine job... The one of Oct. 1st scolding me for being a "spoiled, jealous little boy" was sweet in parts...

He felt utterly worn down and insecure when he imagined his bride playing in a crystal cup of snowy mountains, a magical place styled by some as "the Switzerland of South America." Gliding around the mountain, atop a soft snowpack, layers of clothes naturally peeled off in the warmth of high-altitude sun at Farellones. Her accommodations at the modern stone lodge of the Ski Club Chile offered a slope-side gathering place to forge unique comraderies. There, while lounging on the sun deck, college-aged kids sporting Ray-Ban® Aviators tapped their cigarettes in hammered copper ashtrays and toasted their exchange of ideas over the top-selling cerveza, Corona®.

Believing she might not love him as much as she'd led him to believe, Buster launched a pre-emptive attack to raise her one on the jealousy score.

If I loved you less, then I would care less whether or not you wrote but would find solace in such pleasures as some soldiers enjoy...

That risqué business was no secret. Troops of the Louisiana Maneuvers that August and September descended upon New Orleans in more ways than one. In a battle for bragging rights, unprintable stories emerged.

The Grasshopper and Other Bugs

Call it "jealousy," or "little boy," or anything else...If I hadn't felt that way—and still do—I would have been a fool to marry you under the circumstances...

Proof that love is not categorically a positive emotion and feelings aren't easy to process for many men, he marshaled his will to twist the knife, stopped short, and changed the subject.

Now, let's not quarrel or call each other names any more, darling. Life is too short for there to be any bitterness between us...

It occurred to Buster that, as much as he complained, he was yet to inform Robin how these war games launched.

Ask around today. You'll find most civilians have never heard of this rising tide preceding the attack on Pearl Harbor. When it was all said and done, lessons learned in the maneuvers would lift all boats of the Allied forces.

Last night at 9:00 P.M. the final orders came out telling us what we were to do today...Immediately upon receipt of information as to the communications set-up, I had to dash around and inform the troop radio sergeants of what was expected of them—when they were to open station, what frequency to use, what codes were in force.

He turned in about midnight. Two and a half hours later he rolled his pack, pulled on his boots, made for the car, and opened the squadron radio net.

At 3:25 the long line of scout cars rolled out of camp. It was cold—about 40 degrees—and the pale half-moon on the wane gave an eerie light to that column of death and destruction...the air became colder and colder...that wet, creeping ghost of a mist goes right through your clothing and chills you to the marrow...Around 6:30 we pulled into our bivouac area to have breakfast and await the start of the problem...

While she skied and played golf, Buster faced another five days of filth and sleeplessness. A moment of envy welled up in a thought shift to home life.

...It is nice to know that Bud and Dorothy are settled and happy...

For both of her daughters, Lelia wished the happiness of a little apartment and a taste of home life before their men were called.

...I, too, wish you and I could settle down and enjoy married life. It is the one thing I look forward to more than anything else. However, we cannot always have just what we want—and even if we get it, it is better appreciated if we have to fight for it. This present strain caused by the Army is going to be either the eternal making or the breaking of our marriage. It takes courage on both sides to stick it out...

How was it possible Bud and Dorothy came to be "settled and happy"?

Settled and Happy
Chapter Four

By my standards, "settled and happy" is a relative term.

For Bud and Dorothy, it was true for one reason. Their years-long "dating game," much of it star-crossed and over long distances, was over. That's how they came to feel authentically "settled and happy" at a time in history when few young couples could.

Their dating game was in keeping with the definition of high school sweethearts, except for the fact they'd never stepped foot into the same school. Their adolescent love bloomed under the knowing noses of respected family connections. *Montana* family.

The short, but relevant back-story is this:

Bud hailed from one of Missoula's "pioneer families." His then twenty-one-year-old grandfather, C.H. McLeod, arrived in 1880 by rail and stagecoach. Imagine this streetscape: three general stores, a drug store, four saloons, and a barber shop lining a rutted dirt track. He took a clerkship that paid $1,000 a year in a business that he would eventually come to own, the Missoula Mercantile. That's what happens when a man marries the owner's daughter.

Bud's dad, Walter, was born in 1887, two years before Montana became a state. So began generations of Montana McLeods, well-networked due to their powerful sense of place and belonging. Their comfortable homes "in town" juxtaposed nicely with the family's lakeside summer cabin northeast of Missoula at Seeley Lake. A special place where young love naturally blossomed with temptation and opportunity.

On Dorothy's side of the house, William "Bill" Dixon and "Auntie Alta," Lelia's sister, settled in Missoula as newlyweds in 1908. Cow paths still meandered through town at a time when an inflow of settlers arrived from the Midwest, in Bill's case Indiana. The warm spirit of friendliness and cooperation in the tight-knit community drew folks dedicated to the common good of all.

Walter McLeod and Bill Dixon circulated among a group of like-minded "builders." Authentic Chamber of Commerce businessmen who, while building a better city, were simultaneously building their families and successful businesses.

They lived their lives like a case study in American civics. It explains how the Dixons and McLeods came to be devoted friends.

As Bud came of age, his parental marching orders aimed him toward prep-school at the old and respected Episcopal-affiliated Shattuck Military Academy in Faribault, Minnesota. The straight-line distance from his boyhood home to Shattuck was over a thousand miles east, in a different time zone. That experience may have been the reason, when it came time for college, he chose to enroll at the University of Montana, his father's alma mater. By then, his grandfather had devoted a half-century of service to the cause of higher education in the state.

Returning to Dorothy's story, T. Wayne and Lelia's commitment to a quality education sent her to Emma Willard, a preparatory school for young women in upstate New York. She enrolled one year behind Robin, at Smith College, in the class of "cute '42s."

Year to year, Lelia agonized over what to do with Dottie (as Dorothy was affectionately referred to by family) during school vacations. She'd explained it in a letter to Robin: "It's about any port in a storm. We are at our wits end to know what to do with Russell [their youngest] and Dorothy during vacations."

Uncle Dix and Lelia' eldest sister, Auntie Alta, answered prayers of salvation. Over the impossibly long school break, June to September, Dorothy made herself at home in Missoula.

Before dating came up, it's safe to assume Bud and Dorothy hung out with a gang of young Missoulans. I imagine it then came down to Bud wanting to date just one girl in the group, Dottie. The sudden chemistry might have surprised them both while comparing favorite ice-cream flavors, or some similarly simple thing.

I estimate Dorothy spent no less than six summers in Missoula, from the time Lelia and T. Wayne boarded her at Emma Willard preparatory school, in 1934, up until Smith College booted her out of the class of "cute '42s" in 1940, two academic years short of her college degree.

Bud transferred to New York University in the fall of 1940. He'd finished three years at University of Montana; one year of classes remained. The leap to the East Coast would place him within a train ride of the Smith College campus in Northampton.

Except their signals got crossed.

In a letter to Robin, Dottie made sense of the ill-fated scheme. "I told Bud I wasn't planning to return to Smith and Mother told me I wasn't going to any expensive Katie Gibbs—Guess she's trying to get me married off to Buddo—and the sooner the better to my mind."

The timing of her personal choice, to trade her Smith diploma for executive secretarial skills earned at Katherine Gibbs, would drop her in Bud's New York lap. Except Lelia burst that dreamy bubble. Appalled and disgusted, she demanded Dorothy's return to Chile.

Uncle Sam tangled the courtship further. Bud was among the sixteen million men between 21 and 36 to present himself to register for the draft on "R-Day," October 16, 1940.

An arrangement at colleges and universities throughout the country allowed students, like Bud, to register without having to return to their home precinct. As a college student, he could ask that his training be deferred until the end of the school year. Other than that, once a man put his name on a Grey Poupon-tinted Selective Service registration card, the rules were plain. He would stand ready to join the armed forces on short notice, carry his "government i.d." at all times, notify a local selective service board if he intended to take an extended trip, and obtain permission to leave the country.

The rules laid out a personal checklist for Bud in June 1941. He knew to a T what Uncle Sam expected.

Buzzing with boyish excitement, Bud wrote to Robin:

"I'm awaiting a reply to a letter inquiring the date of my call to active service. How truly wonderful it would be if the reply would state sometime in August! Then I could fly to see Dorothy! But considering past questionnaires, and present conditions, this hardly seems possible...I received such a nice letter from your mother inviting me to visit them. It is so kind of your mother and father...If it weren't for this world mess, Robin, I could sail down with you and stay a goodly time."

On June 11, Bud graduated from N.Y.U. with a Bachelor of Science in the "School of Commerce, Accounts and Finance." I question his attendance at commencement. With post-final-exam tunnel vision, he was off to the races on a flight that tracked from New York and then Miami, to finally arrive at Santiago Airport by way of Pan Am on June 16.

Coincidentally, on the same day, a rosy cheeked, posture-perfect Robin walked the line in the Smith College graduating class of '41.

Lelia dismissed the notion that Bud made the trip with the intention to marry Dorothy. Or she played dumb. Either way, on June 22, a civil wedding ceremony was recorded at House #71, the home of the senior Skinners in the "City of Stairs."

It was the same Sunday in June that the Reverend Dr. Willard Soper pronounced Robin and Buster husband and wife at the Huguenot Memorial Church in Pelham.

In South America, church weddings by a minister were not binding. To include Bud's side of the house in the nuptials, the newlyweds laid out a convincing plan. Upon their return to Missoula, Bud's Episcopal pastor would conduct a church ceremony. Lelia's sister, Auntie Alta, would arrange an evening reception at the newly reopened Hotel Florence, where Bud's dad was president.

Not to be cruel, only to be factually correct, I found no evidence of a church wedding for Dorothy and Bud. Details of what the bride wore, who attended, the flower variety that adorned the bouquet, and the altar were never written into the society column.

The Missoulian of Sunday, July 13 published a two-paragraph announcement. Placed middle of page ten, just above "marriage permits" issued by the clerk's office, it ran with a small heading: "W. Herbert McLeod Married in Chile." "Word was received here Friday that W. Herbert McLeod…was married to Dorothy Skinner of Rancagua, Chile, on Thursday of this week."

A similar article appeared in *The Independent-Record* of Helena a week later, Sunday, July 20:

"Of interest to his many friends in Helena, is the news of the marriage of W. Herbert McLeod…to Miss Dorothy Skinner of Rancagua, Chile. The marriage took place Thursday, July 10."

Both papers botched the actual wedding date, June 22. Did it matter to the lovebirds?

No.

They took up the mantle to be "settled and happy."

On a Pan Am flight out of Santiago, July 20, the newlyweds embarked on a milk-run. Flights were confined to daylight in South and Central America because there were neither lighted airports nor radio beams to keep the planes on track. They bounced along the east and northern coasts of South America, through Central America, and eventually set down in Los Angeles for Dorothy to "get" her trousseau.

Point of fact, this was a spree to *purchase* a trousseau. Essential, in 1941, to a bride's ability to set up housekeeping, it included items like bedding, kitchen linens, and personal attire. For some, like Dottie, everything from cotton undies to a tailored suit, a warm coat, and a fashionable chapeau were part of the package.

In San Francisco, Dorothy met Bud's California relatives. That's where Walter McLeod presented their wedding-gift, a 1941 Mercury *Comet* convertible. Suitcases and trousseau boxes shared space with the spare tire beneath a rounded sloping trunk. What didn't fit there landed in the full-width rear seat. Since she didn't know how to drive, Dottie rode shotgun. Along the northern route of the Lincoln Highway, they sped top down, cooled by the wind in the hot mid-summer sun. With the push of a knob, the electrically operated automatic top rose snug against wind and weather over the Sierra Nevada range.

They rolled into Missoula on Monday, August 10.

Three days later, Bud's mother and sister co-hosted a Thursday afternoon tea. Sunday's edition of *The Missoulian* reported more than one hundred fifty guests called to greet the bride. Bouquets of gladioli decorated the living rooms. A centerpiece of pink roses adorned the service table, where Auntie Alta hovered.

As required, Bud checked in with the local Selective Service board on his return to Montana. He hoped to get into business for a time, before being called.

The stars aligned. *The Missoulian* of Tuesday, September 9, reported his departure aboard the *North Coast Limited*. On the "crack train of the Northern Pacific...famed for its 'Great Big' baked potatoes" and meals as low as fifty cents, he traveled to New York City.

It was from New York State that Dorothy wrote, four months into their marriage, they were finally "settled and happy." They'd shuffled off to Buffalo? Rochester? Possibly Watertown.

Watertown, seventy miles north of Syracuse in the foothills of the Adirondacks, evolved as a hot spot. The Chamber of Commerce modestly claimed the business outlook as "very bright" in an area Buster candidly described as "God-forsaken" in August 1940. He was present and accounted for as a fledgling in the Squadron A Armory National Guard when New York's St. Lawrence Valley hosted three weeks of First Army maneuvers. At the conclusion, Lieutenant General Hugh A. Drum had seen enough. He appealed for conscripted troops and production of needed weapons by "national obligation." Within weeks, FDR signed Proclamation 2425, the Selective Training and Service Act.

Settled and Happy

Between Labor Day 1941 and the spring of 1942, Pine Camp (known today as Fort Drum) nearly *quadrupled* in size. Twelve thousand troops arrived, with many from Fort Knox, Kentucky as part of the newly created Fourth Armored Division.

Ten miles outside the Fort, competition was keen for housing in Watertown, the same way it was for newlyweds around Fort Devens, or any other fort for that matter. Defense industrial activity created employment opportunities for men like Bud.

When Dorothy's convincing letter arrived c/o Braden Copper at the office in Sewell, Lelia and Robin acknowledged her blissful "settled and happy" domestic setup. The rush was over. Bud was working. Dottie kept herself busy nesting in a home where they enjoyed all the comforts. They made new friends. Life was good, except for this looming question: When and where would Bud be called to serve?

Above all else, Dorothy's due date in March revealed the June newlyweds had wasted no time to start a family.

For Buster, mid-October categorically represented football season. Even though only three years had passed since his own last rumpus within the walls of Princeton's ivy-walled Palmer Stadium, he reminisced like an elder over the days when he eagerly looked forward to stepping out of class and onto the practice field. He put it like this in a note to Robin on October 16:

...when battles were fought for fun and hostilities ended at the sound of a whistle! Won't it be grand when sportsmanship and friendship return again to all the earth?

A recent letter from the senior Bedfords unveiled a plan. They would soon take a room at the North Carolina vacation destination of Pinehurst, about fifty miles west of Fort Bragg. Three famous golf courses, a polo club, tennis, and lawn bowling amounted to a side show. As devoted mollycoddlers, solace for Buster is what mattered most.

It's a striking fact that mission-based organizations also chose Pinehurst to deliberate over serious war-related matters. For example, Rotary

International leaders opposed worker strikes in defense industries and the American Red Cross tackled a strategy to implement its largest training program ever.

Hosiery manufacturers met to discuss distribution of yarns to substitute for silk.

Why?

By executive order, FDR cut off trade with Japan, sole silk supplier to the U.S., at the end of July. Back-stocks of silk in the U.S. were commandeered for parachutes and other national defense purposes. Resourceful brides-to-be sought parachutes that failed rigorous inspection, then upcycled the rejected folds of white nylon and silk to fashion wedding dresses.

If Buster knew anything of the planning that went on inside the halls and walls of Pinehurst, it didn't concern him that Sunday afternoon.

```
FT BRAGG
20 OCT
1941
N.C.
```

Pvt. N.F. Bedford, 2nd SQ. HQ. 101 Cav., A.P.O. 306, Fort Bragg, N.C. USA – October 20, 1941 (airmail)
Marked "#8"

Sunday, October 19
My Dearest One,

As I write this I am sitting peacefully at Pinehurst beneath the shade of the waxy green leaves of a giant magnolia tree, symbol of the Old South. The afternoon is only pleasantly warm when me sits quietly, reminiscent of the unhurried richness of the Southern way of life which I can feel through the polished surface of this resort town built with Yankee money.

Bostonian James Walker Tufts was the Yankee philanthropist to whom Buster referred. A first-class health resort intended to be a retreat for New Englanders grew from a previously harvested pine forest in the Sandhills of North Carolina.

Settled and Happy

War is far away. Two hot baths, a haircut, shampoo, massage and manicure have removed most of the traces of the accumulated dirt of three weeks in the field.

Besides Robin, his heart was full of football action. In Durham the day before, he sat with several thousand soldiers among 25,000 fans assembled to watch Colgate's Red Raiders in their attempt to overthrow Duke's Blue Devils. On their home turf, the Devils took down the Raiders, twenty-seven to fourteen.

It does not seem possible that less than forty hours ago I was covered from head to foot with the fine red clay dust of the Carolina secondary road-net, sleepless, exhausted. Still less does it seem possible that in another twelve hours I will be up in the darkness of the early morning, shivering and cursing...Every day I can feel myself slipping...

In keeping with ancient military tradition, every man blindly fell in line. Buster didn't seek anarchy, but in a country where the best minds had been devoted to civilian pursuits and industrial organization was pre-eminent, he asked this:

...Where is that co-operation of great and small which made democracy work by virtue of the very mass and excellency of ideas produced by people of all classes...

And their places of provenance, too.

What is democracy and where lie its virtues if it is not a co-operative enterprise to which all contribute?

It's the kind of lesson he taught holding court at the head of the dinner table when I was a kid. Mindful, rational thinking.

...If I had only to choose my pursuits with no consequences attached I should say only that my heart cries out to be free of all this mess...

Eighty-plus years later, with consequences of climate crisis, political polarization, a global pandemic, and an intolerable Russian regime, the hearts of more than just Buster's children, grandchildren, and great-grands cry to be free of their mess, too.

The future to me looks chaotic...Somehow, crazily, perhaps childishly—I can't help remembering the Boy Scout Oath—"On my honor I will do my best to do my duty to God and my Country..." To you, who perhaps will suffer equally or maybe more from my attitude, I can only quote those lines—immortal to me—from Sir Richard Lovelace's poem "To Lucasta, On Going to the Wars:"—"I would not love thee, dear, so much, loved I not honor more."

He mapped out an action plan. What if his low vision, 20/70 in each eye, did not meet the physical requirement to serve as a Signal Corps officer? He assured Robin of a Plan B in the offing. His call of duty meddled with her future as much as his.

If I am not successful, I am going to do my best to get out of the Army, but I shall not return to law school until the war is over. My next step will be toward getting a job in an airplane factory, producing airplanes...

Bolstering national defense while furthering his own future ends was inspired, yet self-serving.

I should like to get the feel of making things with my own hands, to gain some knowledge of the technical aspects of making an airplane...to learn the nomenclature of the parts and machines, and processes which go towards making aircraft.

Were he to seek a career in...Air Law or any type of patent law...the skill set would be knowledge gained. A building block; confidence in problem solving.

Next, I would like to join a union.

To Lucasta, Going to the Wars
By Richard Lovelace

Tell me not (Sweet) I am unkind,
That from the nunnery
Of thy chaste breast and quiet mind
To war and arms I fly.

True, a new mistress now I chase,
The first foe in the field;
And with a stronger faith embrace
A sword, a horse, a shield.

Yet this inconstancy is such
As you too shall adore;
I could not love thee (Dear) so much,
Lov'd I not Honour more.

Why? Newspaper headlines reported on a wave of national defense strikes. Several hundred million dollars in Army and Navy orders were tied up because of them. Walk-outs affected more than metal mining. Uninterrupted steel production was necessary for the U.S. to arm itself adequately. Parts production and assembly of planes, jeeps, trucks, and tanks were impacted. This wasn't an argument over working conditions or wages. It was the posturing of union bosses; labor dictators who wanted the U.S. government to compel non-union workers to join. On that topic, FDR called their demand "too much like the Hitler methods toward labor."

To impress all seriousness upon Robin, Buster articulated how his experiences equated to personal power with respect to managing labor-related disputes.

...Unions are going to make or break this country after we finish taking care of Hitler, depending on how their energies are guided...Now that my plans have been stated, I guess we ought to get around to your plans...

I imagine Robin sipped a breath of air and her throat tightened. She continued reading.

Maybe I was too selfish in asking you to marry me so soon...

What was he playing at? They were among scores of young couples, including almost all their friends, for whom marriage proved too compelling to resist. Many accelerated their wedding plans. Come what may, they vowed to face the future together. Now he fished for reassurance of her love.

Perhaps you would have had a more enjoyable trip as a single person...I don't quite know how to say it, but I don't want you to do anything your heart doesn't tell you to do.

His words washed over her like a set of waves, each successively larger than the last, leading up to this final blow:

If you don't see your duty as I see mine, if you feel you would be happier at home in Chile, than you would be with me wherever I might be, then stay there until your heart calls you back to me.

It was a bold statement and a chilling prompt. After writing it, he might have stared blindly at the page with tears in his eyes, praying the resolute kick in the pants would force Robin to get clear on her own feelings and priorities. Those that now, for reasons soon revealed, seemed contrary to his.

He closed the letter, sealed the envelope, marked it number eight, bid his parents goodbye, and returned to base camp, despondent. His powerful love for her left him uncertain and confused as to where he fit in. So began the waiting game for her response.

Before dropping it in the mailbox, Nat scribbled optimistically on the outside of the envelope:

"Official order just issued making Buster Squadron Radio Sgt. Dad."

Yet to receive Robin's response to his sobering letter from Pinehurst, Buster began note number thirteen, dated Sunday, November 2, with a light-hearted story of how he'd spent the weekend in Greensboro, North Carolina.

...When we arrived in town things looked pretty bad, for all the hotels were filled and there were soldiers everywhere...On a long shot, I called up the home of one of my Princeton classmates.

It was an outside chance worth taking. Buster's chum was up north in grad school but Mrs. Cone, his mom, did what any Southern mother would. She insisted that Buster come stay at their home and bring his friends, too.

Three of us descended upon her to be shown the most generous Southern hospitality. A suite of rooms and bath apiece...

Locals were encouraged to be kind to the men on maneuvers. When she insisted Buster borrow her Cadillac, he respectfully accepted, "Yes, Ma'am." With decadence worthy of the wheels, the boys dined on steak and oysters for lunch.

We went to a football game last night between two local colored colleges who wore uniforms similar to Notre Dame and Princeton—The Notre Dames won.

Dating back to an era immediately preceding the Civil War, the earliest "colored colleges" (located in the North) were devoted to the education of African Americans in the United States. More followed, at a time when segregation limited equal access to education, long before the Civil Rights Act of 1964. It took an act of Congress, in 1965, to create the acronym HBCU, "Historically Black Colleges and Universities."

Lauded by Presidential Proclamation as "vibrant centers of intellectual inquiry and engines of scientific discovery and innovation," it seems to me it wasn't until the election of vice-president Kamala Harris in 2020 when all fifty states woke. VP Harris, a 1986 alum of Howard University (est. 1867), is one of many HBCU grads, including the likes of Martin Luther King, Jr., Supreme Court Justice Thurgood Marshall, multi-media mogul Oprah Winfrey, and director Spike Lee.

It didn't matter to Buster that "the Notre Dames won." He was delighted to be in the stands watching the game he loved best.

After the game we went to a dance given in honor of the 101st. Not great, - all the local Junior League was out at the Country Club dance for Officers.

Social climbing.

After doing some shopping we came home early, talked to Mrs. Cone for an hour, then went to bed. Nice smooth white sheets! Oh boy!

Southern hospitality dictated a hearty home-cooked breakfast. The three musketeers would wake to the sound of Mrs. Cone's clanking skillets and the smell of sizzling bacon. They filled their plates with scrambled eggs, hominy grits, buttermilk biscuits, and thickly sliced bacon, bowed their heads with thanks, dropped linen napkins in laps, and ate like plantation owners.

Truthfully, his mention of a *"swell southern breakfast"* only popped up incidentally in a P.S. to Robin, but that's how I imagine it went down.

Heavenly as the three-day leave seemed, Buster was haunted by the sinking of the USS *Reuben James*. Three days earlier, on Halloween, torpedoes fired by a German U-Boat ripped into the port side of the destroyer as the vessel escorted a convoy in the North Atlantic near Iceland. All seven officers plus ninety-three enlistees died; forty-four survived. The *James* was the first naval warship lost to hostile action.

Standing before 7,000 men at the maneuver critique on Friday, Buster recorded General Drum's remark…*the situation has turned from "serious" to "grave."*

Woodie Guthrie captured the story in a ballad written immediately after. His chosen lyrics to the now famous song, *The Sinking of the Reuben James*, humanized the loss with these questions:

> *Tell me, what were their names?*
> *Tell me, what were their names?*
> *Did you have a friend on the good Reuben James?*

Drum looked at the news as adequate proof of the seriousness with which they trained. Buster viewed it differently.

There are pretty reliable rumors that the last two weeks of manoeuvers will be called off because the Army General Staff…is being held in Washington during the crisis.

The Army General Staff were the bandleaders for the field combat action. Their fertile military minds were all detained in D.C. Without leadership to test troop organization and technique of the Red and Blue Armies in the weeks leading up to Thanksgiving, what was the point?

I don't like the looks of it, and I won't be happy until you are back here with me…

Upon Buster's return to Fort Bragg from Greensboro, a letter from Robin, dated October 27, awaited him. He turned around note number fourteen dated November 8.

Due to your visit to Santiago you apparently missed my letter from Pinehurst… It means so much, dear, to know whether or not you are still with me and are coming back soon to help me do my part—and do your own, too.

In the letter intended to befriend his mother-in-law, dated September 11, Buster instructed Lelia in no uncertain terms: "…return her to me by early December at the latest." Writing to Robin on October 19 from

Pinehurst, he waffled when he cast this barbless hook: "Stay there until your heart calls you back to me."

That romantic platitude was scuttled with the sinking of the Reuben James.

The weather is cold now. At Fort Devens there has been snow already. Even down here we have reached the long winter underwear stage. But this certainly must be mild compared to Russia. If half the Germans don't die of pneumonia it will surprise me...

More doleful than angry, he resigned to the gray chill of winter in the Northern Hemisphere. Robin's story was entirely different. Her cheeks held a color no rouge could imitate. Springtime in the Andes was everything and more than she expected.

```
FT BRAGG
 10 NOV
  1941
  N.C.
```

Pvt. N.F. Bedford, 2nd SQ. HQ. 101 Cav., A.P.O. 306, Fort Bragg, N.C. USA – November 10, 1941 (airmail)
Marked "#15"

Saturday, Nov. 8
My Darling,

Your sweet letter of Oct. 31 reached me this morning, doing my tired old heart a world of good...But honey, all the thrill of the first part of your letter left me when you said that you would not be back for Thanksgiving...if your parents still insist that you stay longer with them, I am afraid that I must insist you come back.

Respectably, Buster disliked "insisting" and preferred she make her own decisions. He pleaded instead.

I <u>need</u> you, dear, and I need you much more than your parents do...I want a good home life built around <u>you</u>, just as I want to share the first excitement of return to civilization with <u>you</u>...I've been as unselfish as I could and I'm awfully glad that you have had a good time while I have been living the life of a monk down here...so

Six Weeks for Boat Mail

now it is up to you to come back and be my wife or else stay down there and remain a daughter merely. The choice is yours.

Enough to raise the hackles of any self-respecting woman, it must have struck Robin as a wallop of an ultimatum. Though, it begs the question, why would a June bride *not* make the effort to create the joyful marriage memory of a first Thanksgiving as man and wife. The holiday fell three months from her departure from New York; one day short of nine weeks since her parents met the S.S. *Elena* in Valpo.

For one reason or another, Buster appeared to be mad at her and/or himself, ever since. Simply put, his duty and love of honor meddled with his feelings and hers.

He proposed making Thanksgiving reservations at Pinehurst. If she would fly back to Miami in time to catch the Seaboard Air Line Railroad to the Southern Pines train station, his parents would be there to meet her.

...From Pinehurst you can drive back to Pelham with Mother and Dad, get the car, and go up to Mass. to find us a place to live.

The affidavit awaiting her autograph slipped his mind. Along U.S. Route 1, fiery fall foliage provided cover for speed traps from New York to Massachusetts. Five days in the clink would be a blot on the Bedford name should she blow through some small town at a gas-wasting speed of 28 mph.

The main part of your baggage I guess you will have to ship by boat...

When Saturday's letter didn't make the mail, he wrote a Monday morning note to underscore his feelings. He reasoned if they missed their first Thanksgiving as husband and wife it would be by Robin's choosing; not the fault of the Army.

Our first year of married life would be so terribly incomplete...

Surprise Correspondent
Chapter Five

On receipt of her soldier boy's letter from Pinehurst, a distressed Robin responded. Was it the notion, "you would have had a more enjoyable trip as a single person" that caught her by surprise? Or was it his suggestion to "stay there until your heart calls you back to me" that slapped her into action.

After reading the contents of envelope number eight, I imagine she gazed into his face. The black and white portrait, neatly propped on her bedstand, was his gift on her twenty-second birthday, the day she wrote in her diary, "Today we decided to get married June 22nd."

She'd set fairytale intentions with Buster, to be settled and happy in a home they'd call their own. Now she imagined Buster dreadfully chilled, suffering filth and sleeplessness, dark shadows heavy beneath his eyes.

As she grappled with forces of his circumstances, she wrestled with unsettled affairs of her own. An inner impulse called her back to revisit his letter marked number ten, written October 25.

My Sweetheart,

Please don't worry about me darling! So far I have managed to get along quite well in spite of any temporary physical discomforts and I have yet to be even slightly ill... occasional nights without sleep are of little moment to one who has spent many a sleepless week grinding away at some important problem while in college.

Six Weeks for Boat Mail

Robin wasn't the serious student type who would squander anything more than a single sleepless night on schoolwork. She'd booked <u>one</u> all-nighter at Smith, writing an observation paper on "social malice." Creepy subject matter. Thoughts of serial killers might have kept her company through the darkest hours before dawn.

The fact is any sleeplessness on her part while in college was attributable to dating behavior; an over-scheduled social calendar that propelled her toward college campuses and ski slopes across New England. And, eventually, to Florida where she met Buster in 1939, over Christmas vacation her junior year at Smith.

To prove he hadn't gone completely haywire, Buster bucked up to console her with a sanctimonious explanation of the war situation. With his finger on the pulse of U.S. military leadership, he offered this:

If I were you I shouldn't worry too much about the U.S. going to war or at least about the immediate effect on us personally...we are not ready to make a declaration yet as we can do the Allies more good by remaining neutral...even if we do declare war it will be chiefly a Naval and Air battle, for we do not have enough shipping to send and supply more than two divisions abroad—and won't have for another two years.

There were about 15,000 men in an Army division. It would take thousands of *tons* of supplies to outfit 30,000 troops sent overseas. Food rations, clothing, tools, tents, maps, petrol, oils, lubricants, fortification, and barrier materials such as lumber and barbed wire, weaponry and ammunition of multiple varieties, trucks and tanks, repair parts, medical supplies, and, paramount to Buster, all the component electronics to support Signal supply and communications.

However, I am a little worried about your being stranded in Chile...

Coincidentally, the cover of *LIFE* magazine published Monday, October 20, 1941, depicted a photograph of a Pan Am Clipper. His desire stirred to have her board that plane and get home.

Surprise Correspondent

On a cold Carolina morning, sixteen days before the 101st Calvary would break camp and head north to Devens, Buster penned the contents of envelope number fifteen.

Meanwhile, a new character unexpectedly wrote his way into Robin and Buster's story. On letterhead stationery pulled from a desk drawer at The Hotel Carrera, in Santiago, an amorous admirer scrawled sentiments across the page.

Located in the civic district of the capital city, adjacent to the Chilean presidential palace, the Carrera opened in 1940. It stood out as a skyscraper by Chilean standards; seventeen floors, replete with a roof garden restaurant and pool for guests. There, it is rumored, women bathed topless in the sun. Far below, on the street front, bronze doors opened into an art-deco-themed lobby where murals, marble pillars, and crystal lamps appealed to an upscale clientele.

Letterhead Hotel Carrera, 516 Merced, Santiago de Chile[1]

Mrs. Roberta Bedford
Braden Copper Co.
Sewell % Sr. Skinner
November 10, 1941

My Darling,

If fortunes with a smiling face
  Strew roses on our way,
When should we stop to pick them up
  Today, my friend, today.
But should she frown with face
  Of care
And talk of coming sorrows
When should we grieve if grieve
  We must
Tomorrow, friend, tomorrow.

---

1 Correspondence on Hotel Carrera letterhead remains true to the style (and misspellings) written thereon.

Did Robin believe these poetic words were assembled by her pen friend? Maybe. But it was an easy discovery to learn they were pirated. Charles R. Skinner (no relation to T. Wayne) arranged a collection dedicated to his wife and children, first published in 1909. It was titled *The Bright Side, Little Excursions into the Field of Optimism*.

And so you see my dearest I've gotten that mañana attitude, and little seems to care since I've met you. A bit disconcerting I know, but when one is in the state of mind as I am, a civil and sane epistle can hardly come from an otiose land. The paramount thing to me, my little cactus plant, is that your feelings are sincere and that if your mind and heart may be a bit esoteric it is really going to hurt.

Who is this guy?

His letter, addressed to "*Mrs.*", is enough to let one cat out of the bag. His "little cactus plant" did not hide the ring on her finger.

Everyone who's ever been in love knows terms of endearment are often peculiar. To Buster, Robin compared to a little white flower. He said so in a soulful letter written October 8:

"When I plucked it from beside my bed-roll here in the pine-wood, its petals were so soft and white I couldn't help thinking of you. Its very feel to the touch made me want to be with you again, to feel the soft warmth of your skin, to hold you close, my head on your breast, close my eyes, and know the complete peace and relaxation that only your love can give me."

The Hotel Carrera correspondent continued.

I sincerely and truthfully say, as I've never said before, that your tropism has propensity'd me towards you which I know is nonsensical, but quite axiomatic. I've never felt as I do right now and if our love for one another is only perennial, at least they can't take that from me.

In some form of tropism, this halfwit poked out from under a rock. In two sentences the heart on his sleeve revealed, to me, a dopamine-drunk wife poacher, botanical illiterate, and perennial loser.

It is now a bit after three in the afternoon and I've just hung the phone on the hook after being reassured of my happiness, future and love. My nickname for you is quite explicable for your vision in my mind, your voice, your joviality, your pedantic, all fill my heart and spine with shivers that make me jump a mile. It is hard to explain but I am sure you see my point.

Did she?

To be quite truthful I am still a bit dubious as to your sincerity—why I don't know—but things of happiness, splendor and good luck that happen to me always seem to show a spark of skepticism...From now till Thursday seems so far off my sweet that I guess I had just better make the best of it and see if I can line some sort of a future out for us. You know I almost seem to enjoy the thought of working now that I've got something really to work for...Good buy my dearest, till later, Love David

"David," the suddenly-too-familiar stranger, counted the seventy-two hours until he'd see her again. How does a person line out "some sort of a future" with a married woman in three days' time?

For now, Robin holed up like Rapunzel in the "City of Stairs" with considerable distance between them. The descent from the El Teniente mining camp was an arduous undertaking. From Sewell it was seventy kilometers (43 miles) of twisting and turning along a narrow-gauge rail to get to Rancagua. Santiago was another eighty km (50 miles) by a "train carriage" known to be overcrowded and smelly. For the senior Skinners, quarterly pilgrimages to escape the altitude and take care of business were necessary. Any other excursion had to be deemed essential.

Meanwhile, Buster and other lionhearts of the 101st bolstered themselves for the big showdown under the command of Lieutenant General Hugh Drum. The Blue Army would face off against the Reds in the first of a two-phased final Carolina maneuver.

```
    ⟋ FT BRAGG ⟍
    ⟍  12 NOV  ⟋
         1941
         N.C.
```

Pvt. N.F. Bedford, 2nd SQ. HQ. 101 Cav., A.P.O. 306, Fort Bragg, N.C. USA – November 12, 1941 (airmail)
Marked "#16"

Wed., November 12
My Beloved,

Left camp at 2:30 A.M. on the big manoeuver. It is bitterly cold. I have on two pair wool underwear, two complete uniforms, sweater, field jacket, overcoat, and am wrapped up in a comforter...

His unit awaited word of *"the big work"* that the Army General Staff planned for that night. The rumor mill failed with respect to an early end to the maneuvers. The sinking of the USS *Reuben James* fortified the purpose and mission of the war games.

Our assignment is to locate enemy tanks and report their locations so that they can be destroyed before they attack our forces. We are expected to be "killed" or captured, but if we are successful it may mean victory for our side. The success of our whole mission depends on my radio—whether we can get back the information before we are done for by the enemy...

Anyway, I hope to find you at Pinehurst when I get back. If I don't I shall be bitterly disappointed...But, you couldn't let me down that way honey, it wouldn't be you.

This will be my last letter until I see you dear, so remember how terribly much I love you, take good care of yourself, and hurry back to me.

Your own loving, Buster

Letterhead Hotel Carrera, 516 Merced, Santiago de Chile

Mrs. Roberta Bedford
Braden Copper Co.
Sewell % Sr. Skinner
November 15, 1941
My Darling,

This spirs and spimm of enthusiasm, happiness and work for the past two weeks is hardly inexplicable for my Dearest you've changed my whole outlook, and I now have something for which I really want to work. I know of no other and more effective method of telling you that I truly love you and want you to be close by----and a day for you to have faith in me and keep my faith in myself...

I have shown spasms of poetry the past two weeks, and there is a childhood diddy banging around in my mind which reminds me of my father (for he taught it to me one day while we were sailing) and relates directly to you. It is John Keat's poem and runs like this—

"A thing of beauty is a joy forever
It's loveliness increases
It shall never pass into nothingness"

I hope that I am not too emotional, but damn it all I just have to tell you that I want you more than anything else in the world.

So did Buster.

It is typical of me to involve myself into complications but with you behind me, I am sure that we'll be able to work out our problems.

News reports revealed he had, indeed, involved himself in complications. As one among many youth hostlers from the U.S. on an extended South American tour that "summer," he'd raced, by invitation, for "Club Andino" in the "all South American Competitions." For ten years, ski clubs in Chile, patterned after Scandinavian Clubs, became a driving force in popularity of the Andean sport, fashioning its modern reputation for the most glorious ski terrain anywhere in the world.

David's dramatic story swirled in newsprint.

An avalanche, caused by an earthquake, blocked the roads from the village of Farellones to la ciudad de Santiago. David and another brave American soul forged through blinding snow, long-lost trails, and Andean fog to beat a track from the Andino Club lodge back to civilization. Sustained by coffee and crackers, their survival was attributed to an affable dry-goods merchant. Ginger ale mixed with two-hundred-proof alcohol kept the boys from developing pneumonia.

Better than Buster's bouillon, Robin vividly imagined David's heroic quest. He'd beguiled her with his climactic survivor's account.

Six Weeks for Boat Mail

Only Saturday afternoon—seems like a month since I've seen you...

Evidently their Thursday rendezvous on November 13, one week before Thanksgiving, went according to plan. An eleven-minute walk along flat city streets separated his place at the Hotel Carrera and hers at the Crillón. There I imagine they might have sipped pisco sours in the glass-roofed lounge.

She'd since returned to the mining camp, forcing the ski celebrity into a two-day emotional void. He turned to what's recognized today as compulsive shopping. With forty shopping days until Christmas, he'd be ahead of every other man on the planet and most women, too.

...I am buying—Lord knows which what—ditties and things...a couple rugs (Indian) and some Alpaca slippers for preasants if and when I ever return to the States. Crazy—I'll say...

I told you to come down—that there would be a party—well there is one oh! OH! And promises to be very good. Be smug and stick in the mts. So that I'll have a misserable time without you—go on, see if I care.

It's impossible to know for certain if Robin's good sense prevailed, or Lelia flatly denied her the privilege. To me, David lined up as the farthest speck in the universe.

Went to the football game last night...

A soccer match, not to be confused with American football that Buster so loved.

It was really very interesting and the parades and demonstrations were magnificently priformed. Wished all the time that you were with me...David

The long Thanksgiving holiday weekend in Campamento Americano, November 20 – 23, rolled out a brass-tacks plan to obtain Robin's necessary certificates of health and vaccinations. Her December 3 departure from Santiago was set without any wiggle room. Accidentally on purpose, it seems she neglected to tell David.

On the Pan Am Clipper, she would travel by air via Argentina.

Surprise Correspondent

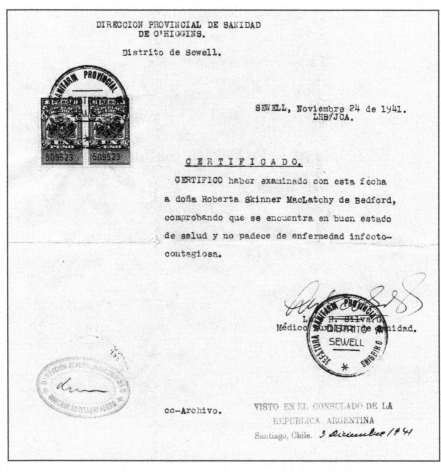

Travel from Chile to Argentina required a Certificate of Health.

For Buster, Phase I of the "big" Carolina Maneuver commenced on November 16.

History tells us a five-day maneuver was the standard length established by example in Louisiana. But it's a fact General Headquarters (GHQ) had no <u>set</u> time limit. As it happened, Phase I Carolina raged straight through Thanksgiving Day and on into Friday, November 21. General Drum's First Army opened with a coordinated attack at dawn. In a most decisive victory, the "Battle of the Pee Dee River," was all over by 0840.

Resigned to the fact that Robin let him down, Buster joined his parents for leftovers on an abbreviated furlough at Pinehurst.

Six Weeks for Boat Mail

> **Fórmulario No. 3**
>
> El poseedor de este certificado deberá revacunarse el año 19...
>
> **República de Chile**
>
> **SERVICIO NACIONAL DE SALUBRIDAD**
>
> Provincia _O'Higgins_ Localidad _Sewell_
>
> **Certificado de Revacunación contra la viruela**
>
> Doña _Roberta Skinner Maclatchy de Bedford_ de _veintidós años_ de edad natural de _Estados Unidos de A._, domiciliado en _Sewell_ calle _____ No. _____ ha sido REVACUNADO con _viruela_ con resultado _de esta fecha_
>
> Fecha _Noviembre 24/941_
>
> Firma _____
>
> NOTA.—Este certificado no tiene validez alguna en la República de Chile si no lleva la firma y timbre de la persona encargada de controlar el resultado de la vacunación.
>
> *Servicio Gratuito*
>
> **DISTRITO SEWELL**

No charge for Robin's vaccinations in the mining camp.

D-Day for "Carolinas Phase II" began at 0630 the morning of November 25 under clear, cold skies. Unbeknownst to anyone it was to be the Army's last peacetime training exercise. Two days into what would turn out to be a final dress rehearsal, the AP out of Washington reported the U.S. put the issue of peace vs. war in the Pacific squarely up to the Japanese Government.

A Japanese aircraft carrier strike force weighed anchor on November 26. Across the rolling gray seas of the North Pacific, they headed for the Hawaiian Islands.

Desperado
Chapter Six

A bold attempt is half of success. The proverbial meaning was lost on David, but he naturally embraced the approach as most young men do. In six pages of single-spaced type, the rag bond paper ran out on page four. Pages five and six, on onion skin, were nearly pecked apart by heavy metal keystrokes. Misspellings, compounded by especially messy typos, got worse. Several hand corrections stood out in light blue ink. So did the Roman numerals written in the top left corner of each page. The feeble attempt to fix everything, including his future, fell to pieces.

Letterhead Hotel Carrera, 516 Merced, Santiago de Chile
Mrs. Roberta Bedford
Braden Copper Co.
Sewell % Sr. Skinner

November 30, 1941
My Darling,

It is now Sunday morning and I am still brewing over the disappointment of not seeing you this weekend.

Robin descended from the mining camp with parental escort. Now within touching distance, Lelia smelled trouble. In and around the Hotel Crillón, on the busiest streets of Santiago, she attempted to keep Robin on a short leash.

Six Weeks for Boat Mail

Truly I've never been so disappointed...but I realize that we are and will be under extreme difficulties for the next several months to come. The past several weeks have been the most dragged ones... not to mention how difficult and hard this weekend has been after setting my heart on one last fling with you here in Chile.

Now after expressing my immediate feelings there are several others which I too wish to put accross. First and most paramount is that I demand complete confidence, truth and honor between the two of us. I'll promise to keep my end of the bargain and I am sure that you will do the same. Remember if there is anything from the most minute to the extreme you are expected to come to me directly rather than by finess.

Truth, honor, integrity is a three-legged stool. The "complete confidence" he demanded? Tippy at best.

Second — as we've already talked over is that I believe that it is only fair to all concerned that you live with your husband long enough to prove to yourself that you either love him or not.

I understand now why Robin primed me at age seventeen with advice worthy of a movie scene: "When a man proposes marriage, tell him you'll think about it." On the roadmap of life, misplaced ardor coupled with inexperience often leads to a wrong turn.

Third—is that I believe that we should see each other in New York upon my arrival...to be truthful I'am really scared that things will involve themselves in such a manner that it will be impossible. Anyways the show in New York is up to you... and your complications. I shall arrive via C.S.A.V. the 22nd of December and if you can't meet the boat lets at least have a letter there so I shall know what to do and how the land lies.

An elementary arithmetic computation informed me if David planned to arrive in New York on December 22, his departure date was, give or take, just four days away. Aboard the S.S. *Imperial*, a CSAV (Compañía Sud Americana de Vapores) diesel-powered cargo vessel, he would travel at seventeen knots among containers filled with Chilean exports—copper, copper ore, fruits in refrigerated holds, and wine delivered in time to celebrate Christmas in North America. Berths for 164 passengers were a cheap ticket for youth hostelers to return to the States, although German U-boats prowling the Atlantic coastline might handily change that itinerary.

Forth—deals with me and what I am planning to do. As you already know my education in a formal manner is finished so we can count that out at the present time...

As one of five children that endured the Great Depression, a college degree did not rank among family priorities. How far did his formal education go?

One year. At Middlebury College. The small liberal arts school in Vermont was working its way up toward prominence. There, he affiliated with the Chi Psi fraternity, volunteered on the "Frosh Frolic" committee, and skied a lot. How old was he?

Nineteen. He'd fallen for an "older woman."

...As for the alturnatives I can really see very few, for if I stay in the States there is a matter of two and a half years as one of Uncle Sams boys and I really don't want to wait that long for you. Then too if I did stay in the States and conformed with the army or navy which ever it may be I shall be walking out of it with thousands of others looking for a job. Not being techinically trained and not having a diploma I fear that I should be the one having the most difficulty...I hope that you don't believe that I am dodging the draft for I am not—only looking out for our future and happiness. I truly love this country of Chile and feel that our immediate happiness lies here....

Why?

...I am thoroughly convinced that there is a big business in the laundry development here in Santiago...But my Darling if you will not be happy here and if you would rather stay in the States you know that I am more than willing to listen...I do have about six months in which I could pick up a mechanical trade...probably get into a defence industry...

But then only two deferments would be allowed and in a year's time he'd be no further ahead that he was right now.

...Consider these facts carefully and face reality when your doing it... Remember it is my life as well as yours and I highly respect your careful judgements.

It's safe to say good judgement is one quality a man appreciates in a woman, no matter their age. The reciprocal clause, using any gender label, holds true, too.

A man in love as I am at this point wants his girl to be all his and feel that no one else has any claim on her...

Buster, of course, shared that sentiment.

...After our meeting in New York—which I am praying will be successful—I believe that you should be with Mr. Bedford for a month y no mas and then visit me and my family for at least a week in Syracuse returning for the final verdict...my home is your home...I hope that you will capitalize on my invitation.

Except he didn't own a home.

My parents I am sure will welcomb you with open arms and you can bet your last dollar—American, gold—that I shall be more than proud to present you to them as my friend, fiancé or wife.

What more can he say to impress?

There is another matter which I wish you would consider and that is in regards to my financial status. I have absolutely no reserve, my parents are not wealthy and when and if we do get married there will be no excess coming from my family. That is mas o menos an unwritten law...

By contrast, the generosity of the senior Bedfords bolstered this bride of 1941 in the lead up to holy matrimony. David, obviously, was privy to the Bedford standard of living.

...Aside from this matter I have absolutely no other statements to make in regards to the help from my family except that as you can judge we are socially excepted in all society—from the DuPont's down—and my fathers status stands as one of the first ten metallurgical engineers in the world...

LOL, socially "excepted?"

...He too is written up in Who's Who is America. Not bragging only stating facts...

Two days later, December 2, the third page of Sunday's letter remained in the typewriter. He sat down and picked up where he'd left off. Testosterone-charged panic set in.

Tuesday noon—Am now waiting for your call and am a bit on end...I am praying as never before that you will be able to make the same boat for to me nothing would be more perfect...

T. Wayne torpedoed that plan when he purchased the ticket to fly. On that point, Robin kept it zipped.

A sneak peek into the turn of events on Monday night exposed so much more. With the half-written letter still in the typewriter, he dared the eleven-minute walk to the Crillón.

... just seeing you last night for the short time that we had filled my heart with spirit love and enthusiasm such that the long voyage home won't be as bad as I expected...It although was a pleasure to have met your mother inspite of the difficulty...I sincerely believe that she is very charming...

There was no way it "was a pleasure" to meet Lelia. She faced facts and, impressed by the generosity of Buster's family, recognized good fortune. In letters sent, she had applauded "nice, engraved invitations" for the betrothed's engagement party held in March, at the Waldorf, six months before.

Her nephew Roy attended the party and wrote to paint this portrait of her future son-in-law:

"...I would term him an intelligent, sensible young fellow possessing a fine appearance and very agreeable personality who will prove a husband striving continuously with his best efforts to make Roberta proud and happy to be his wife and her life most enjoyable."

As Tuesday waned, the blank bottom third of page three beckoned from the typewriter. Bright enough to realize his letter might land under Lelia's nose, David sucked up.

You have a wonderful mother there…she did what any mother in her position would or should do. She was absolutely right in not letting us stay on together even though it was very hard on us…

A buzzkill. Lelia didn't care in the slightest what opinion this nineteen-year-old moral menace held.

I hope that sometime soon your mother and I shall meet under different circumstances…I too am very anxious to have the pleasure of meeting your father and the rest of your family…we shall be able to click in the manner which I am used to.

Then he snapped.

…I am in such a state of perplexity…all that I do know is that I love you more than this Spanish Corona…

How flattering.

Where in hell is your phone call…The suspence of the past few days has been very trying to my nerves and at this point I am literally a nervous reck. Smoked a carton of Camels in the last week.

He holed up awaiting her call while packing his bag. Five and a half hours passed.

It is now five thirty in the afternoon…Still have hopes that I will see you once again before I leave tomorrow at eight A.M.

In under eighteen hours, the Wednesday morning train west out of Santiago to the port at Valpo would be underway, with him on it.

…a large quantity of cerveza has been consumed to keep me from going completely batty.

He rolled page four, onion skin, around the platen and kept typing.

The radio here beside me is playing wonderful orchestrations of the good old American music which we are used to…I am not bucked…I know that everything will turn out in our favor for the inevitable can't be overlooked…

Nor should the *evadable* be overlooked.

...Remember that I am putting all of my life into those two beautiful hands of yours and please don't squeeze them, for my little cactus plant it would truly hurt...Can't stand it any longer—have got to call you. Parden me while I make the attempt. You worn't there...

Lucky for him. Even a fool, when he keeps silent, is considered wise.

Am going to bid you good buy now dearest and I truly hope that I see you on the boat, but if I don't let me know when you will get to New York...Till Leon & Eddies

A clue dropped: their plan to meet at a popular night club on "Swing Street." At Leon and Eddie's, located on a block of West 52nd just off 5th Avenue, mid-town Manhattan, comedians the likes of Jackie Gleason, Bob Hope, Red Skelton, and Milton Berle stood up on "celebrity Sundays."

P.S. It is now II P.M. and I have given up all thought of seeing or even hearing from you before I leave, and to be very truthful am very sceptical about even forewarding this letter...

Posted c/o Sr. Skinner at the office of Braden Copper Company, it would fall straight into the hands of Lelia.

In my heart I am trying to believe that it was impossible for you to get intouch with me but in my mind I am almost convinced that it is something else...Darling only to know what is happening or what is going to happen is all I want to know at this point. Are you returning on the IMPERIAL, going south, going to be home by Xmas, etc...I am very perplexed as to what to do and as to what is going to happen. I am sure that you see my point and will not be angree with me...

Then came proof of a truly nervy nineteen-year-old. It was after eleven Tuesday night when he placed a second call from the Carrera to the Crillón and fabricated this tall tale:

I tried the Susan Brown angle when I talked with your mother and I fear that she reconized my voice...

She had.

I hated to be slighty about it but thought it best...if anything is said please cover up for me...

He back peddled to explain.

I told her that I was calling for Susan Brown to see if you would care to have tea.

Five o'clock tea with cookies at the Crillón to be precise.

Your mother responded by asking if it was David who was calling and I foolishly said no that it was Mr. Pagliuco—Jack Pagliuco, a chap here in the pension whom you've talked with, and I don't believe she believed me...

David foolishly dug the hole deeper.

I later called and asked her if I could see her for a few minutes, for I really wanted to talk with her...much that I hate to admit it she was inexcusably rude to me...

Like a mama grizzly she bit his head off.

Someday I'll expect an apology when the circumstances are different. Not blaming her—blaming ourselves for beeing so stupid on the telephone...

He shifted the blame to entrap Robin in *his* foolishness.

...You've got me sweety and don't misuse your position. Never forgive you if you did—complete honor, trust, confidence and love in each other.

David T. Stagg, September 1941
Villarrica Volcano Ski Resort

Christ the Redeemer
Chapter Seven

On Saturday, December 6, the first of three thousand odd vehicles passed through one of several gates at Fort Devens. On return from Carolina maneuvers, twenty thousand troops of the First Division, as well as other units stationed at the post, were elated to be back and looking forward to the holidays.

Nat and Ethel, anxious to see their son, took a room at their favorite haunt, the Colonial-era Groton Inn. As devoted patrons, they were treated well, which explains why they'd chosen an apartment at the Inn for Robin and Buster's post-honeymoon love-nest. It was ideal until August, when Robin sailed for South America and their reluctant son moved back into the barracks awaiting a decision on his application to Signal Corps School.

That Sunday, December 7, Buster joined his parents in the familiar dining room at the Groton. They began the post-maneuver welcome-home luncheon by toasting his return over giant Gulf shrimp with zesty cocktail dipping sauce. An enormous, mid-day meal crowded the nine-and-a-half-inch oval dinner plate set before the young soldier: full-cut sirloin steak, baked potato, and green beans. As he wiped up every morsel, the Groton's familiar green and maroon coat of arms revealed itself. A fighting lion atop a shield, seemed fitting for a man just back from "war."

About two o'clock that Sunday, December 7, feeling relaxed and happy, the young radio sergeant bid farewell to his folks and prepared to roll five miles south to the fort. He flipped the ignition switch. Breaking news piped through speakers of the car radio. From the island of Oahu, in the Territory of Hawaii, the Imperial Japanese Navy stunned the world. Mayhem at Pearl Harbor unfolded just before eight o'clock that morning (about one o'clock Massachusetts time). That's when the first of several Japanese torpedoes slammed into the USS *Oklahoma*, one of eight battleships moored on the east side of Ford Island, along "Battleship Row." Before the Bedfords laid their dessert forks down, *Oklahoma* foundered and capsized. The heavily armored oil-burning "dreadnought" ("dread," meaning fear and "nought," meaning "nothing") went down in less than twenty minutes; 429 crew members died. The loss of life was second only to that of the USS *Arizona* where, still today, "black tears" of oil bubble up to slick the water's surface at the national memorial site.

Back at Devens, most soldiers, enjoying their first day of liberty, listened to beats on their personal portable radios. Stunned by the breaking news, large groups clustered not believing their ears. Sharing looks of shock and disbelief, they pieced together fragments of information relayed from the world's newest battlefield, waiting for more shoes to drop. On orders of the Post Commander, guards doubled up at every Devens entry point. All persons, including Buster, were halted and asked for credentials to gain entry. More orders scrapped all visitor passes.

Prospects of extended leaves to spend holidays with family dwindled when authorities announced neither leaves, nor furloughs would be granted until further notice.

Robin's exact whereabouts on the return trip from Chile were uncertain. Buster had left the method of transportation up to his wife and her father. When T. Wayne agreed to foot the bill for the Clipper, Buster felt tremendous relief that she would not travel by boat up the Atlantic coast.

Except for this.

Robin's desire to see more of South America sprouted out of a seed her mother planted three years before, "…the East Coast is by far more interesting than this West Coast…" Buster tried to reason, "Is the trip worth the expense in view of the short time you would have to spend in Buenos Aires and Rio and the limitations on your wanderings as a married woman travelling alone?"

He underestimated her.

"Couldn't you put the money to better use in the future to your more lasting benefit?" He suggested a new fur coat, "which I am unable to afford at the present time." Then appealed to the practicality she lacked, "the savings…deposited to your own bank account (would) give you an added feeling of security should anything happen to me."

He relinquished his position begrudgingly and left it up to her…"Of course, it is your father's money and he may feel that its use for travel purposes is the best possible use."

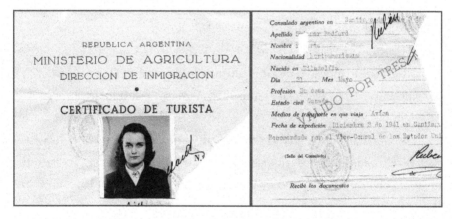

Robin's return to the U.S. commenced December 3

Tattered scraps of paper provide evidence as to the few facts that set the stage for their reengagement.

Looking like a bad-ass female spy, Robin's Certificado De Turista was proof of her departure from Santiago on December 3.

Other than her independent spirit, what inspired her?

Months before, the launch of a new flight map by PANAGRA (Pan American-Grace Airways) smartly targeted a North American audience. Brilliant posters lit up travel agency offices coast to coast. Gimbel's department store picked up an advertising thread to catch Robin's eye: "simple, charming, wearable dresses" for one low price of $4.95. Smart American styles in ten exclusive "Carnival in Rio" prints, "perfect for everyday wear, North or South of the Equator." Special edition pigments mimicked a parrot's feathers: <u>Panagra</u> blue, Peruvian red, Mayan green.

Nose deep in the travel section of the newspaper, Robin percolated and planned her post-graduation "summer to play in" while Buster carried out his khaki-colored duties at Fort Devens. With their newly expanded service, PANAGRA's flight schedules offered scintillating destination options. In miles served, the airline ranked ahead of all other U.S. airlines, second only to the Pan American Airways international system, with which it was associated. The monopoly on intercontinental routes was theirs.

American Airlines, Eastern, T.W.A., and United placed third through sixth at a time in our nation's history when, domestically, those air carriers had the sky almost to themselves.

Because of the all-new routes PANAGRA rolled out, Germany's two lines, Lufthansa and Sedta, were ultimately displaced. This represented a big gain in terms of Western Hemisphere defense and solidarity.

Why?

The German pilots, many of them Luftwaffe reservists, could no longer sketch railroads and harbors or study topography from above. To state the obvious, one bomb dropped by a lone airplane would snarl Panama Canal traffic for weeks.

With an eye toward adventure stoked by Lelia, Robin departed Santiago aboard the Clipper. The trans-Andean flight took her over the hump of the "Cordillera de lost Andes," the longest continental mountain range in the world. Foothills fell far below minutes after takeoff. The flight path on the five-hour hop to Buenos Aires blew by the top of Aconcagua, Inca-speak for "stone sentinel." At 22,840 feet above sea level, it's the highest peak in the Western Hemisphere, wholly located in Argentina, just east of the Chilean border. As one of the Seven Summits of the world, it holds a special place on the bucket list of every passionate mountaineer, where Andean condors, the largest raptor in the world, soar on strong thermic currents.

One hour later, the plane emerged from 150 miles of snow-capped peaks and the Pampas opened up. Flat as a tabletop, vineyards of Mendoza's famed Malbec wine, grain fields, and waving grasslands stretched for seven-hundred miles to the shore of the Rio de la Plata. There the flying boat landed safely in Buenos Aires where uniformed PANAGRA officials assisted her through customs.

Lelia's hand in this had everything to do with laying out an even-steven opportunity for both daughters to see the east coast of South America. In her heart of hearts, she wished to accompany Robin on a mother/daughter sojourn to see the sights together. In silence, she honored her responsibilities to T. Wayne and their son Russell. To leave now, expecting to return any time soon with a war on, was absurd.

In Buenos Aires, a confident Robin whisked off in a cab with a driver who presumably ignored all speed limits, because that's how they rolled in a city devoid of traffic lights. In just under an hour, she arrived at the front door of the nine-story Plaza Hotel, so named because it overlooked the historically significant Plaza San Martin. This, the finest hotel in South America when it opened thirty-two years before, was still considered the best in the capital city. For three dollars and change per day, her room included a private bath.

Today, after several changes of ownership, it's known as the Marriott Plaza Hotel Buenos Aires.

Her accommodations, at the northern end of Calle Florida, the best shopping district, placed her steps away from store window displays filled with exquisite jewelry, perfumes, and specialty items like fine furs, alligator handbags, and evening purses found in ladies' fancy good shops. Compared to the top-dollar establishments she'd patronized with her in-laws in New York, here she happened upon bargains galore with far less chaos. Along the leisurely promenade, only pedestrian traffic was permitted in the afternoon and evening. A gesture that typified the gracious and leisurely living of this great city.

Robin wandered museums and admired historically significant monuments like the Teatro Colon, the largest opera house in the world at the time. It occupied an entire city block, held an audience of 3,500, and boasted a stage capacity of six hundred performers. Since May, when opera season opened that year, the standard repertoire of French, Italian, and German works were presented. So were Mozart's "The Magic Flute" and Gluck's "Iphigenia in Tauris." Inside and out, architectural influences of Italians, Germans, and the French left their eclectic mark with gilded pieces, pillars, stained glass, and marble statues.

When news of Pearl Harbor reverberated around the world, she'd be safe on the streets of Buenos Aires at three o'clock in the afternoon, 7,500 miles from Honolulu.

Except, culturally, Argentina was a mixed bag.

Let me explain.

In 1939, at the outset of the war in Europe, the country declared neutrality while tens of thousands of refugees fled Germany to escape Jewish persecution. Many ethnic Germans also staked their place amidst Argentina's general population. Some readers believed the party-line propaganda they read in *Pompero*, the biggest openly Nazi-subsidized newspaper in the Western Hemisphere.

At the time, Julien Bryan, American war correspondent and documentarian, studied the situation. He opined, in Argentina, America's "Good Neighbor Policy" was twenty years too late. It was impossible to know what percentage of Argentine Germans were sympathetic to the Nazi cause. Buenos Aires was a known two-way funnel through which vast fortunes in securities and jewels, stolen from safety deposit boxes of occupied countries, were routed for liquidation in the U.S. One path for smuggled goods was by way of Spanish boats arriving in Buenos Aires. Once liquidated, the cash circled through various bank transfers and wound up in Swiss or Hungarian banks where Hitler, Goering, and company stacked up millions.

Moving like a knight in a chess game, Robin cut northeast along Brazil's South Atlantic coast to hunt the history and heritage of Rio de Janeiro. Don Ameche and Carmen Miranda had glittered their way into American hearts eight months before when 20th Century Fox's technicolor film, *That Night in Rio*, premiered.

Though, for the musically curious, bossa nova, that soft sensual fusion of samba and jazz born out of Rio, would not be popularized for another twenty years.

With Rio-fueled energy and the legs of a twenty-two-year-old, Robin bounded up two hundred steps and sidled up against the iconic ninety-eight-foot-tall open-armed monument, Christ the Redeemer, atop Mount Corcovado. A cable-car ride to the top of Rio's Sugarloaf Mountain would remind her of the aerial tramway she and Buster shared skiing at Cannon Mountain almost two years previous, when he first declared his love for her.

Little did she know, a 39-year-old Walt Disney, with 8mm movie camera in hand, had circled clockwise through South America just a few months before. At this point in his career, Walt had already produced several landmark features: *Snow White and the Seven Dwarfs* (1938), *Pinocchio* (1940), and *Fantasia* (1940), to name a few. The man was well on his way to becoming a pop-culture force with name recognition in many countries. In the spring of 1941, when headlines out of Hollywood revealed animators for Walt Disney productions went on strike over labor act violations, two of FDR's "alphabet agencies" stepped in. While the National Labor Relations Board (NLRB) sorted the strike, the Office of the Coordinator of Inter-American Affairs (CIAA) arranged a taxpayer-backed "good neighbor" endeavor designed to counter German influence.

Mid-August, Disney and sixteen members of his self-selected studio staff flew aboard a Pan Am Clipper out of Miami to visit Rio, Buenos Aires, and Santiago. They sketched, took photographs, filmed, and met with artists and musicians. New cartoon personalities emerged in fast, happy, musically intoxicating animated films that followed, *Saludos Amigos* and its sequel, *The Three Caballeros*.

Walt would later report he found the people of South America friendly, and decidedly pro-American.

Departing Rio, Robin scanned the Andes once more from the air, traveling west like a silver screen adventuress on a trans-Bolivian run to Lima, Peru.

Six Weeks for Boat Mail

The PANAGA flight map offered many points to debark and explore, making her exact path hard to pinpoint. Smart marketing pitched an air journey through South America with as much speed or leisure as a traveler wished. Two and a half weeks was the norm. In between the provincial cities, Robin had options to visit points of interest. From Lima, her stopovers might have included Talara, a port city six-hundred miles up the coast in northwestern Peru known for big game fishing Buster would appreciate. Then Guayaquil, the commercial port of Ecuador where her ship had gone aground. From Cali, chief commercial city and "Rumba Capital" of Colombia, it was only three and a half hours to Cristobal, Panama.

Aboard the *Elena*, crewmembers prohibited passenger camera's in "the Zone." From the Clipper? A bird's eye snapshot for Buster would be magnificent! For reasons more important now than ever, photos were forbidden.

Short stops in Central America might have mirrored Dottie and Bud's route on their way to Los Angeles: Costa Rica, an overnight at Guatemala City, then north in an 860-mile, four-hour hop, to Mexico City.

Robin's stateside destination? Brownsville, Texas.

Brownsville was the designated headquarters of Pan American's Western Division, where international flight service from South America terminated.

Eastern Airlines took up business in Brownsville in 1939, which made her transfer to the New York metropolitan area logistically simple.

Passenger receipts confirm Robin flew east on December 20 and paid $7.50 for one of fourteen berths aboard a sparkling aluminum DC-3 "Silver Sleeper." The cabin laid out like a compact Pullman coach, with seven upper and seven lower sleeping compartments. No matter how skimpy the weight of her nightie ensemble, she'd be toasty once sand-

$7.50 was the price for a night's sleep.

Christ the Redeemer

wiched between a feather mattress and goose down comforter in the frigid unpressurized aircraft.

If Robin's little brown Hartmann case topped out at the sixty-six-pound weight limit leaving Santiago on the Clipper, hopefully exceptions were made for international travelers boarding a domestic flight in Brownsville. Eastern allotted fifty-five pounds per paid passenger at the time.

The graceful sky-rider nosed down the field, turned, gathered speed, and mounted the sky. A magnificent view of the seventeen-mile-long shipping channel linked the deep port of Brownsville, at the southernmost tip of Texas to the Gulf of Mexico. Until it was time to settle into the curtained sleeping quarters, writing "inflight" postcards was an option. It's also a fact that Eastern Airlines placed knitting kits aboard their Silver Fleet. Stewardesses invited women passengers to fashion standard squares, six-by-six inches, for the Red Cross. Robin gave it a

New York or Newark?

go. Senior year at Smith, during the London Blitz, she'd knit wooly garments for Red Cross "British War Relief."

From Brownsville to New Orleans, Atlanta, Washington, D.C. and up the eastern seaboard, when she wasn't sipping hot chicken broth or sleeping, needles clicked. Her tidy six-by-six squares, gathered up with others, were sent to Red Cross headquarters in Washington where afghans were assembled for distribution.

Robin's ticket revealed the flight was destined to set down in either New York *or* Newark. At a messy time in metropolitan area airline infrastructure, it begged the question. Which one?

Six Weeks for Boat Mail

Fasten your seatbelt for this baffling bit of aviation history.

New York Airport, originally christened "North Beach," opened as one of the largest and fanciest in the world two years before. Bright and shiny, located east of Manhattan, on Long Island, in the Borough of Queens, the forty-million-dollar joint effort between the city of New York and Works Progress Administration launched construction in 1937. Mayor LaGuardia's bitter intention was to drive Newark Airport out of business upon the completion of his pet project in 1939.

Up until LaGuardia Field opened, Newark Metropolitan Airport was *the busiest commercial airport in the world*. Celebrated aviators like Amelia Earhart, Charles Lindbergh, Howard Hughes and soon to be decorated war hero, Jimmy Doolittle, called it home. Newark's landmark terminal, the "administration building" opened in 1935 with a modern airmail center, air traffic control tower, meteorological bureau, baggage facilities, a terrace luncheonette, and a viewing deck. Planes at the time landed and taxied right up to the first-rate art deco space.

A seminal edifice in the early history of U.S. aviation, today the building is a hidden gem listed on the National Register of Historic Places. If a history-loving traveler has time between EWR connections to find it, it's worth the detour.

Then what?

In a snake ball of greed, political maneuvering, and shortsightedness, Mayor LaGuardia tactically planned his superior project to handle increased plane capacity. Loss of business at Newark led to abandonment. The Civil Aeronautics Authority forbade its further use as a commercial terminal. By the end of May 1940, the once celebrated Newark Metropolitan Airport *downgraded* to an emergency field.

It didn't take long for LaGuardia Field to reach a saturation point. By mid-May 1941, Newark *reopened*, as a co-terminal. This meant, for purposes of ticketing, the two airports were considered the same. Eastern, United, American, and T.W.A. all stopped at Newark before they hopped the short leg to LaGuardia field.

Christ the Redeemer

 Six Weeks for Boat Mail

Which brings me back to Robin.

The aftermath of the attack on Pearl Harbor kept Buster at Devens. Nat and Ethel were a poor substitute but perched dutifully at Newark to meet Robin's flight. Ground attendants manually wheeled portable flight stairs to the passenger door of the Silver Fleet DC-3. A handrail made the five-step descent to the tarmac manageable for a well-rested woman smartly dressed for arrival in pearls and pumps. By way of trolly, her mileage-worn suitcase moved to the central baggage room of the terminal. From there, a porter earned Nat's generous tip of twenty-five cents to load it into the Bedford's four-door sedan.

The travels of Robin's Hartmann <u>trunk</u> were destined to become a story unto itself.

Since the attack on Pearl Harbor, officials barred visitors at Fort Devens indefinitely. Only a small percentage of servicemembers were permitted furlough for Christmas. Buster would be one of the lucky ones. With patriotic fervor, men in camp trained on action and handling of incendiary bombs and prepared and practiced for blackouts. The first drill came by surprise on December 23. Three thirty-second moaning sirens let loose. Observers reported every light on the post was extinguished by the time the third signal sounded. Only one flaw occurred when, like a divine sign, the five-foot illuminated cross at the top of the chapel lit up. It took a few minutes for anyone to notice the mistake.

It was President and Mrs. Roosevelt who set the nation straight when they announced plans to proceed with a post-Pearl Harbor "Christmas as usual" in the capital. On the day of the ninth annual White House Christmas Tree lighting ceremonies, December 24, FDR holed up in the historic Lincoln study with Prime Minister Winston Churchill and the American-British war council. They plotted world-wide strategy and world-wide victory against the Axis. Then, at the appointed time of five o'clock, FDR appeared on the South Portico of the White House. The illumination of bright red, white, and blue lights strung on the tree was the signal for similar exercises in communities all over the country. In a half-hour radio broadcast, FDR conveyed a message of holiday courage and Yuletide cheer to the nation by network radio and to the world by short wave.

Christ the Redeemer

Following the broadcast, a buff, 2nd Lieutenant Buster paused to rest his pipe sideways on the polished sterling rim of a cut crystal ashtray. Beside the log fire burning in the Pelham Manor parlor, he stood under the star-topped tree and finally pulled Robin into his arms. Despite peculiarities that previously appeared to her as near-fatal flaws in his personality, a renewed sense of security and duty flooded her red, white, and blue heart. For him, all that mattered was that his wife, who'd travelled far and alone, was safely home. From this first Christmas forward, they would navigate together as husband and wife.

As for David? Dubious as to Robin's sincerity, he didn't need a formal education to realize what a fool he'd been. When the C.S.A.V. docked in New York on December 22, there was no letter waiting. The meetup at Leon and Eddies didn't happen either.

Japan's dastardly attack on December 7 changed the war's entire strategy and the life plans of most young Americans, including David's. Millions of Americans adopted Buster's way of thinking, "May God see fit that such sacrifice will be sufficient to preserve the way of life I love."

Aviation Cadet David Stagg was married on May 15, 1942 (to an English teacher, no less) and stationed with the U.S. Army Air Corps, Maxwell Field, Alabama. On January 6, 1943, he became a father to his first daughter named Christie. A baby her parents would no doubt explain "came a wee bit early."

David served for four years and then, post-war, returned to Middlebury College, where he graduated in 1948. He took a position with Connecticut General Life Insurance Company (later CIGNA) in its Rutland, Vermont, office.

Twelve years later, one Tuesday at noon, David handwrote a note and typed out an envelope addressed to Mrs. Roberta S. Bedford. It posted from Rutland, "MAR15 4-PM 1960," and began, "My darlin', Congratulations!!!— Your contract #984,948 came through exactly as applied for and now rests in my desk drawer. Will go over it in detail with you the next time we get together…"

In the Nude
Chapter Eight

One week into the New Year, in general hand-wringing fashion, Lelia wrote from Campamento Americano c/o Pelham Manor. The Hartmann trunk, chock full of her daughter's apparel, which suited her for three months' play through altitudes high and low and a change of Chilean seasons, had gone missing.

```
SEWELL
8 JAN
1942
CHILE
```

L.M. Skinner, Rancagua – Sewell, Chile S.A. – airmail

January 8, 1942
Dearest Roberta,

I'll get an air line off to you, as we haven't been able to send an answer to your cable as yet concerning your trunk. Grace Co. is supposed to be searching. I never saw such a dead outfit...

The trunk was supposed to have sailed aboard the S.S. *Santa Lucia* at the end of November. Robin looked for it in New York.

...Dad immediately called Mr. Palmer to whom he had mailed the shipping bill and the keys...

Mr. Charlie Palmer, the Braden Copper office manager in Santiago at the time, was a logistics man. The shipping bill documented clearance of

Robin's personal effects for transport. It specified terms of delivery and would be sent with the keys to the Braden Office in New York. Once on the East Coast, Robin expected to collect the keys and claim her belongings.

...fortunately he [Mr. Palmer] *has a letter from Panagra acknowledging receipt of the bill. So now he is after the Panagra outfit and just as soon as we can find out anything definite we will let you know...*

On top of that mishap was this day-of-departure mistake.

...we weren't able to get any answers from the [Grace Lines] *Lucia Office as to which way you had gone...*

Some imbecile led the senior Skinners to believe Robin flew via Miami; in turn, they misinformed Nat and Ethel regarding details of her arrival. Lelia and T. Wayne had no idea she'd flown the Brownsville route—at least until Robin's surprising cable from Texas turned up.

...we hurried a cable right off to Pelham...mortified that we had advised them you were getting in there Thursday...until they would receive a cable from you from Brownsville (and I hope you sent them one) they wouldn't know why you hadn't arrived in Newark...I'm afraid they would be frantic.

Beside herself with angst, Lelia worked herself further into a tizzy.

I'm terribly concerned as to what you are doing for winter dresses—shoes, etc. while you are waiting for your trunk. What we fear has happened, is that the trunk might have been shipped on the Santa Louisa or Santa Barbara or some of the Grace Co. freight boats, but even then it should have reached New York long before this. It's a good thing Dad had it insured...even then there would be some items that you wouldn't want to lose that...insurance could not replace.

The evening of December 3, Robin's eighteen-year-old brother, Russell, arrived in Santiago, sorry to have missed his sister's rise to the sky aboard the Clipper. Nicknamed "Skeeter" as a kid, he was the youngest of the three Skinner children and Lelia's least favorite. Under current circumstances, he proved to be a muy necesario temporary distraction. For the next five days, he basked in his return to civilization at Hotel Crillón, in the same way Buster had at Pinehurst, including a manicure, but in a city center not nearly so relaxing.

...He [Russell] *stayed down with me until Monday night while I was getting laboratory work done. X-rays of stomach and intestines and stomach (gastric juice and bile) analysis.*

As a biology major, Robin was the only one in the family who would be remotely interested in the detail of her fifty-two-year-old mother's medical tests. Worry had been Lelia's constant and prolonged companion for years. An ulcer would come as no surprise.

We got home Tuesday and it was nice he could be here until New Year's Day.

By virtue of his birthplace (Sewell), her son was obligated and currently served with the Chilean Army. He enjoyed the rest of a full month's holiday furlough in Campamento Americano. It made more work for Lelia, but in the same breath she'd confessed this:

It filled the emptiness in the house after your departure...we are thankful and happy we had you the three months.

That would never happen again. From my perspective, it's surprising it happened at all.

After seeing Russell off on New Year's Day, Lelia felt a terrible let down stepping into the empty nest of House #71.

...He looked better than at the time of his Sept. vacation. Is no thinner or nor fatter...has no idea whether he will be released from the Army on March 1st or will be sent to outlying posts along the Chilean Coast now that the Japs are in the Pacific.

Stuck in an unenviable rut, Lelia ruminated. Adela, her Chilean domestic had left for her fifteen-day vacation six days earlier.

...I am very busy—cooking, washing dishes, etc. It keeps me humping, I can tell you. Last year I had Russell and Dorothy here to pare vegetables, wash dishes, etc. and it was a big help.

Many hands make light work.

...The Japs are sure giving us a tough break.

She followed the news. U.S. Army headquarters in the Philippines recently reported General Douglas MacArthur's forces, desperately outnumbered, were falling back both north and south of Manila under the assault of Japanese infantry, tanks, and dive-bombers. The Japanese had established complete aerial and naval supremacy; the fall of Manila was feared imminent. MacArthur's troops, manning defense lines in the Bataan peninsula jungles in the Philippines, were braced to meet a "large-scale general attack."

Hugs and kisses and we'll cable you when we have definite news of the trunk… Write us about your trip. Mother

Four days later, more light was shed on the case of the missing wardrobe. A little extra war-time reality flavored Lelia's correspondence.

L.M. Skinner, Rancagua – Sewell, Chile S.A. – airmail
Passed by examiner 1885 (examiner # is handwritten)

January 12, 1942
Dearest Roberta,

The Grace outfit finally located your trunk in Valpo. And it went out on Sat. Jan 10 on the same boat it should have gone on the last part of Nov… We can't mention names of boats…

Lelia's self-imposed hush on the content of her letter was something she'd learned during the Great War. The WWII propaganda poster "Loose Lips Might Sink Ships," was yet to be invented by the War Advertising Council, but Lelia understood postal censorship had everything to do with national security. Examiners opened, read, and removed content of any letter they deemed might create a breach. The name of a civilian ship, apparently, fell into that category. In the bigger scheme of world affairs, it was a censor's job, even in neutral countries like Chile, to ferret out spies, uncover enemy-related trade deals, and keep military secrets safe.

Six Weeks for Boat Mail

So much had happened in six weeks' time. Would Robin remember her trunk sailed aboard the *Lucia*?

You can count the number of days for the trip and know what day to expect it. You never saw so much calling Santiago as we had to do—just keeping after them—three or four times each day to get any action, and they insisting they never had the handling of it, etc., and then it was over a week before they located it…

The wayward trunk turned up at the port, *late* in the afternoon on January 9. Time fell short of a man's full, eight-hour workday preceding the *Lucia*'s departure from Valpo. If those baggage handlers adopted a "mañana attitude," even a short backlog in the loading zone would dash Lelia's hopes.

…but after raising cane with them they promised by all that was good and holy, they'd have it on that boat for you… You poor kid up there without your winter garments!

Not so fast on the pity party. Under the circumstances, the senior Bedfords would conduct indispensable shopping and dining trips "downtown" with Robin and Buster in favorite haunts: Saks Fifth Avenue, B. Altman & Co., lunching at Schrafft's on 42nd Street.

What a woman wore at home on Christmas to look charming was a duty as much as a pleasure. A little sweater set made with Chantilly lace was popular at the time. She'd also need proper evening attire and something for a matinee at Radio City Music Hall.

Ethel purchased tickets well in advance at the "Showplace of the Nation," where "The Nativity" pageant, a beloved Christmas tradition, was something to behold from first mezzanine seats. A majestic march of wise men, camels, sheep, and donkeys up and onto the Music Hall stage juxtaposed the spectacle of "Kris Kringle's Carnival." Both lived on in wartime and in peace.

Nat especially liked the preferred seating Ethel chose. The eye-high kicks and dance precision of the Rockettes bedazzled him.

Speaking of legs, I imagine Buster insisted they stretch their own after the show. In youthful excitement he'd take Robin by the hand to the ice-skating pond on the lower level of Rockefeller Plaza. On loan from the Bronx Zoo, four reindeer, the Santa Claus kind, were housed in specially built pens. They lifted holiday spirits of passers-by on both sides of the ice rink.

Bud wrote us a letter saying you were going skiing with Buster at Plymouth.

In that case, the latest fashion ski wear would soon be hers. Plymouth, New Hampshire, was geographically as far north as Watertown, New York, where Bud and Dottie were presumably settled and happy. Had anyone suggested a rendezvous, they'd soon agree to skip it. Plymouth was more than a stone's throw from Watertown, three-hundred miles by car, clear on the other side of Vermont.

You won't be able to read this, as I'm writing while my nail polish is hardening and I can't hold the pen properly.

"Cutex—Tops for Flair and Wear" was the catchy slogan that won Lelia's consumer allegiance. If she didn't frump it, this polish job might just hold up until Adela returned to resume dish detail.

…By the way, I found your brown pen here after all—guess where it was? I had put it in my bag…to take to Coya to write letters…it had slipped way down in the pouch part of that black suede bag that I use only for golf…

She spoke of the Coya Country Club. Today it goes by the Club de Campo Coya; par 72, eighteen-holes, built in Rancagua, 1927. As for Robin's brown pen? It was "best set" like the Parker "Duovac" fountain pen she'd purchased her senior year at Smith for an extravagant $8.75. This was a Parker "Vacumatic," brown pearl with black jewels, a fine gold nib, just over five inches when capped. The fact that she didn't want to lose it indicated sentimental value that possibly transcended dollars and cents.

How I am missing Adela. She still has six days of her vacation ahead of her. The past nine have seemed an eternity.

I'm wondering whether you'll be at Groton until the end of Jan. and where Buster will be transferred. These are anxious days! Hugs and kisses—Mother and Dad.

Until Robin wrote, Lelia would have no way of knowing the young marrieds had abandoned their Groton abode, five miles from Fort Devens.

Erring on the side of caution, she posted the next letter c/o Pelham Manor.

L.M. Skinner, Rancagua – Sewell, Chile S.A. – airmail
Labeled: EXAMINED BY 1932

January 19, 1942
Dearest Roberta,

Our air mail letters coming from the States are sometimes taking 12 days to reach us with censoring. Do ours take that long to reach you or aren't ours censored?

She'd find out soon enough. For now, perturbed over the state of Robin's wardrobe, she threw a bone.

...we sent you a $30 check which was the money deposited to my credit for you substituting. Thought you might like to buy a winter dress to tide you over.

The substitute teaching duties Robin assumed to assist her schoolmarm mother deepened Buster's affection for his wife significantly more than, say, reading about her skiing expeditions. He'd praised her last October, in a letter from Fort Bragg: "Patience with children is not only a virtue, but a necessity. Your own children will profit from it, I assure you."

As the youngest of four children, I believe Robin's well of patience ran deepest for me. Her rules of order were consistent. She treated my mistakes as learning opportunities.

Of course, when Buster asked for character sketches of her more interesting charges, she failed to describe them.

We rec'd your letter dated January 1 telling all about your trip.

In the Nude

In which Robin neglected to acknowledge receipt of their Christmas check.

We aren't receiving our bank statements now for some reason...

Without a bank statement, Lelia pressed the matter of the check. Intended for "starter" linens, she knew Winter White Sales offered the best deals—the enduring brainchild of department store king, John Wanamaker, dating back to 1878.

...Why don't you just get plain ones for the time being and not put a lot of money into the embroidered at present?...especially as we want to get your silver the first thing...we can give you the embroidered for anniversary—Christmas and birthdays...One can't do everything all at once...You may not be able to keep house very long anyway—in case Buster is sent in an expeditionary force outside of the States...

They were anxious to hear. Was he accepted into officer's training?

How lovely it would be if you can have an apt. for a few months...Mrs. Turton is having Mrs. Middleton, in New York, buy and send you a silver sandwich tray like Dorothy's. So if one comes in unexpectedly you'll know who from...Hugs and kisses—Mother

Mrs. Turton was fortunate to have Mrs. Middleton, a personal shopper, stationed in Manhattan. Robin fulfilled Lelia's needs as such, in a cliché, "get what you pay for," painfully slow way. The generous gift of silver sandwich trays, a symbol of everlasting beauty for ever-after happiness, was proof of a long and treasured family friendship. As young mining engineers, both T. Wayne and Franklin "Turt" Turton, started their careers at El Teniente. Their wives arrived as new brides, Lelia in 1916, and Turt's wife, Jeane, two years later. They soon found themselves comparing growth charts and minding shoe sizes of the three little girls and two sons between them.

Then, poof, they were grown and gone.

Lelia puzzled over protracted letter delivery between the U.S. and Chile. At the time, United Press reported on speculation that the Chilean government might be at the point of severing relations with the Axis, though the break would not occur until January 1943, twelve months from now. For the time being, because of Chile's neutrality, she questioned, "aren't ours censored?"

It was rumored the censors could sense hidden meanings like a mouse could smell cheese. Lelia's query was put to rest in her very next letter written February 15. There were too many particulars to redact one line at a time. Instead of handpicking words or phrases to blacken or cut out, *they plucked the whole first page.*

Tucked in the folds of pages two and three, a check for two hundred dollars arrived with a shopping list, c/o Pelham Manor via Registered Mail. It was a long list, upon which Robin was expected to execute.

L.M. Skinner, Rancagua – Sewell, Chile S.A. – airmail
EXAMINED 4774

Sometime in February 1942—page 1 missing

...her [Dorothy] *to go back to Montana. I had been worrying about her in the Western part of N.Y. State by herself, for her confinement. Oh! If I could only be with her for the event. If it weren't for the uncertainty of travel up this coast now, I think I would be tempted to go——but no telling when I could get back to Dad.*

In mid-February, the Chilean government announced measures to fortify its long coastline, which meant indefinite retention of both army and navy conscripts. Russell, who was due to return to civilian life in March, would continue to serve. Chilean military leaders chalked out an increase in new conscripts, effective April.

Lelia advanced the latest gossip from Campamento Americano concerning women and families Robin knew.

Martha had a boy Jan. 24. Carmen a boy Jan. 23—but she had to have a caesarian operation, which went off O.K. but some kind of an infection developed and she ran a fever for about 10 days around 102 to 104 (I didn't write that to Dorothy)...

Good. Certain things are better left unsaid to a first-time expectant mother. For example, days before I was due with baby number one, some donut-cushioned half-wit overshared details of her delivery-related coccyx fracture.

[Mr. and Mrs.] *Staples resigned and are going home quite soon. They were just homesick and never did get over not having another house given them and "a lot of little things" she says.*

The goodwill of Mrs. Staples was to the family's advantage. Dorothy's March due date loomed. Weeks before, in December, the soon to be grandmother, Lelia, embedded at the Hotel Crillón. She'd seen Robin off, met up with Russell, and tended to lab tests. Moreover, with her first grandbaby top of mind, she shopped. It lifted her spirits in a bittersweet way. A knitted bassinette blanket and a knitted bloomer jumper suit with sweater would do. The bedeviled question? How to deliver them. Mercifully, Mrs. Staples agreed to shepherd the tiny parcels, as well as a few items Robin left behind, to the States. Her kindness would ensure their safe and timely arrival.

Or so she believed.

I'm sending your riding boots and golf shoes by them. The golf shoes are inside the riding boots, and sewed to the tongue of your <u>right, white</u> shoe—on the inside, you'll find your fountain pen... I tucked the white socks around it.

Robin's Hartmann trunk came custom equipped with exclusive features like shoeboxes. It baffles me how she forgot the tailored leather footwear. A seasoned traveler, she knew to peek beneath the bed skirt. Logic tells me she shed and left them in a mudroom of sorts. So as not to dirty the floors of House #71.

The <u>secrecy</u> of travel by ship was such that Mr. and Mrs. Staples could not find out when any boat would sail until they paid their fare. They spoke generally of a Dutch boat. Either they knew nothing definite or were afraid to mention it.

To that scuttlebutt Lelia shared news that Mr. and Mrs. Cook would soon leave Sewell for good. Mr. Cook was not a miner; he ran the meat concession in the company store. He could find work elsewhere. Medical attention for his wife was urgent.

She...has been very sick, and in the hospital, undiagnosed. I guess they are flying home...

It's certain that noxious air quality compounded Mrs. Cook's illness. Why? Ore from El Teniente snaked down the hill in huge buckets, an elevation drop of 2,500 feet, over an aerial tramway to the smelting plant in Caletones. That's where the copper was refined using giant, blistering ovens. Toxic fumes from the smelter's chimney settled over the camps. Airborne pollutants led to chronic heart and lung problems. In her case, I wager premature death.

Pity the men in the bowels of the mine, too. A company medical report listing illnesses diagnosed and treated in 1942 made no mention of silicosis. Braden Copper's unwillingness to recognize the malady was compounded by the fact that Chilean law did not consider silicosis a work-related disease.

Stateside, the War Production Board moved to increase the flow of copper from South America. Virtually *all* output from El Teniente was under contract at top dollar, which meant balls-out production and shift quotas to be met. Lelia didn't offer a censor-worthy explanation when she wrote this:

...The Company isn't letting any men go home on vacations...

Turning toward domestics, the need to "make do and mend" was understood during times of war. In 1919, following Robin's birth in Philadelphia, Lelia seized the opportunity to purchase a thirty-pound Western Electric *portable* sewing machine advertised to fit inside a trunk. She packed it back to Chile with five-month-old Robin. Since the five-year certificate of warranty was useless in the mining camp, she personally kept it well-oiled and in good repair. Little tricks, like a quick whisk with a chicken feather, kept the shuttle carrier free of lint and bits of debris. But now her thread was breaking. With a few key parts, she could fix the machine herself. Except, U.S. military use of metals jeopardized their availability.

...get me a couple dozen sewing machine needles for the Western Electric... (flat on 1 side at the top) <u>assorted</u> sizes...

With the electric machine it was necessary to choose the right needle size, designed for coarser or finer thread, otherwise the thread would break. She specified the needles in a wooden tube; Boye Needle Company packaged them like that, with helpful advice marked on the outside: "Buy new shuttle if machine skips stitches or breaks thread." No surprise, Boye also sold shuttles. In fact, Lelia's troubleshooting pointed to the shuttle carrier. Robin would find both at Bloomingdales.

I think I had better have Dorothy go and buy me two pairs low heeled shoes from Uncle Dix...Her foot is nearer my exact size than yours, I think yours is a trifle longer in the arch than mine.

Uncle Dix, husband of Auntie Alta, would surely offer a discount! Robin's feet were not much bigger than Cinderella's; size 6AA, with a hard-to-find AAAA heel.

Call me Bigfoot, but beyond my childhood dress-up years, her shoes were of no use to me.

Haven't you found your silver pattern yet?

She suggested a Lunt Co. pattern; purchased through the Braden office. Miss Otterstrom, one who Lelia often leaned on for help, could get a reduction!

Miss Otterstrom was the administrative glue of Kennecott Copper; she kept the men at the top organized, and their families, too. Often faced with crazy logistics related to the Braden subsidiary in Sewell, she orchestrated magic from her desk in the personnel department, high up in the Equitable Building at 120 Broadway, Manhattan.

It reminded Lelia to ask this:

Have you received Jeane and Turt's sandwich plate yet?

Six Weeks for Boat Mail

> *Our Calvert course starts March 2. It seems school only closed yesterday. Never did dread getting back into the collar as much.*

Not to be confused with a piece of Christian clerical clothing, or the cool, cryptographic neckwear worn atop the robe of the late Justice Ruth Bader Ginsburg, she referred to the "white collar" nature of her work as a schoolteacher. Eight months were required to finish each year's course according to the Baltimore based "Calvert" system developed by a Harvard trained scholar in response to a 1905 whooping cough epidemic. Forty years later this "royal road to learning" reached around the world like its own geography lesson. The noble intent, as published post-war in *The Evening Sun* (Baltimore) on November 6, 1947, was this:

> The ultimate object of education in a free society is to develop intelligent, law-abiding, useful citizens who will do their share in making the communities in which they reside, work and play, better and happier places, not only for themselves and for their own families and friends, but for society as a whole.

For some it was education in an envelope. For students at Campamento Americano, lesson manuals, textbooks, workbooks, pencils, erasers, paste, paperclips, and more were packed snugly and shipped to Lelia in a single box.

If only her personal purchases were that easy.

I haven't the faintest idea how much to send for all this shopping.

She reckoned two hundred dollars would do and, without overthinking it, wrote the check. Wisely, she kept a carbon copy to jog her memory, alleviating any second-guess stress.

…it's quite a big list—things for Russell—Dad and myself…

In fact, it was so much stuff, she considered whether to have Robin acquire yet another trunk from the Hartmann Agency to send it. The "reversible" she wanted would take up a lot of space; Russell needed one, too. Practically speaking, it was the ideal coat to weather winter in the

Andes. The U.S. Army Reversible Ski Parka, first issued in 1941, served the 10th Mountain Division and other troops posted in bitterly, cold regions at altitude. The fur-trimmed hood, a functional invention of the Inuit people, buffered whipping wind and snow and kept frost from building up around the face.

How did the reversible derive its name? Obviously, it reversed inside out, U.S. Army drab to snow white, for camouflage. Not that she needed the camo, but Russell might.

...Let me know as soon as you receive this check, 'cause we only receive bank statements once or twice a year now.

Without Robin's acknowledgement, Lelia would naturally imagine the worst.

Double Ocean Trouble
Chapter Nine

During his time on Carolina maneuvers, Buster had wasted his breath imploring Robin to return early from South America and set up housekeeping. It no longer mattered that competition was, in Buster's words, "keen" near Fort Devens "with all the new wives accumulated by the 101st this summer…"

Lelia acknowledged receipt of Robin's New Year's Day greeting written from Pelham. She did not yet have an answer to her question "wondering whether you'll be at Groton until the end of Jan." Until she knew otherwise, Lelia ran with her gut and penned letters to Pelham.

In point of fact, Buster's acceptance to OCS, specifically the Signal Corps School at Fort Monmouth, symbolized a fresh start. The newly reunited couple scrambled to locate a place to rent along the Jersey shore north of Asbury Park. A classified in the *Asbury Park Press* advertised "Loch Arbour Apartments…Comfort within your budget!"

Robin, accustomed to rising with the birds in their Massachusetts love nest five miles from Fort Devens, would rise and shine here, too. Buster reported to Fort Monmouth on Tuesday, January 13. The morning routine was much the same. While he dressed, she prepared a full breakfast. Soft scrambled eggs plated with bacon and buttered toast, set alongside coffee and juice. Without argument, he'd defer the driving to her. From Loch Arbour, the *Zephyr* breezed seven miles north to the fort. There, he fell into formation and marched to class.

After that, I imagine she was free to do as she pleased for much of the day. If she thought about writing Lelia, she didn't.

It was more than a few hours' drive time between Loch Arbour and Pelham, where Nat and Ethel lived near Long Island Sound. In 1942, neither the Garden State Parkway nor the New Jersey Turnpike existed. The route would have included N.J. Route 18 and U.S. 9 to the George Washington Bridge, which opened in 1931. Opportunities for in-law intrusion were fewer. With limited exposure to Ethel's clucking and judgement, Robin stepped up, empowered to rule her own roost.

On the same day Buster reported to Fort Monmouth, so did Prentice Smith, an Amherst College grad, class of 1941. Though they'd taken different paths to get to OCS, they were both there to level up their rank to "commissioned officer." Prent's motivation to get his commission was to keep promises he'd made to his gal, Phyllis, a Tufts College-educated catch he'd met while at Amherst.

Prent, then twenty-two, stood six feet, 158 pounds, black hair, brown eyes. In his home state of Missouri, he was among thirty-four draftees picked by the local Selective Service Board. In September 1941, he reported to the U.S. Army induction center at Jefferson Barracks, a troop mobilization point near St. Louis dating to the Civil War. There he was pressed into two and a half years of service.

In the eyes of the Signal Corps, both Prent and Buster qualified as candidates for Officers Training. As college graduates, they displayed wits enough to stick with and finish the program.

A rigorous three-month course spanned twenty different subjects: International Morse Alphabet and Radio Procedure, Defense Against Chemical Attack, Weapons, Signal Supply, Safeguarding Military Information, and Rules of Land Warfare, to name a few. Monmouth was equal proving ground for officers, both the enlisted, like Buster, and a draftee like Prent.

At the end of January, Robin's bon vivant "pet" Dizzy married Gina in Manhattan where the Haven Housemates' bridesmaid's circle remained unbroken. Gina, Robin's maid of honor in June of '41, was "attended" by

Joyce, Robin's bridesmaid. The wedding gave rise to a reunion of the "old gang." Dizzy applauded Buster's Signal Corps track while, in the footsteps of his flying ace father, he set his eyes on the sky.

It's possible the china, silver, and stemware displayed on Gina and Dizzy's wedding gift table got Robin thinking about her own sterling. In a breakaway move that would satisfy Lelia, Robin trekked north into downtown Manhattan on Tuesday, February 7. Three blocks from the Kennecott Office, Daniel Rado Diamonds and Jewels sold silverware at a thirty percent discount to the copper company's employees.

Odds are good, with the Braden discount, that Dorothy picked out her silver service at the same establishment. Lelia had written to Robin from Campamento Americano shortly after her wedding, stating that she and T. Wayne wanted to get both daughters "flat sterling service for our wedding gift."

Lelia had suggested "Lunt" silver, but Robin settled on place settings for eight in Reed & Barton's sterling. She chose the pattern, "Fragrance." For an extra twelve dollars, all ninety-four pieces came engraved with a "B," for Bedford. A complimentary cherry-toned zipper chest with tarnish-resistant lining neatly organized the order. For a total of $245.21, Lelia would be satisfied. It inventoried like this:

Eight each: Dinner Knives, Dinner Forks, Salad Forks, Cream Soup Spoons, Butter Spreaders, Melon Spoons, Oyster Forks, Coffee Spoons.

Eighteen Tea Spoons.

Three Table Spoons, what we'd call a "serving spoon" today.

One each: Cold Meat Fork, Berry Spoon, Gravy Ladle, Cream Ladle, Pie Server, Sugar Tongs, Butter Knife, Lemon Fork, Sugar Spoon.

With evening dinner parties in the offing, party guests would lay their oyster forks down at the sound of air-raid sirens and blackout test interruptions. Buster would have done his part to prepare their Loch Arbor apartment with supplies purchased at Lewis Lumber, the largest hardware and supply store in Monmouth County. They sold blackout paper, paint, and panels for covering windows and glass doors, and dependable flashlights, too.

Double Ocean Trouble

At the end of February, Civilian Defense officials rushed to complete preparations for the Jersey Shore area's first blackout test. War hysteria gave rise to rumors that bathing beaches of the Jersey Shore, especially Monmouth County, would be ordered closed that summer. Some folks, spinning yarns out of war conditions, reported that sandy beachfront stretches were wired off and mined and troops cluttered up piers and jetties.

Citing the importance of recreation in a time of war, the chief of the United States Travel Bureau assured seaside merchants, owners of rental properties, and concessionaires of a highly profitable summer season ahead in Monmouth County, vacationland of the East. That was his job.

An air raid alarm sounded just before nine-thirty p.m. on Friday, February 27. Army officers from Fort Monmouth and Fort Hancock accompanied members of the Defense Council on an observation flight over a one-thousand-square-mile area.

This was a test.

How did it go?

Alfred Beadleston, director of the Asbury Park branch office of the New Jersey Defense Council, reported the blackout was achieved within three and a half minutes. Thirty seconds after the alarm sounded, not a single automobile was seen moving with head lamps burning.

It was dark. So dark that a new 1942 sedan driven by a thirty-year-old member of the police reserve hit the rear of a truck driven by an air raid warden. Both were on duty. The sedan shot off the highway and came to rest just short of a telephone pole. Shortly after being extricated from the vehicle with an ax, the reserve officer died of his injuries, which included a fractured skull, broken neck, and crushed ribs.

When two local business owners ignored the zero-tolerance seriousness of defense officials, *The Asbury Park Press* reported consequences. An arrest warrant was issued for the operator of the Paris Hat Shop "where a red neon sign and show windows blazoned forth during the blackout..." The same went for a worker at Rudy's market, where "a night light was left burning even after officials had ordered it extinguished an hour before the test."

The earnestness of the February 27 "local" drill was underscored the very next day in a nation-wide Associated Press news release:

> WASHINGTON, Feb. 28. (AP) — Preparations against Axis Spring raids by sea or air were tightened today with a call for all-night, every-night partial blackouts in a defense zone reaching 300 miles inland from all United States coasts…In collaboration with military officials, James M. Landis, director of the office for civilian defense, asked for immediate blackout of all lights in "critical" areas which "are not capable of being put out at a moment's notice" in case of attack.

The coastal blackout program, sent to directors of the regional Office of Civilian Defense (OCD), dictated "target area" regions. Again, they extended inland _three hundred miles_ from the Atlantic, Pacific, and Gulf Coasts. Robin and Buster didn't need any convincing as to the need. Chilly air and water temperatures brought the appearance of peace and quiet to the Jersey beach front in February. Yet, they knew first-hand the enemy nearly knocked at their doorstep.

How?

At six-thirty in the morning the day of the blackout test, German "unterseeboote", U-578, torpedoed the Standard Oil steam tanker, *R.P. Resor*, twenty miles off the coast of Manasquan Inlet. The inlet, near Point Pleasant, was just twenty miles south of Loch Arbour.

The *Resor*, en route from Houston to Fall River, Massachusetts carried nearly eighty thousand barrels of crude oil. The vessel was navigating to avoid detection: blacked out and on a zig-zag course. U-578 skulked at virtually point-blank range, two hundred yards, when it fired one torpedo amidships. A second ruptured the *Resor*'s oil tanks. Flames enveloped the boat in a roaring inferno and danced like the devil off thick, congealed oil

Double Ocean Trouble

atop the water's surface. Heroic efforts of a little Coast Guard picket boat saved *two* of the forty-one crew and nine armed guards aboard.

The explosion started a spectacular towering fire witnessed by thousands in Asbury Park and surrounding beach-side communities. Visitors flocked to watch flames billow on the horizon for two days.

The term "dark tourism" was yet to be coined, but that's what it was.

And then it got worse.

Earlier that month, the U.S.S. *Jacob Jones* (DD-130) was the first destroyer assigned to anti-submarine "roving patrols" along the Atlantic seaboard. On February 27, standing off New York Harbor with a crew of 141 men, the "Jakie" was ordered south toward Cape May, New Jersey. En route, they encountered the *Resor*'s charred and burning wreckage.

A search for survivors turned up none at the time, but newspaper reports in the *Asbury Park Press* revealed oil-covered and burned bodies of several crew members were later found floating in life-preservers. The fate of others who reportedly escaped in a lifeboat remained a mystery.

Not a man aboard the *Jacob Jones* was aware of a lurking "rattlesnake" when, one day later, the Wickes-class destroyer blew, too.

> WASHINGTON (AP) – The navy announced today that the destroyer Jacob Jones was sunk by an enemy submarine off Cape May, N.J. before dawn on Feb. 28 and that only 11 men of the destroyer's crew survived… Two torpedoes hit… The first one blew up the bow and apparently killed all personnel on the bridge as well as men sleeping in the forward living quarters of the ship. The second torpedo blew up the stern and all the depth charges… The Jacob Jones was the ninth naval ship lost so far in the war, including the Reuben James…

By late Sunday afternoon, March 1, Robin and Buster were presumably among throngs standing in the sand watching a Navy blimp, destroyers, and planes avenge the U-Boat attack, circling about ten miles off-shore. Water spouted high over the ocean surface as depth charges dropped.

Six Weeks for Boat Mail

It occurs to me, if oil in the water didn't qualify as a "fish kill," the depth charges did. Nobody at the time printed *that* news, but oil and tar from sunken tankers was added to the list of war-time hazards along bathing beaches which now, allegedly, grew to include machine gun nests and barbed wire entanglements.

Meanwhile, other imposing military actions were unfolding. On February 19, FDR signed Executive Order 9066, "AUTHORIZING THE SECRETARY OF WAR TO PRESCRIBE MILITARY AREAS." One that had little direct effect on Robin and Buster, but for Japanese Americans living in the "West Coast Defense Zone" the consequences were historic. One of the worst civil liberties violations in U.S. history, Japanese assembly areas and internment camps, would unfold in a mess of complicated geopolitics.

Newspapers—the social media of the day—reported both sides of the story.

For example, in New Jersey, on page six of *The Daily Record*, Long Branch, dated February 19, one woman jockeyed for the position of opinion leader in a "Dear Sir" letter to the editor. She had a lot to say. It spilled over two columns and began like this:

> I sent a letter to every Congressman and Senator, the President and several Cabinet members…My thesis is: Every Japanese—American born or not—must be put into concentration camps at once.

In 180-degree New Jersey juxtaposition, positioned to the left of that page six editorial, *The Daily Record* reported on activities and policies of the "County Good-Will Commission."

> The State of New Jersey Good-Will Commission, through its Monmouth chapter, is getting into its stride and is accomplishing much in cementing the shore's various races and creeds into one unity with a single purpose; that of preserving our American Way of Life…Residents who happened to be born in foreign countries and who

lived here for decades are loyal to the Stars and Stripes and are equally anxious to further the war program.

With no control over the ironic editorial placement, the author of "Dear Sir" continued to make her case. She stirred hysteria, throwing Navy weight around. A means to give credence to her message:

> As the sister of a Commander and wife of a Lieut. Commander in the Navy, both Annapolis graduates, I am more than concerned and am unable to comprehend the lack of panic of our people, especially in Honolulu and California, in realizing this peril and coping with it... Pressure is brought on every Japanese woman to have six children 'for the Emperor' and we must use this war to rid America of them. They are unassimilable [sic] and in a generation or two will be a much larger menace. But, for the present, separate the sexes in camps...

Why?

Like a pyramid scheme, the time in internment would be used as an incubating period.

How do I know the way this woman thought?

She wrote a follow-up editorial published in *The Daily Record* on March 3:

> ...in five years each family may emerge with five more children. Unconfined, in one generation we will have five-times and in two generations, twenty-five times as many Japanese to cope with! This is our golden opportunity to rid the United States of them for good...

Hateful enough to make me wonder what cultural biases her children and grandchildren might harbor today.

I like to believe Robin and Buster attended the Good-Will gala rally at Asbury Park that Sunday, February 22. Buster's coursework in civil liberties and human rights at Columbia Law informed his alignment with Roosevelt's "four freedoms." Freedom of speech and religion and freedom from want and from fear.

On the Pacific Coast, however, the inability to separate the sheep from the goats empowered Lieutenant General J.L. DeWitt, Commanding General of the Western Theater of Operations, to proceed with a plan for wholesale internment of Japanese Americans. And when the Census Bureau responded to a War Department request for a "special tabulation" of the 1940 census data? Japanese individuals and families were plotted into small, efficient geographic areas at the census tract and block levels. The groundwork was laid for their round-up.

Days into Robin and Buster's new routine of all-night, every-night blackouts, Dottie McLeod checked in with an overdue update. Sent airmail c/o Pelham Manor, the grace of someone's tidy pencil neatly lined out Manor Circle. The Loch Arbour address was distinct.

Now nearly nine months pregnant, Dottie lived a life most military wives at the time would envy. In her descriptive letter to Robin, words ripped front and back across two sheets of airmail stationery as if she were running out of time.

As any first-time mother can attest, she was about to.

```
MISSOULA
 3 MAR
  1942
  MONT.
```

Mrs. W. Herbert McLeod – 1330 Gerald Avenue, Missoula, Montana – airmail 3/3/42

Mrs. N. Forrest Bedford
~~1283 Manor Circle~~ *Loch Arbour Apts.*
~~Pelham Manor, New York~~ *Loch Arbour, N.J.*
Via Asbury Park

Dearest Robin and Buster,

I imagine if word hasn't gotten through to you from other sources as yet, you will be very surprised to learn that I am in Missoula and Bud takes up his residence from now on at Fort Knox, Kentucky with the Armored Force Replacement Training Center...until he can be gotten into the Quartermaster Corps, which is being worked upon with vim, vigor, and vitality...

In the same way Buster aspired to the Signal Corps, Bud fancied the Quartermaster Corps, a branch of the U.S. Army responsible for procurement and delivery of many logistical supplies of war. I reason he found the Quartermasters akin to the McLeod family business, the Missoula Mercantile. His father, Walter, presided as President following the retirement of his father. With Bud's degree from N.Y.U.'s "School of Commerce, Accounts and Finance" he understood how to manage supply chains.

Like the Signal Corps, it's difficult to distill all that the Quartermasters were responsible for. Their work was diverse. Soldiers trained to fill specialized roles, depending on where and for what they deployed.

For example, take uniform supply. In the *Pacific* theater, mid-day often waxed hot as the hinges of hell and monsoonal weather left quagmires of mud. The Quartermaster knew the M-1942 "jungle boot" was the ticket for this part of the world where exposure to water, heat, bugs, and fungal or bacterial infections was a constant. Globe trot over to *Europe* and the Quartermaster's order included heavy-duty mountaineer hiking/ski boots paired with "bear paw" snowshoes. That was the footwear for winter advances into cold, snowy elevations where camo reversibles, the likes of what Lelia pined for, were part of the package.

The Quartermasters trained at Camp Lee, six hundred miles east of Fort Knox, in Petersburg, Virginia. In all his "vim, vigor, and vitality," if Bud felt disappointment in not being sent to Camp Lee, he shouldn't have.

In Kentucky, the Armored Force command sifted through qualifications of hundreds of thousands of men pouring into the Army. They sought recruits well suited for a specific niche. They planned to assemble the best qualified in top-notch teams. In so doing, the United States would achieve the finest armored force in the world.

Once selected, if a man wanted to be transferred to a different branch, they'd learn the Air Corps was the only other fighting force so highly regarded. They, too, recruited top young men. It took excellent eyesight and superior physical and mental fitness to meet the high standards set for bombardier, navigator, or pilot in the mightiest air army in the world.

Bud lacked the qualifications to fly, but he'd made the cut for the Armored Force.

Poor Bud received his marching papers about the 25th of January—so we consulted the doctor as to my travelling cross-country by train—and with an O.K. hurriedly packed all our possessions and arrived in Missoula January 31st. It was so marvelous getting back to Montana again Robin, and seeing all the relatives and friends.

Dorothy would be safe and happy living with Bud's parents indefinitely.

…it's so wonderful being with them. They are such dears and so good to me.

If only Robin could say the same about Nat and Ethel.

In the summer of 1939, the two sisters spent several weeks in the company of Mr. and Mrs. McLeod, Auntie Alta, Uncle Dix, and a gang of kids, including Bud and Robin's summer love, Billy Hoblitt. They'd rode horseback, pitched horseshoes, picnicked often, watched the moon and the stars, and listened to *Hit Parade* chart toppers. Much of the fun came to pass at Seeley Lake where fiery sweet memories were cast under Montana's blue skies and brilliant sun, anchored at the McLeod's lake-front cabin. Bud's folks orchestrated much of the magic.

They are doing Bud's old room completely over for little Walter Wayne and me and it is going to be just adorable.

They'd chosen an alliterative <u>boy's</u> name in keeping with their societally driven desire for a son; a familial system that perpetuated patriarchy. "Walter" was an easy pick. Both Bud and his father were christened "Walter Herbert." The middle name "Wayne" derived from Dorothy's father, "T. Wayne."

Mom and I have been having such a marvelous time deciding on new wallpaper (light yellow) a beautiful blue rug—yellow and blue flowered drapery material, a new yellow and blue bedspread with a small floral design, a new lamp, a very nice chest of drawers for baby's belongings, darling material to cover a little slipper chair and material to redecorate the bassinette which Bud's Dad used as a baby.

A slipper chair would do nicely for Dorothy to sit close to baby at play on the floor. Historically such a chair was placed in a lady's bedroom; smaller in scale, armless, lower than a dining chair, and used to assist in getting dressed. A slipcover, in keeping with the chosen yellow and blue floral theme of the nursery, would mask ill-suited "grandam" upholstery. In the years to follow, it would efficiently transition into a child's seat.

We're having such fun and scurrying around like busy little bees. Baby is expected on 21st of this month—the first day of spring—so you'd best drop me a line and let me know your address if you want to know all the details of your little niece or nephew…

Bud spent 10 days here with us before he had to leave for his physical exam in Salt Lake City—Fort Douglas…

One of America's oldest Army posts originated as Camp Douglas in 1862, during the Civil War. Colonel Patrick Conner and his command were there to protect the overland mail and keep an eye on the Mormons. At the time, waters of Red Butte Creek were strategic to the location of the camp, on the foothills overlooking the Salt Lake Valley.

Dorothy's self-described "busy-bee" state paled in comparison to what was going on at Bud's destination in the Bee-Hive State. In February 1941, the Fort Douglas reception center ramped up to initiate young men from Utah and surrounding states into military service. The December 7 attack on Pearl Harbor triggered a huge transformation. Twelve days later, on December 19, officials announced over the AP and UP wires out of San Francisco and Salt Lake that the long-established Ninth Service Command Headquarters, at the Presidio of San Francisco, would relocate to Utah's capital city.

Salt Lake became the nerve center of communications and operations behind the Pacific Coast combat zone. Fort Douglas' strategic proximity to highways, railroads, and airlines placed the Ninth Command along

Six Weeks for Boat Mail

the main east-west stream of military supplies, fundamental to the WWII mobilization effort.

Bud reported to the bustling Fort where he appeared before a medical officer who verified he was physically fit for duty.

At the reception center, military leadership modeled exemplary appearance and conduct meant to instill soldier confidence in their Army superiors. Bud cleared the Physical Profile Test and the Army General Classification Test—the same Otis test of intelligence Buster had passed with flying colors at Fort Devens the previous May.

Exceptional test results precipitated Bud's marching orders to Fort Knox.

...We had such a marvelous happy time together. Doctor Marshall wouldn't let me go with him—so I sat here and moaned my bad luck—while Bud did the same thing in Salt Lake for two weeks—doing absolutely nothing...

In truth, Bud did a lot while at Fort Douglas, but evidently spared Dorothy the details. Every step by the book, Bud was interviewed, classified, and assigned. He sat through an orientation on life insurance, bonds, family allowances, and allotments. Had he not paid attention, he'd be at a loss when interviewed and asked to state his wishes on financial particulars.

Training films, prescribed lectures, blood typing, and inoculations followed. Uniforms, equipment, and "dog tags" were issued. Long considered a messenger of death to identify remains if mortally wounded, the new and improved rounded rectangle of thin metal revealed blood type. With that singular upgrade, an immediate transfusion could save a life.

Finally, transportation to their assigned Training Center was determined; almost all traveled by train.

Check. Check. Check. Check. All that "doing nothing." Naturally there was a lot of waiting, but chatting it up with other men getting put through their induction paces in Salt Lake beat nesting nervously in Missoula.

...The trip home from N.Y. didn't affect me in the slightest—but the time was drawing near and Doc. Marshall is a stickler I guess for keeping his patients on hand.

He is a marvelous man—perhaps you remember him, Robin. He is Mary Marshall's father—one of my old school chums.

Fifty-four-year-old Dr. J.F.S. Marshall was considered one of the Northwest's leading obstetricians at the time. His reputation, for an exacting schedule of work around the clock, possibly stemmed from his time in the Great War. He served three years overseas with a Canadian army field ambulance unit.

In 1919, Doc Marshall arrived in Missoula to settle and raise his own family. In 1922, he was counted among five founding members of the "Western Montana Clinic," a progressive medical group patterned after the Mayo Clinic. In the twenty years since, other Mayo-trained specialists were recruited. Word of mouth pointed all expectant mothers toward Dr. Marshall as the "go to" obstetrician.

...He has over 40 babies arriving in March—so you can imagine what a busy person he is!!

As war neared, soldiers the likes of Buster and Bud had occupied themselves planting seeds of a legacy. Dr. Marshall wouldn't get much sleep in the thirty one days of March.

Bud was able to drive back from Salt Lake with another Missoula boy who has a '41 Studebaker—and exactly the same orders...

For the time being, Bud had no need to consult rail routes and timetables. The stars aligned when he fell in with *that* fellow Missoulan. The slipstream design of the Studebaker "Commander Sedan" looked as though it was moving even when it wasn't—clean lines, art deco styling, easy on gas. It must have been one of the last off the production line before the war.

He was here for two days last week before leaving for Fort Knox. They left early Friday morning and are probably at Fort Knox now. It was just terrible having to part—but just one of those things that must be. I'm hoping after baby is a few months old I can go visit Bud for a while—wherever he may be...

Travel to Fort Knox would take the two soldiers across two thousand miles or more, through Montana, South Dakota, Iowa, Illinois, and Indiana.

Six Weeks for Boat Mail

They'd drop south into Kentucky across the Ohio River and report for training at the Fort, according to strict orders issued for the time and place of assembly.

Plain-spoken as a pregnant woman could be, Dottie let urgent bits roll off the tip of her fountain pen as if she were the family news editor up against a hard deadline.

...We think you two have been so lucky so far being together most all the time—and hope you'll keep on being as lucky. I've received a letter from Mother last week, Robin, in which she said one of your last letters with Buster's fort and town had been gone over by the censor and the fort and town's name cut out—quite a few lines cut out as a matter of fact. She thought it very strange my letter hadn't been mutilated in the same way with Bud's fort...

For the time being, Lelia would at least know Bud's training whereabouts at Fort Knox. The simple explanation for Robin's mutilated letter proved the censors sustained secrecy surrounding ground-breaking developments in electronics at Fort Monmouth. In closely guarded laboratories new codes for the Army were devised. Enemy communications, intercepted by way of "listening posts," were decrypted. Secretary of War, Henry L. Stimson, described a so-called electric eye: "intense study is being given to the wave echoes of radio...the device can see at night through fogs and clouds and tell the location of enemy vessels or planes."

And then Dottie thought to add this:

...We're both so glad Bud has his 2nd lieutenant's commission—and can be a 1st lieutenant in six months. I feel so sorry for boys who have to go in as buck privates at $21 a month...

As a matter of movie and music trivia, Universal Studio's 1941 release, *Buck Privates*, popularized Dorothy's cliché reference. Celebrity stars aligned when The Andrews Sisters, under contract with Universal at the time, performed what would become that sensational WWII morale-booster, "Boogie Woogie Bugle Boy." Written specifically for the script, the pop-jazz-jump song burst forth as a hit. So did the comedy duo of Bud Abbot and Lou Costello. They nearly ad-libbed their way into big-screen stardom.

Double Ocean Trouble

In a now classic drill routine scene, they clumsily tripped up. Japanese military leaders used the film sequence to demonstrate the ineptness of U.S. troops, as a means to boost the confidence of their own Imperial forces.

Fun and games aside, how exactly had Bud McLeod managed a 2nd lieutenant's commission to surpass Buster's post?

Recall Bud attended Shattuck Military Academy, the college prep school in Faribault, Minnesota. There he'd learned rigid military discipline and practiced drills and maneuvers. After graduation, he returned to Missoula and majored in Military Science at the University of Montana. Enthusiasm for that course of study mounted due to war talk in Europe, as foreign affairs snarled. Advanced military training though R.O.T.C. was his fast track to 2nd lieutenant in the U.S. Army Reserve. As a rifle marksman he, like Buster, knew how to shoot.

Enchanted with her current situation, Dottie marveled at her maturity.

…It will feel so strange to think of '42 graduating this June. I feel as though I'd finished college five years ago—Little baby will be almost three months old then.

Few women at the time believed they'd ever be personally responsible for their future standard of living. Enthusiastically, she gushed over the fact that Bud's older sister, Olive, delivered her first baby two weeks ahead of schedule, on Groundhog Day. She described it like the perfect life she imagined for herself.

…It happened just 2 days after Bud and I arrived in Missoula and I was so happy that Bud could be here and see her. Little Mary Sharon was a 6 ½ lb. baby—and is just a month old today. She is simply adorable!!! She has beautiful blue eyes—and lots of dark hair. Mom McLeod and I go over to see her almost every day—and I'm learning so much that I will feel like a veteran when Walter Wayne arrives. (If it should by chance be a girl we think we'll call her Florence Anita—Do you approve?)

Then, with sisterly perception, she spilled a snip of news Robin might want to hear. Billy Hoblitt, Robin's summer of '39 heartthrob, remained a bachelor. He worked for Bud's dad, Walter, at the Missoula Mercantile. The animal husbandry skills he'd honed at Montana State, class of 1939, were on hold. Like so many other young men, he waited for his draft number to be called.

Dottie closed with the next order of business. News of Bud's younger sister, Marsh. Age seventeen, she was the baby of the McLeod family with plans to marry a Montana State graduate, class of 1941.

...Henry (Hank) Hibbard a marvelous boy from Helena age 22 who attended Dartmouth his first two years then finished at Bozeman last June—He's a marvelous skier. It looks very serious and the engagement ring is gorgeous...

Evidence of what materially mattered to a girl in 1942.

...write soon—Loads of love, Dorothy and Bud

On Friday, March 13, Dottie arrived at St. Patrick's Hospital in downtown Missoula, where Doc Marshall attended to the birth of a healthy baby boy, Walter Wayne McLeod.

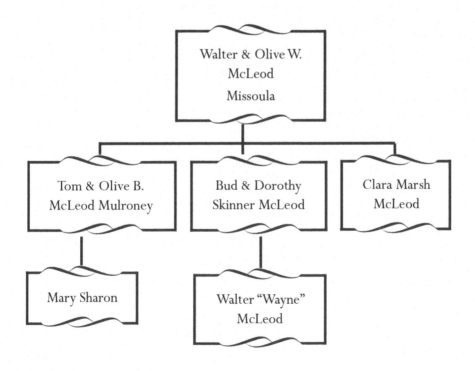

KGEI Radio
Chapter Ten

During his Fireside Chat on February 23, 1942, President Roosevelt asked Americans to pull out their maps of the world. The war map craze had become part of mainstream culture across the country. Every home had at least one. In the aftermath of December 7, United Press capitalized on the market for new and improved maps. For fifteen cents, they included vital areas in the Battle for the Pacific.

Reference globes were handy, but harder to stick with pins.

For Blue Star families, those with sons and daughters in active service, letters held clues. Bits left unredacted by censors added up when matched with "invasion maps" regularly published in morning and evening "tribunes." Inky newsprint graphics, with arrows pointing to action, depicted offensives and areas of resistance.

Five days after Easter, with no mention of the traditional leg of lamb or mint sauce she'd served, Lelia crafted a letter dated April 10. For now, she had war news top of mind. It posted registered mail on April 11, Rancagua. Addressed to *Mr.* Nathaniel Forrest Bedford, Loch Arbour Apartment B-4, it took a ten-day path that began, "Examined by Censor 4427." POR AVION PANAGRA it flew into Miami on April 16 and out April 17. Into New York on April 18, arriving Asbury Park April 20.

But the date of her letter coincided with OCS graduation day at Fort Monmouth. By the time it reached Buster, the tea towels and bed sheets of Robin's trousseau were performing admirably in their Barrington Court

Six Weeks for Boat Mail

apartment, Cambridge, Massachusetts. Located steps from the winding Charles River along Memorial Drive, the table was set to entertain Dizzy and Gina whenever schedules permitted.

L.M. Skinner, Rancagua – Sewell, Chile S.A. – airmail stamped in NJ April 20
EXAMINED BY 4427

April 10, 1942
Dear Buster (and Roberta),

I'm writing to our two "sons" tonight (although possibly they may let their wives read the letter providing they'll get busy and write one themselves). It must be Roberta is putting in all her time in the kitchen…We do so earnestly hope that both newlyweds have more weeks and months together before "foreign duty" calls…

Grim news of "foreign duty" spilled over the radio daily. From her geographic point of reference, the Japanese in the Pacific were far more worrisome than the Germans in the North Atlantic.

On the island of Luzon, General Jonathan Wainwright, commander of U.S.-Filipino forces in the Philippines, inherited the heavy responsibilities of "Dugout Doug" MacArthur (his derogatory nickname) when "Doug" departed on March 11.

That famous declaration, "I shall return," would be immortalized alongside the likes of eighteenth-century naval hero, John Paul Jones' "I have just begun to fight."

History tells us, after three months of fighting, a final Japanese offensive began in Luzon on Good Friday, April 3. The estimated 76,000 troops, short on rations since January, weak from malnutrition and disease, pushed into the southern tip of the Bataan Peninsula. On April 9, trapped by the Japanese, they were forced to surrender.

KGEI Radio

...I feel very sorry for our Boys in Luzon tonight. They have put up such a brave fight!!

In the stroke of her pen on April 10, Lelia revealed she knew of the surrender. But the horrors and atrocities that occurred at the hands of the Imperial Japanese Army in the days that followed? The sixty-five-mile forced hike to San Fernando under the blazing sun, without water, was aptly named the "Bataan Death March." Along the way, scores of American soldiers fell beaten, bayoneted, beheaded.

On a lighter note, Lelia sang praises of her favorite radio show as if ready to stand up and tap dance.

...Every Sunday night over the network we get "Command Programme", which is put on for boys on foreign service. We understand it is only short wave... You probably saw a mention of it in Time... it was in our airmail Time of April 6...

Lelia's "Command Programme" was one and the same as what North Americans knew as "Command Performance." The veritable variety show, new in 1942, originated as a way for popular entertainers to show their support of the U.S. Military. The wide-ranging showcase embraced comedy, sports, popular and semi-classical music, novelty numbers, and Hollywood stars.

...No one draws pay—no one rehearses—but all top flight talent. It is short waved by 17 different wave lengths, 17 times each Sunday...

Her enthusiasm suggested she dialed in several times on Sunday. Buster would appreciate the descriptive detail when she wrote how last week's performance packed a punch: Comedian Fred Allen and his Star Theatre Troupe volleying topical laughs and satiric humor; diva Gladys Swarthout, a colorful forty-two-year-old soprano; *New York Times* Sports Columnist, John Kieran; "A-list" talent of English actress Madeleine Carroll, idolized in Britain and America, famous for several starring roles—Alfred Hitchcock's *The 39 Steps* (1935) among them.

It's a sad fact that Germans killed Madeleine Carroll's sister. While seated at a typewriter in London, her building took a direct hit in October

1940, during the London Blitz. That was a turning point for the talented ash blonde actress. She reprioritized her career to help win the war.

Lelia left off with a mention of comic Henny Youngman. Snappy, irreverent, the "King of the One-Liners," rapid-fire jokes were his forte, to wit: "If you're going to do something tonight that you'll be sorry for tomorrow morning, sleep late."

...Tonight K-G-E-I was announcing Eddie Cantor...

In half a sentence Lelia revealed call letters for the high frequency shortwave station that aired out of San Francisco. She spilled Cantor's name, too, the top-notch emcee for Command Performance. His radio voice, comedic touch, and guests the likes of Danny Kaye and Dinah Shore, boosted morale for soldiers and anyone, the likes of Lelia, who knew where to point the shortwave radio dial.

Was it serendipity, or did she cast her mind back three years to make the KGEI connection?

In 1939 when Lelia and T. Wayne, returned to the States for their first holiday in five years, they rendezvoused with Robin and Dottie in California. First stop on their reunion tour? The Golden Gate Exposition. It showcased the completion of the Golden Gate (1937) and San Francisco Bay (1936) Bridges. Over four full days, Robin noted twenty-seven marvelous exhibits in her diary. Among them: "Air Transportation Pan American..." and "Folies Bergère—Whee!"

From the Exposition grounds on Treasure Island, a compact KGEI studio and transmitter were on display. K*GE*I signified "<u>GE I</u>nternational." Its purpose? General Electric seized the opportunity to capture emerging foreign markets over the airwaves. *Ooh-la-la, oui-oui*! They'd engaged the Folies Bergère chorus girls in a flamboyant song and dance sales pitch to push their branded refrigerators and ranges to consumers.

Then what?

Post-exposition, the station stayed on the air under GE's control. A clear signal reached into Latin American and Asia. As the war escalated, their communication was strong.

The bad news?

GE lacked a news editorial policy. Consequently, the ripped-and-read teletype via the International News Service (INS) was slanted with the personal "non-intervention" philosophy of William Randolph Hearst.

History tells us in the months before the attack on Pearl Harbor, FDR was out to counter Japanese propaganda on international airwaves. But his hands were congressionally tied. Unlike other countries around the world, *an official government radio voice* was <u>unconstitutional</u> in the United States.

Then commentator William Winter, the first "Voice of America," stepped into the studio. Winter contrasted news items and reflected on the majority view of Americans. When his *balanced* reporting reached into Asia and the Pacific, it symbolized one of America's four great freedoms that Buster so loved. Speech!

Over KGEI, Lelia heard the announcer's words the same way, *and on the same day*, our nation's intrepid fighters did. While she sat high in the Andes, they were hunkered in western Pacific bunkers. For them, live rounds fired within earshot.

I imagine she wept when the short-wave broadcast of "the Voice of Freedom" shook her with the news, "Bataan has fallen."

The KGEI bulletin imbedded America's message of democracy: "…what sustained them [the troops] through all these months of incessant battle was a force more than physical…It was the thought of their native land and all it holds most dear to them, the thought of freedom and dignity and pride in these most priceless of all human prerogatives."

…Fortune gives us lots of good "war dope."

Buster's ten-dollar gift subscription was money well spent. The May edition revealed nothing about Bataan, but she learned about other important topics. The world's biggest merchant marine building program, for example.

Lelia went on to describe life in the mining camp in a way she believed Buster would find interesting, and Robin might, too.

...Red Cross is keeping all the women out of mischief here. Beside the Tuesday of work for the British Red Cross, we are now starting in to give Friday, a day for the American Red Cross...

The women reported at nine-thirty a.m. and worked until six p.m.; released in time to fix dinner. But what was the *"mischief"*?

This backstory is relevant.

In the early years of El Teniente, Braden Copper strongly believed that development of a modern nuclear family came with rewards. To a large extent, North American values imposed on everyone led to moral improvement of the entire company town population.

Gender-based roles were such that men, as wage earners, were head of the household. An able wife, educated in domesticity, would devote her energy to hygienic housekeeping and care of her husband and children.

Of course, there were other widely known stories. Those of adulterous women "making mischief" in extramarital relationships.

But *this* was not *that*.

In the early months of 1942, the mine workers went on strike. Their women rallied to the cause. They conducted meetings and schemed on how to strengthen the strike movement, and picketed with their husbands, too.

According to company policy, *that* was mischief.

As a company woman, what did Lelia's personal "hygienic housekeeping" include?

...Adela and I have been at fall housecleaning for a week...I've stretched all the curtains...Tomorrow have a man coming to wash the kitchen ceiling—he'll probably have to do the walls, too, before he's through...

The walls were filthy, another indicator of sick air quality. She'd also made quince jelly, a fall tradition. When ripe, the mouth-puckering quince resembles a rumpled pear with brilliant yellow skin. It's delightfully edible when cooked down into its sweet, blushing rose form and spread on hot buttered toast.

Then came the news she assumed they knew but wasn't certain.

And since this letter was still winding its way from Loch Arbour to Cambridge, they'd know for sure by the time it arrived.

...Walter Wayne McLeod has made his appearance! Born March 13...What a shame Bud has to miss his first months of babyhood. His call would only have to have been postponed about a month for him to have been with Dorothy for her confinement...

Uncle Sam didn't work that way.

She was pretty plucky, Alta wrote...

Lelia's mind wandered to the baby blanket, suit, and sweater yet to be delivered; but instead turned the topic to stretching the usability of their own worn clothes.

...I had the sewing girl, finally, about six weeks...remodeling old garments. She took an extra pair of trousers and made Dad two vests...

He'd wear those to the office.

...Made house dresses for me, uniforms for Adela (also white aprons) changed elastic in girdles, etc., etc. Oh, yes, turned shirt collars and cuffs...

Imagine changing elastic in a girdle.

Imagine even owning one to begin with.

...Russell has just been home again for three weeks. Had jaundice and was in Army infirmary for 10 days before coming up. Lost quite a few pounds but gained back five or six on home food. He returned to Cavalry School last Tuesday. Doesn't know whether they'll be released April 15th...The [Chilean] Army is taking on double the previous number of conscripts...Loving thoughts and hugs...Mother and Dad

Tough as it was for Russell, Lelia's heart also ached for Bud. When he slipstreamed Kentucky-bound out of Missoula early in the morning of February 27, six weeks of training at Fort Knox awaited. He was luckier than most. Raw selectees were sent from reception centers to thirteen weeks of basic training. With R.O.T.C. under his belt, Bud flew over that phase. He knew the fundamentals of soldiering. They'd been drilled into

Six Weeks for Boat Mail

him early on at Shattuck: military discipline, care of clothing, equipment, and the like. His six weeks were focused on techniques peculiar to the Armored Force where a menu of specialized training awaited: light tank, medium tank, mortar, antitank, machine gun, and more.

Bud's six weeks wound down as plans for "Army Day" wound up. At Fort Knox, pressed service dress uniforms came out of the closet under pressure to perform on April 6, the day after Easter. It marked the date in 1917 when Congress voted to enter the "war to end all wars."

On this twenty-fifth anniversary of World War I, at four o'clock Monday afternoon, new and experimental fighting devices rumbled out 4th Street, parade style, between curbs jam-packed with spectators in an eye-popping, two-mile-long display. The greatest armored force firepower display anywhere in the country was underway.

Somewhere in the mix, Bud found his specialized place among experimental amphibious tanks; heavy, self-propelled assault artillery on half-trac scout cars; and several platoons of fast, shifty light tanks, the "welterweights" of the Armored Force. The latter, known for lighter armor and armament, could deliver a punch with devastating speed.

For the first time anywhere in the nation, two brand-new thirty-ton M-4 medium tanks, complete with a high velocity 75mm gun and multiple machine guns, rolled along the route.

Destined to become the most iconic tank of WWII, the M-4 "Sherman" had made its debut.

The charting, formation, and movement of all that military might met with parade success.

Following graduation from the training center, Bud sped home with an assignment into an armored division at Fort Lewis, Washington State. He hoped to return to Fort Knox one day, where those with exceptional ability leveled up at the Armored Force School.

The Sunday, April 19 edition of *The Missoulian* revealed Lieutenant McLeod had been "granted a short leave and will continue on to Fort Lewis later in the week."

Fort Lewis, named after American explorer Meriwether Lewis, served as a major training and personnel center at the time. Communication methods had come a long way since 1804 when the Lewis and Clark Corps of Discovery launched west into uncharted territory at the direction of Thomas Jefferson.

Now, nearly 140 years later, it was the present state of chaotic world affairs that complicated everyone's ability to keep tabs on wandering friends and loved ones.

For Lelia to track the young Bedfords and McLeods was one example. Here is another.

While working as a warehouseman at the Missoula Mercantile, twenty-five-year-old bachelor Billy Hoblitt became too restless waiting around for his draft number to be called. The week after Easter he reported to the Army's district recruiting headquarters where, under strict quotas, he enlisted without assignment. That meant his experience, skills, and abilities would be put to work where, in someone's opinion, they were most needed. Most recruits were sent to Fort Douglas. Billy was one of just three whose compass pointed toward Fort Lewis.

There, five hundred miles west of Missoula, he'd be waiting when Bud arrived at the end of the month. The two boyhood chums were surprised and pleased to be reunited, at least for a little while, in the service of Uncle Sam.

Anyone's patriotic future was impossible to predict. But for Billy, five overseas tours through every theater of war took this Montana-born-and-raised ranch boy around the world. After which he returned to his hometown, married in 1947, and lived to be ninety-six.

Hornet's Nest
Chapter Eleven

During Robin's senior year at Smith, Dottie once wrote to describe their folks as "having cat fits because you haven't written."

More cat fits were to come. Robin let letter writing slide, censors messed with the messages, Lelia was left anxious, waiting, uninformed, and life went on.

Buster and his buddy, Prent Smith, graduated OCS together on Thursday, April 10. They followed the strategic 2nd lieutenant training path U.S. Army superiors laid out. The clock ticked.

Three weeks to the day, on May 1, more coursework commenced. In secrecy they embarked on a specialized subject of study at Harvard University's Cruft High-Tension Laboratory, "Electronics and Cathode Ray Tubes." Vital facts became fixed firmly in their minds.

Buster's parting shot at Fort Monmouth. Dressed in 2nd Lieutenant's attire, he puffs his pipe in the shade of New Jersey's coastal oak-pine forest.

Officer's Candidate School Graduating Class,
Fort Monmouth, New Jersey, April 1942

Vacuum tubes, made of glass, were a fundamental element in "modern" radios to create and amplify an electric signal necessary for the radio to work. In this war, effective communication between air and ground forces relied on them.

Committed to forty-three hours a week in the classroom, it left Buster time on the outside to keep Robin happy, and Prent time to continue courting his future wife, Phyllis.

L.M. Skinner, Rancagua—Sewell, Chile S.A.—airmail

Six Weeks for Boat Mail

April 25, 1942
Dearest Roberta and Buster,

Why don't we get a line from you?...I'm afraid you are ill...We do so want to know if Buster is a Lieutenant...how he's standing Army life, etc.

During Buster's twelve weeks at OCS, Robin sent just *one* letter.

...We were waiting for you to write us whether that $316 you mentioned included linen or whether the linen was extra...to be added to the cost of your flat service. But we never hear a word...Dad had the New York office send you a draft for the $316...Have you received that...?

...and did you receive the $200 I sent you for shopping Feb. 15?

Ten weeks had passed since Lelia mailed the registered envelope with her $200 check for Robin to purchase reversible ski parkas, and sewing machine parts, among other things on the shopping list. After the censors plucked the first page, the remaining contents were good to go. Had Robin made any purchases on her mother's behalf? While Buster attended OCS at Fort Monmouth, she had time on her hands—and yet she wasn't using it to shop for, or write to, her mother.

Lelia felt pressed. Miss Rivera, a nurse-friend of the family who lived in Sewell, was presently on vacation in North America. If Robin would simply get the shopping checked off, packed, and delivered to the capable hands of Miss Otterstrom, Miss Rivera would gladly shepherd the goods onto the steamship when she returned via Grace Lines.

Reminding Robin of yet another embarrassing etiquette misstep, Leila added:

...The Turtons are going up to the States next week...They have never received a thank you for the sandwich tray...

Lelia bumped into Jeane Turton at the automat just the day before.

...I feel rather ashamed.

Then this mess got messier.

Thanks to the kindness of Mr. and Mrs. Staples, Robin's riding boots, fountain pen, saddle shoes, and the knitted baby blanket, suit and sweater arrived in New York the last of March. Unaware of the Loch Arbour address at the time, Lelia instructed Miss Otterstrom to retrieve the package from the Staples' trunks and arrange delivery to Pelham Manor.

Now two steps behind, Lelia remained in the dark on their <u>Cambridge</u> address.

...Will you get the knitted things right off to Dorothy as soon as possible?... When it comes July—Aug and Sept. it will be too warm for a knitted suit...

And by the time fall weather rolled into Missoula, Walter Wayne would have outgrown them.

Signing off with war news, she reported that Russell continued to serve with the Chilean Cavalry. Although the Chilean Navy was among the best in the world, it was small, with nearly four-thousand miles of Pacific coastline to protect. Chile needed him.

I wonder if Hitler will keep hitting at the Russians—where he can be defeated, I think...

News over the AP wire from London reported Soviet pilots and ground batteries destroyed 1,500 German planes in the week ending April 14; one of the biggest scores of the air war.

Lelia prayed the Russians would prevail.

...but if he [Hitler] starts through Turkey to India to join up with the Japs— we will have a long, long struggle.

Obviously, Lelia followed inky war maps on her own kitchen table. Her strategic thinking went like this: Turkey's neutrality was at risk. Both Axis <u>and</u> Allied Nations promised military, economic, and political support. What if Hitler made it through Turkey, to India, and joined the Japanese?

The driving force behind Japan's aggression was a fire-breathing General Tojo, aka Japanese Premier Hideki Tojo, War Minister. A dictator whom Lelia particularly despised. He'd reached out a clutching hand with promises of a "new order" in Asia, in which India could be free of British oppression. Then, the day after Easter, at a critical moment in India's negotiations for self-government with Britain, Japanese planes raided two

Six Weeks for Boat Mail

Indian ports and Japanese warships began attacking merchant ships in the Bay of Bengal.

It may explain why Lelia closed on this cheerful note.

...Our boys are doing beautifully bombing Tokio, don't you think?...Hugs—kisses—Love to both, Mother

One person's revenge is another's social justice. Whichever camp Lelia was in, that one-line closing sentence captured this "never forget" WWII event:

On April 18, 1942, under the command of Lt. Col. Jimmy Doolittle, eighty volunteers on a secret mission divided themselves aboard sixteen American B-25 twin-engine bombers; olive drab; unmistakable white stars on red-and-blue circles displayed on their wings and fuselage. They flew from the deck of Aircraft Carrier USS *Hornet* in the first offensive air action against Japan; retaliation only four months after Pearl Harbor. Bombs fell on strategic targets, including the military, political, and financial heart of the empire: Tokyo!

Cpt. Ted W. Lawson, a pilot, lost a leg but captured the story in his book: *Thirty Seconds Over Tokyo*. In 1944, MGM released the Oscar-winning film by the same name. Box office favorite Van Johnson won the nation's heart as bomber pilot Ted Lawson. Spencer Tracy led the mission, cast as Lt. Col. Doolittle.

When Lelia's letter of April 25 finally caught up to Robin and Buster, they'd already seen the headlines that boosted morale across America. The *New York Daily News* of April 19 pitched it like this: "War Loving Japs Get a Taste of it at Home." General Tojo did not know from whence the storm came, nor where it went.

Meanwhile, in retaliatory rage, a fantastic attempt to avenge the Doolittle raid began when the Japanese immediately set out to produce twenty thousand balloon bombs. Built of rice paper and bamboo, with a small percentage constructed of rubberized silk, they were designed to carry radio equipment and a bomb load averaging about fifty pounds. This unguided aerial offensive would travel the jet stream, intended to ignite raging wildfires in the western U.S. The large-scale launch would not, however, commence for another two and a half years.

It wasn't until the first week of May when Robin's letter, written in mid-February from Loch Arbour, reached the Braden office in Sewell. It answered questions that had plagued T. Wayne and Lelia for months.

Until the next pivot in Buster's military training, letters from friends and family would post to:

Mr. and Mrs. N. Forrest Bedford
988 Memorial Drive, Apt. 485
Cambridge, Mass.

L.M. Skinner, Rancagua—Sewell, Chile S.A.—airmail

May 7, 1942

Dearest Roberta and Buster,

Your long looked for letter finally arrived. We were beginning to be quite worried. We put off writing from air mail, to air mail, each week thinking you would let us know how much we were to send you for your linen... When you didn't receive a letter or a check from us I should have thought you would have sent us another notice... all the boat mail is taking <u>six</u> wks. now...

Water under the bridge. Thank God the censors didn't pluck anything beyond the first page of Lelia's letter, also written mid-February.

Will you look into the parts for my Western Electric sewing machine at Bloomingdale's right away—if you haven't already done so?

She feared she would never get them, and her machine would be worthless. If Robin would only get after the shopping and hand off the goods to Miss Otterstrom to be sent with nurse Rivera, they would be delivered. Snap!

Lelia edged toward panic. W.J. Turner, General Manager, laid out company policy particulars. Company travel from Kennecott in New York

Six Weeks for Boat Mail

to the South American operation declined sharply after war was declared. Baggage no longer traveled unaccompanied.

> ...*Mr. Turner has sent letters to all people working in each Dept. not to order things to be sent to N.Y. Office to be forwarded to Sewell...the Office is being swamped with bags...they can't get them down to us unless some particular person is coming...once in a blue moon...Is that brown suitcase in good enough condition to send back down?*

That case was nearly new! Robin's September 1939 diary entry, written on the eve of her return for Junior year at Smith, corroborated it:

> September 20—Bought new suitcase today. Lovely Hartman [sic]. Had lunch with Mr. Turton from Chile. Packed and left for Albany amid many farewells from Mom and Dad—was pretty hard to leave 'em.

Hard on Lelia and T. Wayne, too. This was the summer they'd tried to pack in enough memories with their kids to bury five years of life without them. Robin's note, watermarked with tears, concluded a three-month coast-to-coast travel extravaganza: from the San Francisco Golden Gate Exhibition to "The World of Tomorrow" at the New York World's Fair.

Since then, the inanimate brown case nearly came to life on par with the *Brave Little Toaster*. It chaperoned Robin between ivy-covered campuses and ski areas all around New England, to Florida where she met Buster on Christmas break, from New York to Santiago, and in a circuitous return, up the east coast of South America, through Central America, then from Brownsville to Newark. When her enormous Hartmann trunk went missing in Valparaiso and failed to appear in New York harbor, the well-traveled suitcase prevailed.

To borrow Indiana Jones' quote in George Lucas' *Raiders of the Lost Arc*: "It's not the years, honey. It's the mileage."

Enough of that. Except to acknowledge, for Lelia, the situation was dire. Nurse Rivera was her only hope to deliver the shopping she'd become obsessed with.

...So glad Buster has his commission...it's grand he will have his three months at Harvard.

Every new military training opportunity for Buster granted Robin more time to settle in as a wife and homemaker. That unpleasant business with David? Over and done, so Lelia hoped. She didn't know and wouldn't care that he married on May 15, five months after he swore his love for Robin and pulled that preposterous "Susan Brown angle."

I had a Mother's Day card yesterday from Bud mailed at Missoula...

Was he home on leave, or transferred? Puzzling his moves made for more worry.

It happened like this. A one-month-old Walter Wayne met his father mid-April. That's when Bud, after completing his six-weeks training at Fort Knox, travelled by way of Missoula, on the way to Fort Lewis. He'd been granted a short leave to visit with family after the Army Day shebang. While in Missoula, he signed a card Dottie handpicked. Sent airmail, it reached Lelia four days before Mother's Day, May 10.

...We haven't had a letter from Dorothy since <u>before</u> W. Wayne's arrival. We don't know whether she isn't as strong as she should be, or whether a letter has been lost. The announcement came yesterday—was mailed March 22nd up there. How I would love to see the little fellow!

It was a comfort to know, even while shouldering new military responsibilities, Bud checked up on his wife and son.

...even if it should be for only a few days so he can see him as a "new babe."

As for her fruitless worry over Dorothy, it's a shame she underestimated Bud's dad. An experienced Walter McLeod took bold steps to diffuse the irritable chaos he expected with a newborn in the roost.

How?

By devising a birth plan of his own design.

Before Dorothy returned from the hospital, Mrs. McLeod shoved off for two-weeks rest at a health resort on the Flathead Indian Reservation, the curative waters of Hot Springs, Montana.

Six Weeks for Boat Mail

Bud, with baby Wayne and Dorothy, at the McLeod home in Missoula.

For his daughter-in-law and firstborn grandson, he employed private nurses day *and* night at the hospital. They stayed on for several days after the homecoming, too.

By all appearances, when Bud passed through, the family was well-rested and ready to sit for a professional photoshoot. Advertised as keepsakes for generations, solo-soldier and family portrait sessions grew to be a lucrative market. Picture perfect, every hair in place, no baby spit-up, Lelia would be especially pleased to run her eyes all over this ideal 1942 family unit, practically of her own making.

One to Grow On
Chapter Twelve

Lelia continued her letter of May 7 in which she clucked approval of her daughter's choice of sterling. She'd spotted the "Fragrance" pattern in a Reed & Barton magazine ad. With a twist of envy, she added:

...It's nice you are in such a nice new Apt...Are you budgeting with the high cost of living? Our living here has been soaring every month since you left...Do you have your car up in Cambridge with you?

It was fortunate that both sets of in-laws, Mr. and Mrs. McLeod and Nat and Ethel, popped for the newlyweds' cars in 1941. The automobile industry halted production in February 1942. Factories re-tooled and trained full throttle toward war production: planes, guns, and tanks.

...but the tire situation sounds serious.

Rubber was essential to defense. As it happened, one of Japan's early successes cut off rubber supplies from Malaya and the Dutch East Indies to the U.S. and Great Britain. Hence, an enormous, government-owned stockpile of natural rubber that existed in 1941 rapidly depleted in the production of tires for tanks, trucks, motorcycles, airplanes, blimps, landing boats, life rafts, gun mounts, gas masks, puncture-sealing gas tanks, hoses, belts, and gaskets. The list went on. Synthetic rubber production was in its infancy.

In a White House publicity stunt, all rubber bones and balls of FDR's two-year-old, shaggy-black Scottish Terrier, Fala, were gathered up for the executive mansion's contribution to the nationwide rubber scrap collection.

Over the AP came this news. The rubber shortage was "so acute" the time had come to halt "Sunday trips, visits to Cousin Joe and petting parties."

In his 1920 debut novel, *This Side of Paradise*, F. Scott Fitzgerald introduced the concept of "petting parties." Young Americans since have euphemized the term. In the parlance of the 1960s, "make-out parties" embodied those coming-of-age moments when romantic love flourished in an atmosphere of budding sexuality.

...I don't dare put in my "two cents" on the views of the war for fear my letters may be thrown out by the Censors.

Censors be damned, she added this:

We feel so sad for the boys and Officers on Corregidor tonight, as the news came over K.G.E.I. Of course it was expected but nevertheless it's sad...

Japanese artillery and air attacks on Corregidor began shortly after the fall of Bataan. Now, after a battering four-week siege, Tokyo rejoiced triumphantly. Like Lelia, the rest of the world looked at it as an inevitable outcome. The War Department issued communique No. 219. It revealed approximately 11,574 soldiers, sailors, marines, and civilians were taken prisoner; "Lieutenant General Jonathan Wainwright, commanding the American-Filipino forces, presumably was among those captured."

Following his order for the white flag of surrender, Wainwright stayed with his men. No special treatment for him. As POWs they suffered the brutality of their Japanese captors together.

...I just can't keep wondering where Buster, Bud and Junior [Bill Dixon, Jr.] may be sent. I am glad for every day that you and Dottie may have together with your "hubbies." Make the most of them and get all the happiness you can out of each other's company.

It was the only advice she could muster. Her mind played an endless loop of war news.

...It's 12:00 midnight and here I sit...Russell didn't get "let out" in April so expect it will be Sept. anyway, before he is released...As you say he will be in the draft now that the age [in the U.S.] *has been lowered...Mother and Dad.*

Around the world people agreed these were uncertain times, but one thing was certain. The month of May marked another trip around the sun for Buster (born on the cusp of Taurus/Gemini) and Robin (a Gemini purebred). Both sets of parents wrote birthday wishes with divergent styles, like chalk and cheese.

A letter written to *Lieutenant* N. Forrest Bedford arrived at the Cambridge address:

```
PELHAM MANOR
  19 MAY
   1942
         N.Y.
```

Mrs. Nathaniel L. Bedford, 1283 Manor Circle, Pelham Manor, New York – May 19, 1942

Dearest son:

Day after tomorrow is your twenty-fourth birthday. You have grown into manhood in wonderful surroundings and you have proved the ability to get the most out of all the opportunities that came your way.

There is nothing that makes a mother more proud and happy and appreciative of the blessing of having such a wonderful son—To me you shall always be a darling boy, who each year is a better and stronger man—dearer and dearer each year. I wish you could be home here with us this weekend...

Buster was stuck in Cambridge. Ethel wished for his return to celebrate in Pelham. Confound the OPA (Office of Price Administration). When they introduced War Ration Book Number One, the "Sugar Book" in early May, Americans in every state across the nation shared the burden equally. So why was it, effective May 15, *gas rationing* ensnared just seventeen states along the Atlantic Coast, Maine to Florida?

Recall the sinking of the tanker *R.P. Resor*. When it was torpedoed in February, eighty thousand barrels of crude oil destined for Massachusetts burned, too. Doubtful anyone standing in the sand watching flames off Cape May considered how the dogged interference of U-boats, wreaking havoc with coastal shipping, would curtail their motoring habits two and a half months later. But of course, it did. For non-essential driving, the basic "A" gas ration card allotted three gallons of fuel a week. Not nearly enough to navigate the two hundred miles between Cambridge and Westchester County, on U.S. Route 1, the Post Road. Travel by way of the Massachusetts Turnpike was fifteen years into the future.

...Daddy joins me in wishing you a Happiest-Birthday ever with lots of health, good luck and wealth and prosperity—which will all come to you I am sure, and right soon. Loads of love, many, many more Happy Birthdays and kisses...Your Devoted Mother and Dad...

A check enclosed, in the amount of twenty-five dollars, came with this note:

Twenty-four and One more to go.

With Nat and Ethel out of the way, Robin planned to don an apron and roll up her sleeves for Buster's birthday.

In the days leading up to the OPA rollout of the "Sugar Book" system, which commenced May 4, newspapers across the nation published instructions. Because she was new to the neighborhood, Robin's first step was to get bearings on the nearest public school. At the local government level, school superintendents orchestrated *who* registered *when* over a four-day window. By applying conventional alphabetical order, even the worst procrastinators moved evenly through the cue. A blessing for teachers tasked, as volunteers in patriotic public service, to register every citizen.

The OPA trusted educators in their ability to <u>legibly</u> handprint on each book: name, age, height, weight, color of hair, and color of eyes. They'd also get the math right. After ascertaining how much sugar a family had on hand at home, that amount was divided by the number of people in the family unit and stamps were torn out for all sugar in excess of two pounds per person.

Barring any language or literacy barriers, the estimated time to complete the registration was five to seven minutes.

One to Grow On

The local school strategy was brilliant. Should a feisty mother with a lot of mouths to feed get out of line, I imagine her lumps would come from friends and neighbors standing in line behind.

Robin embraced the first day of registration in Cambridge. She reported among the alphabetical grouping of last names A through E. The New England Civilian Defense Councils were directed to stand down on blackout tests for the nights of May 4 – 7, so as not to create chaos that might interfere with the distribution effort.

A pound of sugar per person every two weeks supplied what Robin needed for whatever flavor cake and fluffy frosting Buster desired. She didn't need a reminder from the OPA that the first sugar coupon expired at midnight on May 16. After that, it became void automatically. From then on, until May 30, stamp No. 2 would be used. She planned her own birthday confection accordingly.

A Sunbeam Mixmaster, the "world's finest electric mixer" (according to advertisements at the time), hogged proportionally too much counter space in the Barrington Court apartment, but like every modern electric appliance, it was bewitchingly effortless. To whip cream, mash potatoes, create delicate hollandaise sauce, and prepare batter for cakes and cookies took little wrist action. Proper consistencies were guaranteed by way of Sunbeam's exclusive "magic mix-finder" dial.

Lelia posted a birthday greeting for Robin, strategically timed to catch a particular plane en route to North America, where it arrived punctually.

L.M. Skinner, Rancagua – Sewell, Chile S.A. – airmail

May 20, 1942
Dearest Roberta,

I am still awaiting an answer to my last letter but I'll have to send this along, so as to have it reach you by your birthday. I wish I could have you here to make a birthday cake, and we celebrate it together. It seems no-time at all since your birthday last May.

At Buster's request, Lelia imparted *"domestic wisdom"* over the three months Robin spent in Sewell. Presumably, her helper, Adela, got in on the act, too. If nothing else, Robin learned how to bake a cake. Pies and cookies, as well.

I wish those months of Sept., Oct. and November were coming to us again…

Lelia recalled this time last year with mixed feelings. It started with an innocent invitation for Bud to visit Dorothy in the mining camp. The timing of his arrival forced her to abandon her dream to see Robin graduate and marry, yet everything turned out alright according to life's plan.

…So much has happened this last year—your graduation, both marriages, both sons getting their commissions, Walter Wayne's arrival. It makes me feel that the months and years are going by altogether too fast.

There's no denying how time moves faster in an abstract way, causally related to age. With the birth of her first grandson did she suddenly realize how little genuine happiness she'd personally experienced in her fifty-two years? Worry and rumination, the joy-killers of life, dominated Lelia's way of being. Contentment eluded her.

We rec'd a letter from Dorothy…Her description of "Waynecito" was so interesting…I would send hers on to you, but it is so cute I read and reread it and hate to give it up.

A gem in which she took delight, for a change.

I find myself going back to it to discover some new point in her description… She says he is too good for words—no trouble at all, and as strong as an ox. She and he were christened together in the Episcopal Church…

It never occurred to me that Lelia would overlook Dorothy's baptismal commitment as an infant in Sewell. Or, for that matter, Grandmother Marie McLatchey, a Presbyterian "Gospel Minister," did not take it upon herself to christen her trifecta of grandkids. They'd debarked the motorship *Geisha* in southern California's San Pedro Harbor as young children on New Year's Day, 1925.

The embarrassing slip-up might have first surfaced in Missoula, when the McLeods tried to arrange Bud and Dorothy's church wedding the previous August. It was a widely held belief that a bride, wed in a church, was magically destined to live happily ever after.

But there was one matrimonial requirement lacking. Proof of Dottie's baptism.

At the Church of the Holy Spirit, the two-for-one mother-son rite of immersion into the Christian faith went off without a hitch. Dorothy's bridal-veiled church wedding? A long-forgotten promise.

...You are Godmother (although she said you didn't know it yet)...he didn't cry once inside the church.

In Robin's absence, Bud's seventeen-year-old sister, Marsh, held the baby for the sacrament.

...Bud had 10 days at home on his way to Fort Lewis...

Dorothy and baby Wayne joined him enroute as far as Spokane, the celebrated Inland Empire of the Northwest. Out of Missoula, Bud navigated the *Comet* along U.S. 10A. The hard surfaced road avoided treacherous mountain passes by way of the "water grade route." It wound along the Jocko, Clark Fork, and Pend Oreille Rivers where rich mining operations and fruit growing enterprises were backdropped by spectacular mountain scenery. With their own baby on board, Bud and Dottie were enchanted with family-type farms and a bountiful springtime display of weeks-old dancing lambs and suckling calves. An abundance of piglets and chicks proved beyond doubt that small farming operators pushed production levels to help the all-important food for defense effort: milk, chickens, eggs, lamb, and pork.

...They stayed at Hotel Davenport...

When its doors opened in 1914, Davenport Hotel became "The Pride of an Empire." No expense spared with respect to architectural design, décor, and service. An oasis of rest for travelers, it served equally as a business and social center. The Who's Who of explorers, statesmen and stars lingered in luxury. The young McLeods nestled into their chambers; walls charmingly done with delicate pastel patterns on the wallpaper; mahogany woodwork; thick linen draperies; dressing and reading lights, soft ceiling, and sidewall fixtures. The bathroom, separately heated, warmed the room for bathing.

Dorothy found her way to the mezzanine level for a weary mother's indulgence: coiffed hair and a manicure. Adept operators in the salon, who took turns rocking the six-week-old son of a soldier, made it possible.

Or so I'd like to believe.

Downstairs in the basement Bud stepped into the "Pompeiian Rooms." The finest statuary marble and bronze figured into the décor; murals on a background of Pompeiian red; mirrors on all sides reflected into infinity. When the barber, manicurist, and masseur were through, Bud felt like a noble warrior.

Conceivably, with Walter Wayne to bobble about, room service delivered their fine dining experience.

...she returned to Missoula at 4:00 P.M. the following day.

The Northern Pacific mainline out of Spokane swept mother and son eastbound across the Idaho Panhandle and over Lookout Pass, the Idaho/Montana border, amid the Coeur de' Alene Mountains of the Bitterroot Range.

Looking eight decades ahead, it would be laughable to imagine a new generation self-propelling, by foot or on bicycle, along the abandoned railbed at Lookout Pass. For fun, no less. The aptly named "NorPac" Trail is one of many preserved pathways for which credit is due to the nonprofit Rails-to-Trails Conservancy.

To Lelia, both daughters were counted among the "wandering wives" of WWII. Having survived a nomadic youth, she had confidence in their ability to take charge of the life to which they were now assigned. She'd puff up just a little with pride at the thought.

...Bud located a very nice motel and Dorothy and baby were leaving the last of April to be with him...he could be home every night and Sat. noon until Monday morning...

At the time motor lodges advertised "furnished rooms" in newspaper classifieds: "Near Fort. Telephone, radio, bathrooms have tubs with showers, complete comfort. Rates by the week or month. Excellent new coffee shop."

Bud's mother, Olive McLeod, accompanied Dottie and Wayne aboard the Northern Pacific mainline where they reunited with Bud in Tacoma at the beginning of May.

To keep it a *happy* birthday letter, Lelia circled back to their four-day weekend plans.

...Dad and I are going to Santiago tomorrow morning and returning Sunday night. Tomorrow is May 21—the Anniversary of the Battle of Iquique so a holiday...

The five-year "War of the Pacific," also known as the "Saltpeter War," pitted Chile against the defensive forces of Bolivia and Peru. Waged over rich nitrate deposits, the Battle of Iquique (1879) was critical to the naval stage of the hostilities.

Today, Iquique, a duty-free coastal city in the north, is pitched as one of Chile's premiere destination resorts where "Día de las Glorias Navales," "Navy Day," is still celebrated annually on May 21.

We had our first snow storm—lasted about four days last week. I hope we won't get another for two or three weeks. Salto Observatorio reports this will be a dry winter in this central valley (although not in the South)...

She'd roll over in her grave to know many Chileans regard hotter, dryer conditions as their greatest external threat today.

Here is a birthday check of $20.00 to get a new dress or something for your bedroom. Make a birthday cake so Buster can enjoy it. Possibly with rationing the sugar isn't sufficient. We are being rationed for tea—only a teaspoonful per person... Best love and a birthday spanking, Mother and Dad

Home at the Motor Court in Tacoma, Dorothy, Grandma Olive McLeod, Bud, and baby Wayne pose with the 1941 Mercury Comet "ragtop."

Paper Anniversary
Chapter Thirteen

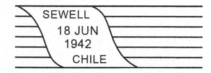

L.M. Skinner, Rancagua – Sewell, Chile S.A. – airmail

June 18, 1942

Dearest Roberta and Buster,

A Happy "First Anniversary." Does it seem as though you have been married a year? We shall be thinking of you June 22nd and wishing you many joyous anniversaries together. You will be very surprised to see how your married years slip by. It doesn't seem possible when you get to be our ages that you have lived together as many years, as your anniversaries remind you—birthdays and anniversaries are two of the sad reminders that your lives are slipping away...

How depressing. Why introduce those thoughts on a first anniversary?

... you won't notice that until you have had about 20. The first ones bring only the element of joy and happiness in celebrating—but later there is the "time" element...

I can attest to the fact Robin never adopted that attitude. She loved a party. So did Buster.

I am sending a check for $25.00 for you to buy a piece of silver for your set.

Six Weeks for Boat Mail

Something practical: a water pitcher or serving tray for entertaining. More to polish. An eight-ounce jar of Wright's Silver Cream set the budget back twenty-three cents.

As she had in her last letter, Lelia marveled at all that had happened in a year's time then took it to a whole new blessed level.

...already one grandchild and another one expected.

When Robin wrote to deliver news of her own pregnancy, she'd tucked photos into the folded letter. Lelia's imagination, tickled by the focal point of a baby-bump beneath an apron, brought some combination of joy and sadness.

Robin full of life in the kitchen.

Buster with the World Map pinned above his desk.

Don't know whether so much can ever happen again in one year, in our own immediate family or not (unless triplets or quadruplets should arrive)...

Impatiently she awaited baby Wayne's portrait.

...coming by boat mail, which takes six wks. now...

Reflecting on her growing family tree, she added:

...I know how happy you're going to be...with Waynecito's little cousin...

Then, abruptly, Lelia's stream of consciousness darkened.

...Too bad about "Penny." Very pathetic also—Hope you can find another you will be as fond of. A dog will be such a nice companion for little "Junior."

A long-eared silky coated cocker spaniel featured on the January cover of *Dog World* magazine influenced the decision. Penny's certified pedigree revealed the red cocker, born February 9, came from a litter of nine with champion lineage. Her adoption took place at the standard eight weeks; a day before Buster completed OCS at Monmouth. The move from Loch Arbour to Cambridge followed.

Penny at play.

More than a "nice companion for little Junior," interrupted sleep and unexpected messes prepared them for parenthood.

How Penny vanished from their lives, leaving chewed balls of yarn and an unfinished box of biscuits, one can only imagine. Pets running loose are no match for city traffic. Was Penny hit, then left to suffer and die alone in the gutter along an aptly named Memorial Drive? That qualifies as "pathetic."

Would they find a replacement for Penny?

Absolutely.

It would not, however, be a small sporting breed with a puppy cut, like Penny.

The Dogs for Defense program kicked off six months before, in January 1942. Initially, canines in training were assigned to sentry duty and certain tactical missions. Over time, the Army identified seven breeds best suited

Six Weeks for Boat Mail

to the program. Those deemed capable, eager to work, and hearty in various conditions.

The mighty roster included German shepherds, Doberman pinschers, Belgian sheepdogs, collies, Siberian huskies, Malamutes, and Eskimo dogs. Or some crossed combination thereof.

Their handlers would conjure empowering names, like Dash, Scout, and Zippo!

I don't know exactly when or how it happened, but Buster bonded with a silky coated Irish Setter named "Red." On tactical K9 missions, it's possible the scent of little critters proved to be an impossible distraction for the pup.

Buster with Signal Corps mascot, Red

Did it matter? No. Red accepted the rank of five-star Signal Corps morale booster, beloved by all the men in camp. The Army had no objection. In fact, it had been said if a list could be made up of all the mascots in Uncle Sam's army around the world, it would read like the sailing manifest of Noah's Ark. When the timing was right, Buster and Red were destined to reunite.

...I do so hope you can be in Cambridge until Nov. so you can be together for Junior's arrival and not separated by as many miles as Dorothy and Bud were...I was glad for Bud's sake Waynecito came ahead of schedule...he would have been in torture on the 21st, awaiting the telegram.

As it was, the news had come as a surprise to Bud on March 13. At Fort Knox, a hearty backslap landed with every Cuban cigar Bud doled out, while exclaiming, "it's a boy!" She closed with an impatient reminder of her crippled sewing machine.

If you can't find the shuttle carrier anywhere send back the old one and I will see if I can have one cast (by that one), buy a new bobbin if you can, also send the old little wheel with rubber on it.

Robin felt downright grateful and relieved to open the envelope containing Nat and Ethel's anniversary greeting. The verse of the baby-blue Hallmark® card projected onto their happy state of expectancy.

> *From every indication*
> *You surely have in store*
> *A most successful year ahead,*
> *And many, many more!*

A short note tucked inside asked nothing of Robin's time and energy.

```
PELHAM MANOR
   22 JUN
    1942
    N.Y.
```

Mrs. Nathaniel L. Bedford, 1283 Manor Circle, Pelham Manor, New York – June 22, 1942

Dearest son and Robin,

This being your first wedding anniversary and known as your "Paper Anniversary" Daddy and I could think of nothing more useful as a gift to you both, than the enclosed small, green piece of paper.

Please accept it with our love and loads of good wishes for a long and happy life.

Devotedly, Mother and Daddy Bedford

Robin's notion to spend it on dinner and a show fell apart when, in a side note, Ethel urged the youngsters to purchase their first "savings bond." It was a gentler way to suggest a "War Bond," so named following the attack on Pearl Harbor. Buster wholeheartedly agreed.

A week later, *The Boston Globe* of June 30 published an urgent plea by Massachusetts Governor "Salty" Saltonstall. Robin relented when his call to action, directed to all citizens of the Commonwealth, convinced her of the patriotic thing to do:

These are days for action. Our boys who are fighting so bravely for the preservation of the things we hold dear in our way of life need our help. We can give that help through War Savings Bonds and Stamps. We make no sacrifice in buying War Bonds and Stamps. We make the best investment in our own future as well as in that of our country.

Bond denominations that began in the amount of twenty-five dollars were destined to become the world's most widely held security.

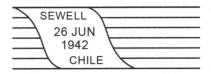

L.M. Skinner, Rancagua – Sewell, Chile S.A. – airmail

June 26, 1942
Dearest Roberta and Buster,

Your letter, written June 11th...arrived last evening...I am so happy the suitcase is underway and I am so grateful to you for all your efforts in trying to secure everything. Sorry the sewing machine parts gave you so much hunt...

I can hardly wait to open the cover of the case, it will be such fun!! Am waiting to see what my "surprise in blue" is...After you wrote me you were "expecting" I could just fancy all the inconvenience the running around had given you.

Every modern woman I know, many employed up until their due date, has run around. Those errands, however, fulfilled their own nesting and newborn needs, *not* their mother's.

The old brown case has made quite a journey hasn't it?...I shall hope it gets to Valpo without encountering any submarines. I'd be broken hearted to lose it...

Miss Otterstrom understood the peril. She boldly acted with the purchase of "war risk insurance" on the old case before it boomeranged back to the Chilean port with nurse Rivera. Five months from now, T.

Wayne's eyebrows would fly off his forehead when the forty-dollar debit for risk insurance (nearly $750 in today's dollars) hit his bank statement.

Due to censorship, neither Lelia nor Robin communicated what they knew of the demise of the Chilean freighter *Tolten*. Neither did Miss Otterstrom. Three months before, early in the morning of Friday, March 13, *Tolten* was the first Chilean vessel, a *neutral* ship, to fall prey to an Axis submarine along the New Jersey coast.

News of the *Tolten* received prominent attention in the Santiago papers. Robin read about it on the front page of the *Asbury Park Press*, dated March 17. The story was all too familiar. A torpedo hit amidships. The vessel exploded and sank in six minutes. One engine-room worker survived. Twenty-seven crewmen died.

Tolten wasn't the only reason Miss Otterstrom took acts of war seriously. Here's another.

That same Friday, March 13, around 3:30 in the afternoon, an anti-aircraft shell struck the crown molding outside the office windows on the thirty-seventh floor of the Equitable Building, 120 Broadway, New York. Though I don't know where Miss Otterstrom landed, I do know for a fact some employees of Kennecott Copper were thrown from their chairs.

Like some yet-to-be invented cinematic effect, eyewitnesses reported flaming red balls, blue smoke, and the smell of gunpowder.

Still shaken to the core by Pearl Harbor, thousands of persons fled from nearby buildings. Fire apparatus, emergency squads and more than two-hundred detectives raced to the scene. Ranking Army, Navy and Coast Guard officers quickly joined them.

An explanation of the accident revealed that automatic anti-aircraft weapons, located along the East River, accidentally discharged. Seven of the rounds were believed to have arced into the river, possibly the Upper Bay or even clear over Lower Manhattan into the North River, southernmost portion of the Hudson. The eighth blasted the decorative cornice at 120 Broadway, where it was later reported a few bricks were knocked out.

Putting that drama aside, Lelia percolated on maternity dresses; to be purchased with plenty of adjustment so as not to look tight in the last couple months.

You will never want to have one remodeled or wear it after confinement...one tires of the clothes worn during that time...

She also advised on baby's needs.

...Get your layette together far enough ahead of time, so you won't be having to shop at the last, when you won't feel like it. The little "Vanta" wool garments with tape ties are so convenient for dressing baby.

Vanta Baby Garments had been around for years. Department stores widely advertised the popular label. Attention-grabbing Vanta display ads in the likes of *Ladies Home Journal* drew new mothers to brand loyalty through "teaching moments" that capitalized on naivety. An advocate for the "no pins, no buttons" approach to dressing baby safely, Lelia marveled at Vanta's innovative "twistless" tape fastening.

How I wish I could help you shop for Junior and what's more—be there with you while you will be in the hospital.

Lelia had wished, then missed, all events surrounding Robin's graduation and wedding. And now the birth of Robin's child added one more demoralizing, long-distance blow to the list.

We had the dearest letter from Bud telling all about their home and how happily situated they are—I'd send along the letters, only it takes 6 wks. by boat mail now to New York...

She'd already read every word a hundred times. When Bud raved about Dorothy's swell cooking, a charmed Lelia re-read that paragraph a hundred more.

It was Bud who began this next letter from Fort Lewis to the Bedfords in Cambridge with news he'd already shared with Lelia.

Paper Anniversary

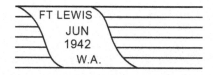

Mr. and Mrs. W. Herbert McLeod – Fort Lewis, Washington – airmail June 1942

Dear Robin and Buster:

You were exceedingly kind and thoughtful to remember our anniversary...

Tongue in cheek, there was no excuse not to remember it, married as they were on the exact same day, oceans apart.

Now for one year and nine days the Bedfords and McLeods have been embarked on that famous sea and my, how truly wonderful it is...

Bud let loose, bursting with happiness over the news Robin was expecting.

A baby gives indescribable joy. Our Wayne makes us tingle with pride each morning and every hour through the day and night...

Not every hour. While Bud slept through the wee hours, Dorothy nursed, and nodded, propped up in an upholstered rocker. KGVO Missoula signed off the air before midnight. White noise on the radio soothed mother and son.

The two little cousins will grow up together and when our long looked-forward-to reunion becomes a reality, what fun we'll have...

A waterfall of questions followed. Wives' tales were useful to determine the sex. Did she "carry" high or low? Were cravings sweet or salty? What names did they have in mind? The due date?

We'll fairly gobble up every bit of information you can give Aunt Dorothy and Uncle Bud...

Bud hoped October 7, his birthday, to be "the big day."

You certainly surprised us, and thrilled us.
Little Wayne now weighs twelve (12) pounds, and is a perfect specimen and gentleman.

Six Weeks for Boat Mail

Then this gush, which, surprisingly, had little to do with McLeod family pride:

We think that he is a combination of the Skinner family. He has Dad Skinner's smile, Mom's blue eyes, and his own Mother's sweetness and disposition...

Enthusiastically schmoozy. It's a sad fact I never knew my aunt Dorothy, but later in life, I cherished my first cousin, Wayne, for the same qualities he possessed as a baby.

Wayne seldom cries—he spends his conscious hours observing all that goes on around him...smiles and crows a great deal of the time...You and we are awfully fortunate. So many people pine for a dear little child but are unable to have one. It is a great blessing for us...

A blessing to be especially thankful for in the days preceding medical miracles.

Needless to say, we certainly shall be glad when this war has ended. At the present, however, we are as comfortable and as well situated as we possibly could be in an indefinite location.

A cut above the motel room they'd occupied last month.

We are living in a little bungalow-type house...

It was the modest dream castle of a technical sergeant, located in a semi-rural district, four miles from Fort Lewis. When war forced the move of the sergeant's young family shortly after construction, the young McLeods chanced upon it.

This part of Washington is quite heavily wooded. Wild flowers and Scotch broom grow in abundance, and in the distance Mt. Rainier, a perfectly gorgeous and towering extinct, snow covered volcano, looms into the clouds.

Far from extinct, a quick check with the USGS today reveals Mt. Rainier is an actively monitored volcano. Dangerous and potentially destructive, it lies forty miles southeast of Tacoma.

You will be amazed to learn that we have a brood of bantam chicks...

Paper Anniversary

Before moving, the sergeant sold his little brown banty to neighbors down the lane. Like a horse back to the barn, the hen stubbornly insisted upon returning.

...She solitarily roosted in our garage...and unobtrusively pecked about the ground during the day. Finally, she lay eggs in a little pile of coal briquettes...

Unfamiliar with the finer points of raising chickens, Bud and Dorothy observed the broody little hen, who set and set on the clutch without result. Bud's dad, Walter, knew enough to suggest they slip some fertilized eggs into the nest.

Now we have five chicks, three yellow, one gray, and one brown and black striped bird. Our brood gives us a great deal of pleasure and fun...

Bud stated his idealistic hope for the future, then rested his pen:

Some day we hope to have a little country home in the Bitterroot Valley, where we may raise a few chicks and a few ducks and other things...

Dearest Robin and Buster,

Bud was unable to finish this letter to you over the weekend, so I'll see what I can do...

Dorothy thanked Robin and Buster for Wayne's wrapper and booties; they matched his big blue eyes. She dashed off several pages, gushing over adorable attributes, comparing him to a *Good Housekeeping* baby. That meant long eyelashes and, except for the bald spot in back, loads of blonde hair. He laughed lots and sucked his thumbs with great glee.

I'd like to send you lists of things for Baby—and bits of advice for you, Robin... It seems rather strange for "baby sister" to give out advice, doesn't it?...The Great Event will arrive before you can realize it—and then you really will have something to show for all that kicking—and jig dancing in the little "pouch"—as we used to call it...

We hope you had as nice an anniversary as we did...we took a lovely weekend trip to Mt. Rainier, staying overnight at Paradise Inn...over a third of the way to the summit—There was a great deal of snow—and we saw many bronzed skiers—including several soldiers from the ski troops stationed in that area.

Six Weeks for Boat Mail

It so happens the first regiment of ski troops, the 807th Mountain Division, came together at Fort Lewis in November 1940. Army units all over the country sent their best skiers. To teach an experienced skier to shoot was easier than the other way around.

During the winter of 1941 – '42 a thousand-man regiment gathered at the Fort. Contingents were sent to Mt. Rainier where conditions and terrain simulated the European Alps. Soldiering and skiing merged in on-mountain drills. The Army rented and occupied the Paradise Inn, elevation 5,400 feet. For higher altitude expeditions, the lodge served as "base camp." Dottie corroborated that ski soldiers made turns on Rainier nearly into the summer of '42.

We found some little odds and ends in the cute gift shop at the Inn—We wanted to have them sent from the Park...

But they didn't have, nor could they remember, the Cambridge address.

You move around so frequently—we just can't keep up with you.

Dorothy went on, like new mothers do, marveling at how busy she'd become.

I just wonder what I ever did with my time before Wayne arrived.

Sadly, she'd never experienced the satisfaction of working outside the home.

I'm still on my three hr. nursing schedule 7 – 10 – 1 – 4 – 7 – 10...in addition to that Baby started his Pablum two weeks ago at 9 A.M. and 6 P.M.—plus his orange juice and water...

Mead Johnson launched the first pre-cooked baby cereal, Pablum, in the 1930s. Vitamin and mineral fortified, it was considered a nutritional science breakthrough.

But orange juice?

Yes. Afflicted with scurvy, a baby loses its appetite and becomes anemic.

Speaking on health, one patronizing physician had this to say: "It has become quite customary for mothers to give babies orange juice, which is the richest known substance in nature, so far as concerns its content of vitamin C, except for paprika—and paprika is not a food for babies."

Paper Anniversary

In line with the war program for improving national nutrition, cod liver oil rounded out Wayne's bill of fare. For bone health, that foul-tasting vitamin D supplement was known to prevent rickets. Nowadays, a quick click on the internet informs us health benefits of omega-3 fatty acids range widely at any age, from boosting immune and brain function to reducing anxiety, depression, and inflammation.

So – o –o I'm feeding him something every 1 ½ hrs. of the day—And if you don't think that keeps me busy I have his bath and laundry daily...

The tip of the iceberg.

But I love it all—and baby is so well and healthy...Bud is kept very busy—from 7:30 to 6.

With the Fort just four miles away, most days Bud circled through at noon for a lunch she had waiting for him.

He likes the Armored Force very much – next to the Quartermaster Corps ... He commands four other tanks besides his own – and comes home just black whenever he goes out on daily manoeuvers or overnight problems...

Their hopes? To stay put for the winter.

Robin...I've finally learned to drive—I have a license...Bud was very patient and still is...an excellent instructor. Our little wedding car is holding out beautifully and we've enjoyed it so much.

With its powerful engine and wide white walls, the 1941 Mercury was known for elegant drivability, with low rpm cruising even at highway speeds. Walter McLeod chose it for what he knew his son would appreciate under the hood. Once she got the hang of shifting gears, I imagine Dottie's joy derived from a sense of freedom, whisking top down around town. Since becoming a mother, her love for chart toppers on the *Hit Parade* hadn't changed. The way she looked at it, the AM radio responded to the ignition switch. When the car was on, the tunes were, too.

Before closing we both want to congratulate Buster on his promotion...We think perhaps he'll be an engineer instead of a lawyer when the war is over...whichever it is—we wish you all luck and happiness...

Our best love to you both, Dorothy, Bud and Wayne

Othello
Chapter Fourteen

It had been almost a year since FDR called out the Nazi's in his Fireside Chat of September 11, 1941, as "a menace to the free pathways of the high seas." At the time, Germany believed it would win the war by preventing delivery of war supplies and fuel from the U.S. to Britain.

Then came the attack on Pearl Harbor. The game changed in a flash for U.S. military forces to contemplate a Pacific theater. January to August 1942 came to be known as the "Second Happy Time" for German U-Boats along the coastal waters of the Atlantic. Their marauding went nearly unopposed as evidenced by Robin and Buster's experience at Loch Arbour. The demise of the Chilean ship, *Tolten*, too.

Reporters rearranged words in news stories under redundant headlines which had to do with submarines, torpedoes, sinking, and abandoning ship. Passengers, overboard, lifeboats, oil-soaked, burnt flesh, survivors, lives lost, still missing were common testimonial themes.

Seamen predominated on the victims' rollcall and the Red Cross responded. Seventeen chapters were set up along the Atlantic coast to specialize on the war's "new front" at sea.

The old brown suitcase survived to and through the Panama Canal and down the coast of South America. One more leg of the journey remained.

Othello

L.M. Skinner, Rancagua – Sewell, Chile S.A. – airmail

July 24, 1942
Dearest Roberta and Buster,

The suitcase arrived in very short time from New York, having caught the <u>last</u> boat that left that port. All boats now sail from New Orleans…

Four months had passed since the sinking of the *Tolten*. Evidently it took that long to adjust the fixed schedule between the ports of New York and Valpo.

…So it was very fortunate that brown suitcase along with Miss Rivera's baggage, was shipped just when it was…

From the port of Valpo to the mining camp it didn't go so well. Lelia's yardstick, by which to judge, was Miss Rivera's luggage. From Valparaiso the nurse's possessions wound their way through Rancagua, then up the narrow-gauge rail to Sewell in the usual three days' time.

As Lelia's luck would have it, the old brown case hit a snag.

She explained.

…All the parcels belonging to other people had to be taken in charge by the Rancagua Welfare Dept…it was about a week, <u>setting</u> down <u>there.</u> I was fit to be tied!…

When the suitcase finally rolled into Campamento Americano, she discovered three pairs of Russell's suspenders and a bottle of Chlorazene gargle tablets were stolen out.

The poor kid needed the suspenders…

They needed the gargle tablets, too. Chlorazene was a powerful synthetic antiseptic first introduced by Abbott Laboratories in 1916. Medics used it to clean battle wounds in WWI. Gargle tablets suggested an antibacterial mouth rinse.

 Six Weeks for Boat Mail

In more ways than one, the thievery left a bad taste in Lelia's mouth.

I can see the war inferior goods in the girdles and Russell's reversible…in war times one has to expect that.

She spoke from experience; military essentials had taken precedence over civilian desires in the Great War. Likewise, in March of 1942, the War Production Board issued Regulation L-85, rationing natural fibers: cotton, silk, nylon, wool. Lelia's inferior girdle was proof of restrictions on rubber-based stretch fabrics. However, less elastic did not mean the modern woman could be expected to do without.

Why?

Throughout the country, many women engaged in strenuous civilian defense and Red Cross work outside the home. Others took full-time jobs in defense industries, taking the place of men called into military service. To keep their health equal to the task, proper diet and well-fitting foundation garments guarded against body fatigue.

I like the dress very much, also the nightgown is so pretty! Which of those was the surprise you spoke of?

They were the only items in blue. Which one wasn't on her list?

It made Lelia sick to shell out five hundred pesos duty on the contents; sixty-two cents in today's dollars. On top of that, when the infernal sewing machine parts didn't reach the New York office in time, she was forced to hire a sewing lady. Her petite frame called for hemming of the dress and slacks, as well as shortening of the sleeves on her blouses and reversible.

Three weeks had passed when Lelia picked up her pen again to explain and attend to unfinished business in her letter, dated July 24.

<u>August 15</u>:

I am so ashamed this letter has never gotten finished and underway. I was sick with grippe for 10 days…

Influenza. More bad news followed. The day Lelia got out of bed, it was adios Adela! Fired. Boom.

She got impossible!

To replace the devoted domestic would take time.

Ten months, in fact.

I was just nearly dead keeping up 8 hrs. in school and trying to get the meals and keep the house clean...

Just then, the Chilean Army released Russell. Now she had another mouth to feed.

Dad and I like salads — soups, etc., but Russell wants potatoes — vegetables, meats twice a day.

The question remains why, still today, is a life skill tied to survival all too often a woman's concern?

I sure thought of Dorothy with her house to keep and little "Waynecito" to bathe — feed — wash for every day...is about as busy as I was the past month.

I keep thinking about you also...

What motherly advice did she offer?

Don't lift heavy things these last months or you might lose the baby, and don't get overly tired.

On the heels of "women's talk," the mail examiner possibly missed the next one-liner. It slipped from the tip of her pen without redaction.

Our boys are doing awfully well in the Solomon Islands, aren't they?

Unraveling this Solomon Islands' moment, here's the fast backstory: That spring, while the Bedfords and McLeods slapped each other with birthday and anniversary wishes, U.S. forces celebrated strategic victories at the Battles of the Coral Sea (May 4 – 8) and Midway (June 4 – 7). The tide of the war at sea

Dorothy and baby Wayne stretching his legs.

turned with the fury of full-scale attacks. Major offensive campaigns of the Japanese Imperial Navy were curtailed after important warships were sunk.

Lelia tuned to KGEI for the latest. On August 17, Navy Communication No. 107 issued details of the surprise attacks and landing operations that commenced early morning, August 7. Boom. Flash. Under MacArthur's command, the Solomon Islands campaign ignited twelve hundred miles northeast of Australia. Eighteen Japanese seaplanes were destroyed before pilots climbed into cockpits. Under protection of U.S. naval guns, transport-borne amphibious forces of the Marine Corps landed on islands in the Guadalcanal-Tulagi area. They defeated enemy resistance speedily; Japanese prisoners were taken. As U.S. troop transports and cargo ships unloaded according to plan on August 7 and 8, Japanese land-based aircraft from nearby Rabaul, site of important Japanese airdromes on New Britain Island, attacked American forces. In close-range fighting, U.S. warships drove them off; at least eighteen more enemy planes were destroyed. U.S. troops suffered only minor damage.

Then, during the dark of night, August 8 – 9, a Japanese force of cruisers and destroyers attempted to attack U.S. transports, cargo ships and supporting forces, only to be intercepted and engaged by U.S. cruisers and destroyers. Heavy fighting followed; the Japanese were forced to retreat.

In the Solomons, a vicious six-month battle waged. Dense vegetation, unfamiliar terrain, heat, mosquitos, and tropical disease made for a nasty stay. As Lelia signed off with hugs and kisses, this question plagued her:

When and where would her sons-in-law deploy?

Meanwhile, at home in Massachusetts, the young Bedfords were relaxed and happy. Buster, and his buddy Prent Smith, completed their Harvard Defense Training course on Electronics and Cathode Ray Tubes July 23. Nine days later, the two men marched into the study of Ultra-High Frequency Technique: a three-month full-time course at M.I.T.

The week of August tenth, Buster proudly waltzed his seven-month pregnant Robin along the Charles River to the Cambridge Summer Theatre.

Othello

Brattle Hall, historically conceived by the Cambridge Social Union in the mid-nineteenth century, was situated less than a mile east of their apartment. For years the auditorium served as a multifarious gathering place. Now, with tire and gas rationing, theatre companies gladly rented the stout barnlike structure, steps from Harvard Square. There they played to a discerning audience within walking distance from home or the railroad station. With a maximum capacity of 235, there wasn't a bad seat in the house. Tickets topped out at one dollar and sixty-five cents. Buster, no doubt, sprung for the best.

Today the historic theatre is an epicenter of independent film, home to The Brattle Film Foundation.

That evening of August 1942 celebrated Black actor Paul Robeson, starred in the U.S. premiere of *Othello*, a Shakespearean tragedy. Racism, love, dangers of jealousy, betrayal, revenge; all themes laid out over which Robin and Buster would dual wits.

For the unenlightened, Robeson was known as an athlete, actor, singer, scholar, and activist; well worth praising for his contribution to the Harlem Renaissance. Buster admired Robeson. For starters, he was a football star. Born in Princeton, New Jersey in 1898, this son of an escaped slave attended Rutgers on a four-year academic scholarship and worked his way through Columbia Law. As a revolutionary champion for human dignity, democratic rights, and economic justice, the man deserves eternal applause for far more than his stage presence.

Deep bows by actors and wild applause by the audience followed culmination of the fourth and final scene, titled "The Bedroom." All were standing, but no one rushed out.

Why?

They heeded bold blue typeface in the program:

"The audience is urged to join in the singing of 'The Star-Spangled Banner' with the company at the end of the performance."

After which everyone felt uplifted and unified as they filed out through the Brattle's heavy exterior wooden doors.

Six Weeks for Boat Mail

A well-placed Good Humor advertisement in the theatre program had patrons acting in a manner like Pavlov's dogs. I imagine when they stepped onto the street that August evening, a jovial man attired in a non-military white uniform stood at the ready with a loaded, four-barrel coin changer clipped to his belt. The ring-a-ling of his truck's brass bells called the crowd in a direct line to his iconic refrigerated truck.

Patriotic "Bomb Pops" didn't hit the frozen confection market until summer 1955, but that summer of 1942 I imagine a woman seven months pregnant might crave a vanilla ice cream bar wrapped in a smooth chocolate coating on a stick. Buster would be the man to indulge her. And himself. He loved ice cream.

L.M. Skinner, Rancagua – Sewell, Chile S.A. – airmail – Censored [Last page missing]

Sat. September 12, 1942
Dearest Roberta and Buster,

> After exercising a lot of patience my sewing machine parts finally arrived!

How?!!

A wee package, tucked in a company trunk, shipped with the Turton's baggage. Lelia spent a full Sunday afternoon finagling the shuttle carrier. When she made the screw too tight, the upper thread tangled and knotted, instead of locking with the bobbin thread.

One good reason why, save for a needle and thread to secure a button or mend a split seam, I don't sew. High school home-economics (mandatory for a girl in the 1970s) forced me to piece together Simplicity's simplest apron pattern. Bobbin thread baffled me. My fingers were better suited to untangling a bird's nest of nylon filament fishline.

> ...I was so afraid they might go astray or be lost—being such a small package...

Othello

When she finally loosened the shuttle carrier screw, Lelia was ecstatic. Nine months had passed since Robin's hunt for parts was supposed to have begun in New York. With the machine in working order, the matter was finally put to rest.

We heard a rumor this afternoon that <u>air planes</u> are not going to carry letters and air express, except for Gov't use.

Lelia didn't have all the facts, but it was true that the present volume of overseas airmail far exceeded the facilities to deliver it. A bulletin from the Postmaster General explained it. If ordinary airmail demands to foreign countries continued at the present rate, military necessity may require that transport be limited to official mail and V-mail.

For the present time, the restrictions <u>excluded</u> non-military service areas, including good neighbor countries in Central and South America.

Long before war broke out, the far-flung members in Lelia's circle of family and friends learned there were no guarantees that a letter bearing airmail postage would go by air. It was true now, more than ever, airmail often landed on a boat.

...But we receive boat mail only once in six or eight weeks so I am keeping my fingers crossed that it may be only a rumor...it seems like the dark ages...in the pioneer days in Chile it took only 31 days...when I came down a bride.

The year was 1916, twenty-six years before. The thought opened her eyes to the changes that had occurred in her sphere of work, company town community, and expanding family since.

Heart over mind, she reflected on Robin's arrival at Valparaiso a year ago.

The weather is just about as warm as when you landed in your pretty thin weight blue suit and hat, my but you did look so sweet and pretty!

How nice that Mother Bedford is taking so much interest in Junior's arrival. I envy her being able to go and buy pretty, pretty little garments. When I go to Santiago I want to see if I can find something sweet and dainty to send up—but there is scarcely anybody going to the States anymore...

All who traveled flew with bags crammed full. Furthermore, according to Mrs. Turton, the baggage allowance had been reduced.

I'm just going to be thinking of you now day by day.

Robin's due date loomed.

Are you going to go to a Boston hospital? Too bad it had to be war times that you picked out for your first arrival.

Pot calling the kettle black, the WWI Armistice was signed on November 11, 1918. In a near miss, Lelia delivered Robin six and a half months later.

Then and now, compassion is—or should be—the rule toward every young, anxious, first-time mother-to-be. Naturally, niche product markets capitalize on that fact.

For example, take this miracle drug, "Mother's Friend." The Georgia-based Bradford Regulator Company manufactured the emollient used by generations of pregnant women dating to the 1850s. In 1897, they pitched it this way; "Childbirth relieved of pain and danger! Happy mothers and perfect children!...Positive assurance against 'Rising Breasts' and other ailments of pregnancy...shortens the time and agony of labor."

Eventually Bradford Regulator got caught up in the Pure Food and Drug Act of 1906 which, among other things, prohibited the sale of misbranded drugs the likes of "Mother's Friend." Even so, in 1919, Robin's birth year, newspaper advertisements stretched it: "a truly wonderful penetrating application for the abdomen and breasts. It softens and makes elastic the muscles, rendering them pliant to readily yield to nature's demand for expansion...The usual wrenching strain, 'bearing-down and stretching pains are counteracted.'"

In Chile, Lelia would have missed the ads or medically dismissed them.

At this time of Robin's pregnancy, the Bradford company effectively relied on new mother testimonials "promising ease and comfort to expectant mothers." Though I have no evidence she used the "exquisitely prepared emollient."

An online search today reveals unanimously positive reviews for the lanolin-based Mother's Helper. Caveat emptor (buyer beware), lanolin is derived from sheep's wool. What modern woman wants to smell like an old fisherman's sweater when there are a bazillion other yummy, plant-based belly butters to choose from?

The best that I can hope for you is that it will be a perfectly normal delivery and not too long...

Fortified with some hypnotic drug like amytal, and a little gas anesthesia during the final minutes, Robin wouldn't recall much of her experience with little Bobby. But who doesn't perk up when a mother recounts the story of an eventful childbirth? For years after my birth (1957), Robin regaled listeners with the fact that I nearly dropped onto the linoleum floor in a wheelchair race to the delivery room. Likewise, thirty-five years later, my youngest all but delivered himself in fourteen minutes flat, hospital curbside to crowning head.

Both of us exceeded Lelia's hope for a "perfectly normal delivery and not too long."

It seems to me that I have been cheated out of everything that a Mother would wish... (That's what going to a foreign country to live brings about.)

What other practical advice did Robin's mother muster?

...put your rings into the hospital safe...Don't entrust your valuables to the nurses...better still leave them in your bank vault beforehand. Am glad you are getting all the sunshine possible and have someone coming in to help you with the cleaning, etc. I think the names you have selected very pretty. Am glad the Bedfords like them.

She went on to name each toddler living in Campamento Americano and all the expectant young couples, too.

When I see one of them, I just can't help thinking of "Waynecito."

She silently gauged them, as any grandmother would, against Dorothy's colorful descriptions and a short stack of black and white snapshots.

Six Weeks for Boat Mail

...I'm glad we'll get acquainted with "Jr." at the same time as Waynecito so we won't be partial to our "first grandson." He hasn't gained as fast as he should have. Dorothy had plenty of milk but it couldn't have been as rich as it should have been...

Wayne's birthweight, 6lbs. 10oz., was on the lighter side of "average." In six weeks, he'd gained nearly three pounds: 9lbs. 8oz. On the scale, he fell within the "normal" range. Her niggling spawned angst in both the new mother and mother-to-be.

Is it a foregone conclusion that Buster will go to Florida? It will be nice to be in the South during the winter months...

Foregone conclusion or not, *the censors* objected to Lelia's reveal about Buster's assignment in the Sunshine State. The last page, where she would typically sign off with hugs, kisses, and random add-ons, went missing.

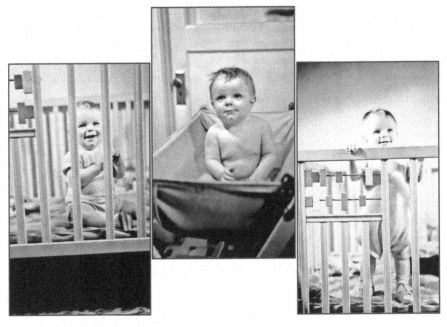

The many sweet expressions of Wayne's chin-dimpled face.

Accelerated Training
Chapter Fifteen

Buster and Prent were set to complete their three-month "Ultra High Frequency Technique" certification at M.I.T. on October 31. The two 2nd lieutenants remained in the dark on the exact location of the secret place of their next order of training. Life-changing events unfolded for both during the last four weeks of classwork in Cambridge. They'd need time to plan and execute a major move south to the undisclosed location in Florida, to which Lelia referred in her censored letter of September 12.

On October 6, Buster's wish for a healthy first-born son, of an only son, of an only son, came true. The operator put the call through to Pelham Manor promptly, where Nat and Ethel picked up the receiver. A cable to T. Wayne, c/o Braden Copper informed the Skinner grandparents of baby Robert's arrival.

As for Prent, his engagement to Phyllis was announced at a Sunday afternoon tea on October 25th. Six days later, on Halloween, best man Buster hurried the groom out of the war training room at M.I.T. and drove him directly to the Tufts College campus six miles north. At precisely four o'clock, Prent and Phyllis were married in the Goddard Chapel.

For Lelia, the whereabouts of Robin and Buster got lost in another training shuffle. She posted her next letter c/o the senior Bedfords at Pelham Manor.

Six Weeks for Boat Mail

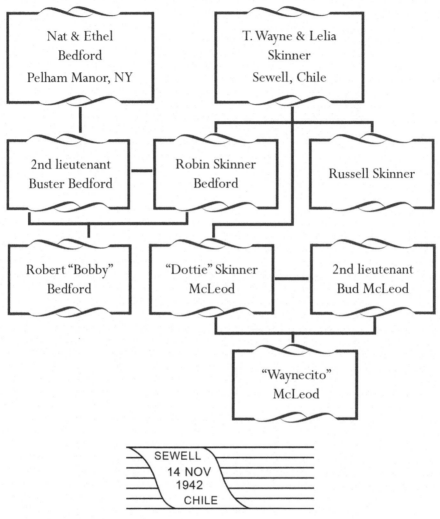

L.M. Skinner, Rancagua – Sewell, Chile S.A. – airmail

November 14, 1942
Dearest Roberta and Buster,

I have a hunch you haven't received my last letter to you because about the time you should have been leaving the hospital, 18 days after Robert arrived...

Wait, what?! Eighteen days post-birth "confinement" for a normal vaginal birth without complications?

Accelerated Training

In that regard, we are not our mothers' daughters. To cut them some slack, the field of medicine had worked steadily for nearly a century to overcome what Oliver Wendell Holmes, Sr., wrote about in 1843, "childbed fever." A septic infection of the uterus.

I wrote asking you what baby carriages cost today, so I could send you a check...

It didn't seem all that long ago that Lelia purchased baby Robin's stroller. Made of nicely varnished reed and upholstered in corduroy, it had good springs, reversable gears and rubber-tired wheels. In 1919 it priced out just shy of thirty-seven dollars.

With the war on, Lelia speculated a 1942 model would cost considerably more. Not true. A rubber-tired English-type "coach" sold for twenty-five dollars. So very "English-looking" that one would expect a young Mary Poppins-like nanny at the business end of the handle. Of course, like Lelia's girdle, the rubber on the tires would be inferior.

For that matter, factories turning to war work created a crimp in the supply chain. And as the birth rate climbed like the war debt, bassinettes, highchairs, carriages, cribs, and playpens wholly sold out in some retail establishments.

No word has come so I think probably you didn't get the letter...

She resigned to the fact that, war or no war, mail went astray.

Various people here remark that some of theirs haven't arrived in the U.S.... Auntie Rhea wrote she sent me two, between Aug. 1st and last of Sept. and we didn't get either of them. I thought possibly they were boat letters and would reach us a little after the eight or nine weeks boat letters require today—but here it is about 14 wks. and neither of them has arrived...

Three and a half months was a long wait to receive what would, by then, be "yesterday's news."

The war news is glorious these days isn't it? I only hope the African situation can keep up as brilliantly as it has started out, without Hitler sending too much opposition during these winter months.

Six Weeks for Boat Mail

Minding the censors, Lelia knew better than to elucidate on *Operation Torch*, the all-out British-American invasion of French North Africa in early November '42. But I wonder if she got the real dope over KGEI. Recall the S.S. *Santa Lucia*, the boat that eventually delivered Robin's trunk to New York in the spring of '42. Presto chango, by August, the U.S. Navy pressed the *Lucia* into wartime service to be commissioned a month later as USS *Leedstown*. She made a fine troop transport, one amongst the large convoy in support of *Operation Torch* with a crew of 538 and 2,505 servicemen aboard. Then what? Just five days before Lelia wrote this letter, two German torpedoes hit the transport rear amidships. All abandoned ship. The *Leedstown* settled by the bow with a heavy starboard list and sank off the Algerian coast two hours later.

Just think—Robert is over a month old! I hope your milk is rich enough and that you can keep it for seven or eight months at least. Your description of him was quite vivid.

She anxiously awaited the first vivid snapshots, too.

Your camera was a good buy all right! I expect they are almost impossible to get now and you will use it so much with little Robert...

The camera she spoke of was, at one time, mired in this intercontinental family drama:

Home movie cameras were a new sensation; the Skinner family learned all about them at the 1939 World's Fair, in New York. A promotional pamphlet pitched it like this: "This Eastman Exhibit, beyond the shadow of a doubt, is the greatest photographic show ever staged." T. Wayne fell for the new technology. Upon her graduation from Smith, Robin's parents congratulated her with the gift of a 16mm "movie Kodak."

Fast forward to fall of 1941. In Chile, Robin's disheartened father escorted her to trade in the "movie Kodak" for a 35-millimeter camera.

Why?

Buster already owned an 8mm Bell and Howell.

When purchased, he'd had his choice of any movie camera on the market, including the Kodak T. Wayne picked. The 8mm was a practical

Accelerated Training

decision. Film cost for a 16mm was *three* times that of an 8mm. It made no sense to have *two* movie cameras under one roof. Slides and prints were equally, if not more, important for purposes of waving around.

Duplicate snapshots could be shared!

In the end, Buster threw up his hands with this remark: "If your father and you feel differently, that is your business and I am sorry that I meddled in his affairs. I shan't do so again." He put his foot down: "Any film for that 16mm will be film that he gives you or film that is bought out of your own amusement allowance. I won't have any part of it."

Enough with the curdled Kodak moment. Robin and T. Wayne settled on a Zeiss-Ikon Contax 35mm. Lelia turned back to war news.

Last night's radio news said the 18 and 19 yr. old boys will be taken in Dec....

Following Russell's mid-August release from the Chilean Army, he registered in October to serve in the U.S. The nineteen-year-old pledged to American Embassy officials his desire to return to the States in March. He set his sights on the Navy.

The papers had to go to Washington and I suppose will lay on the desks up there for wks. maybe months before they get back here. I wish his education were further along so he could be something higher than just a private...

In the Navy, if he could get past the intelligence test, he'd rank an apprentice seaman crowned with the regulation "Dixie cup." The iconic sailor's hat purported to have many uses. Sun protection, flotation device, and dog dish, to name a few. Recruiters promised rapid advancement in rating and in pay. He'd learn life skills and a useful trade. How to cook in the galley for starters.

In Lelia's opinion, the boy needed to get back to school the minute the war ended.

Eye-catching posters of the U.S. Maritime Service summoned recruits, "Apprentice Seaman Training" preparing young men for a career in the American Merchant Marine. They were sure to swivel Russell's head.

Yo Ho, Yo Ho! He'd never go back to school!

I bought some knitted little garments for Robert and a little shawl blanket, very light weight, to wrap around him.

Now she wrestled with the method of delivery.

Tell Buster I expect he's about the proudest Daddy, ever! By the way was Robert born on the 7th of Oct.? We couldn't tell from the cable. The date doesn't seem to appear on them anymore. And when is Buster's birthday? I never did know and always keep forgetting to ask.

Lelia signed off with love and enclosed a check for fifty dollars with a silent prayer that this PANAGRA envelope would not go astray.

As the Thanksgiving holiday approached, the senior Bedfords laid out the welcome mat at Pelham Manor. Their home in Westchester County fell between Cambridge and Buster's next assignment at an undisclosed training camp on an island further south.

Nomadic apartment living had, so far, minimized the hassle of packing and moving household goods, which, as far as I can tell, amounted to china, silverware, stemware, their linen largesse, a Sunbeam Mixmaster, and the Turton's gift of a silver sandwich tray. There was also the matter of ski gear.

But what to do now that they'd bumped up against the baby clutter years? Breastfeeding made travel easier, but a bassinette, pile of nappies, and presumably a portable diaper pail crowded the rear seat. Space in the *Zephyr* was limited.

Two years before, in 1940, Mayflower® Transit Service became the first trucking company in the industry to operate in the Lower 48, as authorized by the Interstate Commerce Commission. Direct agents signed on and mobilized all over the country to move military personnel and their families under the (now iconic) screaming green fleet emblem of a full-rigged ship. Instinct tells me Nat stepped up to smooth logistics of the move. Ethel, meanwhile, set herself afire in recompense for Buster's disappointing Thanksgiving furlough at Pinehurst a year ago, when the Carolina maneuvers ran unexpectedly long and Robin failed to show.

This year's celebration was to be symbolic of the good life for which men all over the world were now fighting. From years of practice, Ethel could lay a holiday table in her sleep. Working up from the starched white base of a floral-scrolled double damask tablecloth, she chose her most cherished tableware possessions. In some pieces she found courage in their endurance, symbolic of the hardest years of her personal history as an immigrant. Bounteous and peaceful, with a centerpiece of richly colored chrysanthemums and tall candle tapers, this table epitomized American fortitude and faith.

That Thursday, 26 November, families gathered around their radios promptly at eleven o'clock a.m. Eastern War Time. All eyes in the Pelham Manor parlor fell adoringly upon seven-week-old Bobby, as President Roosevelt delivered Proclamation 2571 with an opening quote from Psalms 92:1, "It's a good thing to give thanks unto the Lord." The Bedfords and their King James Bible certainly thought so. For the next thirty minutes, every radio network across the nation broadcast the "White House Thanksgiving of Song and Prayer."

Five days after Thanksgiving, just as Robin and Buster re-packed the *Zephyr* to hit the road, nationwide gas rationing went into effect. Fuel supply was not the problem. This had everything to do with preventing wear on passenger car tires. Twelve hundred miles or more loomed ahead. A 1942 "C" ration sticker, pasted in the lower corner of the passenger side windshield, was their ticket to drive the distance.

The "C" mileage ration sticker came with seventeen check boxes laid out like a drop-down menu starting with "Official Gov't or Red Cross business." With that, a "C" ration person was entitled to drive more than 470 miles a month. Buster checked the third box from the bottom: "Members of the Armed force to duty." The box above his was meant for others with an equally vital job: "Construction, repair, maintenance services or production specialist."

History lovers today are captivated by the massive WWII construction effort underway at the time. It involved billions of dollars and the buildup of thousands of facilities nationwide. Installations to support training, operational, and logistical activities of the forces, including Buster's Signal Corps, were booming. So were the buildup of airfields, naval bases, and plants for production of aircraft, artillery, and ammunitions. "Special Projects" were another kettle of fish. Among them, the "Manhattan Engineering District."

Six Weeks for Boat Mail

That entity scouted for what would become the consequential site chosen for "Project Y."

Military officials were drawn to the specific attributes of Los Alamos Ranch School, an established college preparatory institution in New Mexico. Its isolated location in the Jemez Mountains near Santa Fe, sixteen miles from the nearest town, was ideal.

By Thanksgiving 1942, box after Army box had been checked off in the evaluation. Access to the mesa on which the campus was built could be "controlled." Existing school buildings met immediate housing needs. Much of the surrounding area was already owned by the Federal Government. Dr. J. Robert Oppenheimer, the slender, pipe smoking thirty-seven-year-old theoretical physicist chosen to direct Project Y, agreed. So did members of his staff. Work commenced on the former campus of Los Alamos Ranch School.

A slender, pipe-smoking Buster with baby Bobby

About the same time, a slender, pipe-smoking Buster landed nearly two thousand miles east of Los Alamos. On Jupiter, the southernmost barrier island off the east coast of Florida, lay a brand-new top-secret Signal Corps radar training installation.

L.M. Skinner, Rancagua – Sewell, Chile S.A. – airmail

December 19, 1942

Dearest Roberta and Buster,

We have been off on our quarterly jaunt down out of the altitude…

Accelerated Training

A five-thousand-foot descent from Sewell to Santiago placed them well below the toxic air of the mining camp. Lelia took the lead checking off to-dos, which included a visit to the dentist for prophylactic cleanings and to have Russell's gold crown switched out for cosmetically pleasing porcelain.

...Your location there on the Island sounds so ideal. What a wonderful find! I just envy you...

Under the pressure of war demands, the Corps had opened a new school just a few miles north of West Palm Beach. On a tract of 11,500 acres, nestled amidst inaccessible swampland camouflaged with a thick forest of palmetto, fern, and bamboo, Camp Murphy sprang up like a troop of mushrooms in the spring of '42. When it opened, July 5, its exclusive mission was to train Signal Corps <u>radar</u> technicians year-round.

At the onset of winter tourist season, in a highly desirable resort town well known to celebrities today, the young Bedfords found a steal of a deal. A furnished home for $125 a month, plus utilities. They shared the place and split the expense with another young couple, Lois and Ray. Mail delivery posted to Hobe Sound.

Fort Monmouth was not conducive to military exercises when the temperature dropped. General George Washington and the Continental Army made that chilling New Jersey discovery at their encampment site in Morristown, where they spent "the hard winter" of 1779 – 1780 during the Revolutionary War. With a tropical rainforest climate at Camp Murphy, the Corps could accelerate training rates. Buster upskilled in the clandestine radar program, sworn to keep the true purpose of the base classified. Civilians employed as laborers, secretaries, and nurses, were sworn to secrecy, too. When technical class was dismissed, the sound of target practice and the filth of combat exercises created the impression it was like any other military installation.

Nightly blackouts were the rule and U-boats still skulked offshore. However, when the Richmond Naval Air Station, located southwest of Miami, was commissioned the previous September, the Nazi's "Second

Six Weeks for Boat Mail

Attention-grabbing action along the coast. Robin and Buster (center), with Prent and Phyllis Smith, and Hobe Sound housemates Lois and Ray.

Happy Days" ceased. Since then, Navy patrol blimps had successfully escorted thousands of surface vessels in convoys and, to date, only one ship had been destroyed. The lighter-than-air (LTA) craft maneuvered with grace, which made them fun to watch. They stood still in the air, flew forward and backward, and rode securely as a boat at the drop of a sea anchor. Equipped with depth charges and a machine gun, LTAs could take out enemy craft from above, or drop a rubber life raft with food and first aid.

While Buster trained, Robin wrestled the way all new mothers do, with Bobby's every uncharted cry. Gertrude, a nursemaid the senior Bedford insisted on hiring, inserted herself with experience.

...You want to look out Gertrude doesn't spoil the baby for you...It takes very little standing over a baby when he cries before he will demand it.

Lelia's true colors beamed green. Envy shot like an arrow from four thousand miles away.

And by the way Roberta, you want to consult a Dr. right away if that one bottle a day still sours...Babies don't spit up soured milk normally.

Wait, what?

It's common for healthy babies to spit up. It is the reason burp cloths were invented. When breastmilk (or formula) meets acidic stomach fluid it's naturally curdled in appearance when baby "burps."

...That is an old Grandma's whim or possibly a Negress' whim, don't listen to Gertrude about that.

One good thing about letters? Robin had the option to quit reading and toss the unsolicited advice aside.

...You know when you nurse a babe only three or four times a day, one's milk becomes weaker and less in quantity...so you want to watch his gain. You may have to begin and give him all bottle feedings shortly...

Every successful nursing mother knows it's a simple matter of supply and demand. At eight weeks, a two-to-three-hour breastfeeding schedule would be sufficient for Bobby's weekly gain. Introduction of a bottle was step one toward weaning.

With no wartime obligations outside the home, had she consulted a doctor on that point?

You should not go in swimming so soon after confinement. The muscle fibers in the uterus do not return to normal before six to eight weeks after delivery...and also you ought not to be in the ocean for your milk. One has to be so careful of any chilling...

While I imagine Robin moving like a porpoise through the waves, Lelia's words tangentially raised this question for me. Whatever happened to the frozen confection "ice milk?"

It's one example of how laws around food labels have changed. Millennials will have no recollection of ice milk. When the Sealtest® Light 'n Lively label vanished from grocery store freezer cases in 1994, it was of no consequence to anyone. The name refreshed in the form of what we know today as reduced, low, and non-fat ice cream choices.

I wouldn't suppose a Dr. would consent to your going swimming until you had completely finished the nursing period even if it were seven or eight months, or didn't you consult a Dr. about that point?

No! Enough of that. Lelia went on to lecture about baby weight gain. Dorothy, of course, hired a specialist. Not surprisingly, she suggested Robin find one, too.

The specialty of pediatrics had grown in recent years. It came to be organized under the American Academy of Pediatrics in 1930 and quickly became one of the most important and progressive branches of the medical profession.

The conundrum was this: All the nation's healthiest physicians under age forty-five would ultimately be commissioned for military service. That fact was announced in May 1942 at a meeting of the American Academy of Pediatrics in Cleveland. Pediatric specialists numbered among those swept up and dispatched to war-time medical units when the U.S. Army committed to double the number of doctors in service by the beginning of 1943.

...A young babe rarely cries if the feedings are properly adapted to his digestion—so if he cries for an hour or two straight there may be something that isn't just right.

Beware the witching hour.

This letter of Lelia's was so full of advice scripted across three sheets of PANAGA airmail stationery it's surprising there was room enough in the envelope for stuffing and cake recipes. She'd already weighed in on Bobby's fussing, spit up, weight gain, and the condition of Robin's uterus and chilled breast milk.

What else?

This family planning moment.

Accelerated Training

...By the way when one is only partially nursing a babe, pregnancy can occur very easily...be cautious, because you have no idea what it is to have to take care of a 12 or 15 month babe and a new one besides.<u>That's when</u> a mother doesn't know which way to turn.

Fourteen years later, I was the red-faced, colicky "surprise" that wriggled into Robin's arms one year and five days after my "near-Irish twin." Just short of age thirty-nine at the time, Robin would turn to Buster and ask, "what are we going to do with another baby?" He'd reply, "we're going to love her."

And they did.

Flip the Calendar
Chapter Sixteen

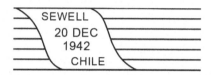

L.M. Skinner, Rancagua – Sewell, Chile S.A. – airmail

December 20, 1942

Dearest Bedfords,

A Merry, Merry Xmas!

First order of business for Lelia was to let Robin and Buster know this letter, written and mailed on the heels of yesterday's, included their Christmas check.

...might be less danger of it getting lost.

Letters are going and coming so irregularly these days...even so, we are so much more fortunate in regards to letters than in cases of families having to send them to Europe...

Americans couldn't comprehend why it took weeks to get a letter through to war-torn Europe. The reasons varied. Letters typically piled up at an embarkation point waiting for a convoy to be assembled. That alone could take weeks. Censors, too, had a hand in the delay. Mail to a boy transferred to a new post took longer; hence proper addresses were stressed: name, rank, serial number, unit to which he belonged. Most important was the "A.P.O.", the Army Post Office number. The transposition of two numerals in the A.P.O. would send a letter meant for Italy to Iceland. Other reasons? Mailbags were known to go down with a torpedoed ship; several boats carrying over 100,000 parcels of mail were sunk. Often the mail was held up purposely, concealing the whereabout of certain units from the enemy.

Feeling "triste," Lelia recalled it had been a full year since waving Robin into the sky aboard the Clipper. At the same time, she marveled at the miracle so quickly conceived and delivered in under ten months following her daughter's return to the States.

...A year from now he'll be able to sit up and take a little notice of a tiny Xmas tree and toys. Bud writes that Waynecito squeezes his rubber fish and dog and rattles his rattle with great enthusiasm.

Seven months later, Robert would do the same. She hoped Buster would be around to see it. Except Bobby would be deprived of squishy playthings. All the major toy manufacturers had turned to war production: gas masks, life rafts and hospital field supplies.

Ethel Bedford cradles eleven-week-old Bobby at Hobe Sound

Six Weeks for Boat Mail

Wouldn't it be lovely if we could all be at the same dinner table for Christmas turkey?...If I can't get to see Robert and Waynecito by Xmas 1943 I'll be disappointed! But, oh dear, even though we were in the States, how could we work it that we could have both grandsons on Xmas day?

One solution? Destination travel. It was right under her nose when she speculated on plans for Buster's folks.

I am just wondering if the Bedfords won't try to go to Florida for the holiday season, to get out of the cold, northern weather...you have ample room to have them with you, and of course they would love to be with "their baby" at Christmas.

She wished the same for herself.

We would love to hear all about what Buster's new work is in Florida, but I don't know whether you could tell it in a letter...We just hope you will enjoy all the Florida grapefruit and other delicious fruits and nuts for us!!...

Chile's citrus industry was terrorized by Jack Frost. Low yields in lemon and orange groves were not unusual. Growing conditions were worse for the larger "pomelo." Lelia stooped to canned Florida grapefruit, if she could get any. The order she'd placed through the company store in Sewell last July, at the peak of the Chilean winter, was yet to arrive.

On the gastronomic upside, Swift's Premium holiday hams were readily available. Though she preferred turkey at Christmas, a Swift® meat packing plant in La Plata, Argentina, seven hundred miles or so to the east, made it possible for Lelia to bake a brown-sugar-cured ham in clove studded splendor. A platter garnished with spiced pineapple rings, if she could get them, made a ham-dandy presentation.

Frankly, I imagine she found little energy for holiday fanfare with only T. Wayne and Russell to please.

While Ethel amused Bobby, Robin was free to busy herself in the kitchen with housemate, Lois. In early November, the government's <u>voluntary</u> "Share the Meat" program kicked off, buying time for the OPA to grapple with logistics of War Ration Book Two. Under the voluntary program, beef, pork, veal, lamb, and mutton were limited to two and a half pounds weekly for each member of the family over the age of twelve, incrementally less for the youngsters.

The king of the feast, *turkey*, was exempt. In fact, *all* poultry was fair game. So were several other nutritious meats: hearts, livers, kidneys, sweetbreads, ox joints, pork feet, and varieties of tongue. The list went on.

Here's a family secret. In my youth, beef tongue inventoried among the animal organs Robin occasionally asked for at the local grocer's meat counter. Sure, it's a "cut of beef" and well known today for culinary uses all around the world. Except a three-pound tongue with 25,000 tastebuds is, on a phallic scale, the equivalent of a geoduck clam. Glazed or braised, visual overtness made it impossible to get past my mind and into my mouth. So, when *I* unloaded the groceries, that butcher-papered parcel went straight to the basement refrigerator, out of sight and mind behind the Miller and Schlitz.

Lelia made out the Christmas check for fifty dollars, to be divided.

...Five for Robert and $22.50 for each of you two. I'm putting the entire amount in one check...Since Robert is too small for toys, I don't know any better use...take him to a baby specialist and have him check on his weight gain and his formula feedings and see why he cries...

Then, as if she'd worked up an appetite envisioning Christmas turkey, Florida grapefruit, and Swift's famous pork products, she shared Waynecito's food fare, too.

...such a nice variety—say from four or five months on. His latest desserts are Jell-O — apricots, and they are giving him cottage cheese—imagine it. And he had vegetable soup so young!

The best of everything throughout 1943 to all three of you, and hugs and kisses from us all...Mother and Dad

On New Year's Day, beacon lights of the Statue of Liberty illuminated the dawn of a new year. Three flashes and a prolonged beam messaged the familiar rhythmic pattern used in the first four notes of Beethoven's Fifth Symphony. It signified the Morse code symbol "V" for victory.

Silent, yet thunderous.

Six Weeks for Boat Mail

Lady Liberty, darkened for two years in conformity with blackout regulations, lit up a teeming, war-time harbor. By way of shortwave radio broadcast, a description of this shining "Light of Victory" reached to points around the globe. A program of song and music performed by stars of opera, stage, and screen, relayed America's message of freedom to men in the armed forces in all parts of the world.

Lelia would catch it on KGEI. The likes of Robin and Buster tuned in at home. Uniting the nation, NBC transmitted the show over 139 stations across America.

With the Hobe Sound post office box penciled into her address book, Lelia's Happy New Year greeting skipped Pelham Manor and flew directly to Florida. It opened with more head banging over mail service.

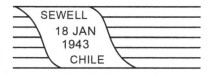

L.M. Skinner, Rancagua – Sewell, Chile S.A. – airmail

January 18, 1943
Dearest Children – Three;

Roberta's letter of Jan. 3 reached us Jan. 15...Scarcely seems possible that between Florida and Chile, with a three days flight, the mail would be taking that long, does it? I want this to reach you before you leave for the Gulf Coast.

Robin's January 3 letter hinted at another move. Her "Gulf Coast" reference was censor-defensible. Not counting tidal pools, the southern coastline stretches just over 1,600 miles where water laps at five states: Florida, Alabama, Mississippi, Louisiana, Texas.

Hope you leave a forwarding address at your present P.O. because this is the last letter I can get to you before you leave your lovely "Island Home"...Your Xmas sounds wonderful, especially the enormous turkey. In all my married life I have never had the privilege of stuffing one that size. The ones we get here weigh only 9 or 10 lbs...

If the butcher sold a bird any larger, it wouldn't fit in the standard, undersized oven at House #71.

Tomorrow I'm doing up a pkg. consisting of the little while blanket shawl... sweater...and a couple knitted little sun suits...

She also folded in something innovative for Bobby's layette.

...The Chileans use these little panties that button on to the little bands, over the diaper (instead of rubber panties) and the American mothers who have attempted the style also like them very much.

Coincidentally, in the Sunday Tampa Bay Times of January 18, a page thirty-seven headline read, "Even Babies May Have to Forego Rubber Panties for War Effort, OPM Chief Says"

> NEW YORK – (AP) – Copper pennies, nickels and even babies' rubber pants may disappear because their materials are needed for war...

Rubber baby panties were heaped with dog toys and several dozen other household items in the "acceptable salvage" pile staged curbside for collection day.

Surprisingly, the Chilean invention sounded like the innovative "Biobottoms" brand of felted lambswool diaper covers I used on my babies fifty years later. Brilliantly breathable, they fastened with flexible hook-and-loop Velcro® tabs. My environmentally-sound choice was weirdly based on a Marthas Vineyard honeymoon experience that placed me standing in an old town dump, turned landfill, hunting antique bottles. A colony of seagulls anchored an ocean of dueling diaper brands, Huggies™ and Pampers™.

...I wanted you to try them for use on top of the diaper as the moisture doesn't soak through, they say...

Bonus. Unsoiled clothes and crib sheets meant less laundry to wash and hang out along the clothesline. Not only that, if a washer broke, spare parts to fix it were impossible to find.

Six Weeks for Boat Mail

...We want you to remember that in case Buster gets sent to foreign soil, that the latch string always hangs out for you and Bobby. We would be more than delighted to have you with us, and we would just love Bobby to death.

"In case" Buster got sent? Lelia retained a flicker of hope. Her son-in-law *might* be spared deployment. Of the world's evil triumvirate, (Hitler, Mussolini, and Tojo) her hatred was particularly bitter for Hideki Tojo, the then 58-year-old German-educated General turned dictator. That stand-alone reference, "Tojo," became what would, one day, be considered racist slang, as did "Butterhead." The expression, adopted by U.S. Marines in the Pacific at the time, was born of their enemies' yellow skin tone.

Merciless propaganda took the form of wallet-size hunting licenses; multiple formats, all bearing a similar message: "JAP HUNTING LICENSE" ... "ON YELLOW BELLY JAPS" ... "SEASON OPENED DECEMBER 7, 1941—NO LIMIT" ... "GOOD UNTIL EXTERMINATION (NO CLOSED SEASON)" ... "AMMUNITION FURNISHED BY UNCLE SAM."

Should Robin choose to pull the "latch string" in Campamento Americano, Lelia understood household order and routine would turn to toddler chaos. But this amounted to a one-life-one-chance moment to weigh the anchor of regret on missed opportunities with her own children. To be sure, she imagined gaining an edge over Ethel Bedford in bonding with baby Bob.

As for Russell, three months had passed since his last visit to the American Embassy in Santiago. While waiting for news from

Snapshots of Robin with Bobby pulled Lelia's heartstrings.

Flip the Calendar

Washington on his passport, he took an engineer's helper job with Braden Copper. As a water marker, he measured fluctuations of water levels inside the bowels of El Teniente at the payrate of thirty-five pesos a day.

...It at least gives him something to occupy his mind with, and gets him out of the house into the fresh air...

Above and below ground, smudged air was anything but fresh, but at least he wasn't under her feet.

Robin's little brother, Russell, age twenty, 1943

I expect when they get short of boys in the U.S. army and navy Russell will hear...If he can't get off by March 1, he will have ten cat fits, because he said when he finished the cavalry in Aug. that he didn't want to stay in Chile a day longer than March 1...

Lelia carried on, satisfied that Robert now gained weight according to schedule. As if he would be in college next year, she added:

How wonderful he has an educational fund already started!

With that, a hint of rivalry reared its ugly head. In carving a customary path well known to White privileged America, Wayne, now ten months, was already registered at his father's alma mater, Shattuck. The Episcopal-affiliated military boarding school in Minnesota.

Likewise, expectations for Robert's future fell in Buster's footsteps and the legacy of Lawrenceville. Lelia did the math, which placed her grandson in the prep-school class of 1960.

How far off that seems, doesn't it?

Though she knew it to be no time at all.

I wish Waynecito were down in the Fla. sunshine with Bobby, instead of up in that rainy, winter climate of Tacoma...

Between rain showers, Dorothy managed to get Wayne out for his airing almost every dreary day; temperatures averaged in the forties.

...She can't find any help there, to help her with the work...

Except for a high school girl. She came over one night a week for Dorothy and Bud's date night.

You spoke of one sheet having been left out of my letter...

Yes. Her letter from Sewell dated September 12. Four months had passed.

...It must have been—possibly by accident in the censoring—because I never have sent a letter that I don't sign off...I don't know how they would have to leave a sheet out unless it were by mistake or oversight...I almost never refer to the war in my letters for fear something will be cut out...Hugs and kisses to you both and a big squeeze for Bobby... Mother and Dad

Circuits of Victory
Chapter Seventeen

In the Sunshine State, folks "ate local" and appreciated the year-round nutritional advantages they had over those living in most other parts of the country.

Or world, for that matter.

Buster angled whenever he had the chance. For three glorious months, the young Bedfords "guarded their health" with an abundance of fresh fruits, vegetables, and fish.

During the 2nd lieutenant's stint at Camp Murphy, all indicators pointed toward a family leapfrog over the Florida peninsula to a location along the Gulf Coast. Then to everyone's surprise, orders were issued for this station: Rome Air Depot.

Facing a second move in under five months, Robin begged to keep the family together. How about an apartment in upstate New York?

No.

The "RAD" installation, authorized by the War Department in June 1941, was ordered top prior-

Buster, the proud provider.

Six Weeks for Boat Mail

ity following the attack on Pearl Harbor and ready for "takeoff" February 1, 1942. Located about fifteen miles northwest of Utica, New York, its mission laid out like this: maintenance, aircraft storage, equipment repair, and shipment to units throughout the United States, European, and African theaters of operation.

Despairingly, Robin re-packed their belongings. She was also duty-bound to scissor OPA Form No. R-1301 from the local paper. This "consumer declaration" was a widely publicized step number one to apply for Ration Book Two. It obligated her to document quantities of such food items as coffee, canned fruits, vegetables, soup, and juices. Other than coffee, there wasn't much to declare. Provisions in the pantry were scant. Their penchant for fresh food had many advantages, including less mess to box up and move.

On February 22, when nationwide registration commenced, Robin made the dutiful run to a school in Stuart Florida, twelve miles northeast on U.S. Route 1. Lucky for her, *where* ration books were *issued* had no bearing on *where the stamps could be used*.

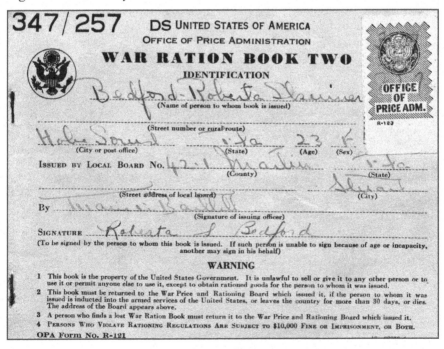

Robin's Hobe Sound souvenir.

Circuits of Victory

On the same day War Ration Book Two became active, March 1, the young family uprooted from Jupiter Island. Robin and Bobby were planted like cut flowers with Nat and Ethel in the middle of a New York winter.

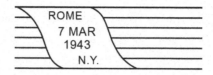

Lt. N.F. Bedford, Rome Air Base, Rome, N.Y. – March 8, 1943 (postage FREE)

Sunday, March 7, 1943
My Darling,

Tonight at 10:30 I at last have time to write you a note after an extremely busy day...

He rationalized the decision to cloister his wife with his parents.

...even if you were here I would have had no time to be with you...I have landed up to my ears in work.

Buster ranked as one of seven 2nd lieutenants. He chronicled the new assignment for Robin.

The 883rd is a Signal Company—on paper. Actually, it consists of seven second lieutenants and sixty-six privates, most of whom have had no training at all.

Lieutenant Frank Hefton, a November graduate of Officer Candidate School, led the lucky seven leadership team as commanding officer. Another lieutenant, one Buster knew from Camp Murphy, was expected to arrive soon. The other four, still wet behind the ears, were more recent grads of OCS.

...All the officers are nice chaps, I am glad to say, and I know you will like them, but they are already leaning heavily on my collection of notes for information and on me for judgment in getting the unit started.

The twenty-four-year-old's notes and "experience" derived from Harvard, MIT, and Camp Murphy following his OCS graduation from Fort Monmouth, nearly a year ago. Enormous responsibility rested with him to explain, educate, and guide. Slightly out of character, he acknowledged personal fallibility.

I wish that I knew a great deal more than I do, believe me.

While building this outfit from scratch, the unit would supply radios and radar equipment for aviation activities. What rewards came with hard work and the push to train sixty-six privates?

A first lieutenancy is open for a Radar Officer...we also have openings for a Captain and a Major!

He was invigorated over the thought of a promotion for good service. But others, assigned from the outside with a higher rank, might dash that hope. It's how the system worked.

The host mission of Rome Air Depot, "RAD," fell to the 100th Aviation Squadron, under the Army Air Corps Material and Technical Services Command. Once again, restrictions prevented most operations from being talked about. Whatever they were up to, RAD appeared to be a Signal officer's holding pen.

Rumor has it we will not be in Rome long, but will move to New Orleans within a month to start our real training...

The Gulf Coast!

I hope you will be able to come up Saturday for the weekend. I will phone you Thursday night when I know how our organization is progressing...Kiss Bobby for me. I love you dearly, B.

There is no evidence Robin made the two-hundred-fifty-mile trip that weekend. Buster's phone call on Thursday night preempted her dash north. When the 883rd bugged out, headed south, his wife and five-month-old son would move, too.

With his parents help, the young family re-settled into a furnished, three-bedroom, two-bath bungalow on North Broad Avenue in the Seventh Ward of New Orleans, a quintessential Creole neighborhood. Then, under

Circuits of Victory

Silky coated Red, family pet and beloved mascot of the 902 Signal Company.

orders of Uncle Sam, Buster re-packed, kissed Robin and Bobby, and yo-yoed further south.

From street view, the rental home was an easy six tiled steps up from the sidewalk to the bungalow's modest pillared porch. Atop the gabled roof sat a boxy cupola with wooden slats. During New Orlean's sweltering summer months, ventilated air flow, from windows wide-open in the downstairs, breezed through to the louvers up top.

Buster's "arrived safely" telegram sent from Orlando, May 2, came by way of a Western Union delivery person on Monday, May 3. Robin was glad to receive it. His first stamped envelope from Orlando wouldn't arrive for days.

Western Union, Tour = Orlando, Fla. – May 2, 1943
Mrs. Nathaniel F. Bedford
1557 North Broad Ave.
New Orleans (NRLNS)

= ARRIVED SAFELY TRIP NOT SO BAD WILL WRITE YOU TONIGHT LOVE = BUSTER.

Six Weeks for Boat Mail

He wrote three letters, dated May 2, 4, and 6, on official U.S. Army insignia stationery. Stuffed into one envelope, they weighed less than half an ounce combined; two three-cent stamps paid the airmail postmarked May 9.

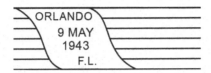

Nathaniel F. Bedford, 2nd Lt. Sig C 0-455263 Officers Mail Rom AAFSAT, Orlando, Fla. – Via airmail May 9, 1943
U.S. Army letterhead

May 2, 1943
My Darling,

Here I am, back in a G.I. barracks again, living like an enlisted man. Well, if I learn something it will be worth it...I haven't heard much favorable comment yet from the Signal Corps Officers who have been here for a couple of weeks...

Why?

In an imperfect military, changes were always underway, and the cheese had moved. At this fuzzy moment, it seemed Buster's peers had a two-week head start. He reserved judgement. Once his month-long assignment launched at this station, he'd see for himself.

The trip was not nearly so bad as it might have been. Although I was never able to get a Pullman berth, I had the good fortune to meet a Signal Corps Tech Sgt. who invited me to share his lower.

Both stretched out and slept.

The train was late getting to Jacksonville...it didn't make much difference...

He explained the *express* train, his railway connection to Orlando, was even later.

...I finally landed in Orlando at 2:45 on a local that stopped at every cow pasture.

Circuits of Victory

For most, it's a forgotten fact that Florida's landscape is naturally a vast area of grassland. Over the last half-century, the sprawl of a 1970s Magic Kingdom and subsequent theme parks, as well as age-targeted retirement communities, have taken a big bite out of those wide-open spaces.

...Sundays are very dead here and the process of registering was short and simple for a change. My chief annoyance was the fact that my checked luggage never got through. Please hurry my laundry along as I am short of shirts and may have to buy another if it doesn't come thru soon.

He'd left behind a heap at a time when business boomed too big for laundry operators. For one thing, civilian clothes were filthier than ever, greased up on the job in factories. And at the substandard hourly payrate of twenty-five cents, the laundry business couldn't compete with wages offered at New Orleans based Higgins Industries. They'd won a War Department contract of $40,000,000 to build boats. Mr. Higgins himself was cooking up a plan to pay trainees fifty cents an hour. Once they learned how to weld, well-compensated essential war work was theirs. A very forward-thinking Andrew Higgins also offered equal pay, based on the position, for men, women, African Americans, and the elderly.

For seven or eight cents a pound, Robin would have the laundry service wash, fluff, and tumble his attire. She could only "hurry things along," by ironing in the starched military creases on her own time while Bobby napped.

...At least I have a lake with alligators (and presumably bass) right at the door of the barracks...

One did not need laundered garments to fish.

That evening, Buster steered clear of the twenty-five-cent slop in the soldier's mess. He wandered off base. For eighty-eight cents he scored a big steak dinner at a local diner. With his sophisticated palate and stomach satisfied, the walkabout began. He assessed the surroundings like this:

...Orlando is a lovely town, nice homes, clean and inexpensive.

Six Weeks for Boat Mail

Once the sun went down, hunkered in the barracks, there was little to do except write, study, and sleep. He would do plenty of the latter while he could.

What about classes?

...interesting, profitable, but the auditorium is hot and stuffy.

Ashtrays on every desk hint as to why the room was stuffy.

The last eight days, entirely in the field, would take place down around Leesburg...*where the bass come from...*

He was eager to get outside.

May 6, 1943

My Beloved,

Time tears on and the first four days of school have now been condensed into a few pages of notes in my notebook. The course still looks as though it has opportunities to me, but I think they rather lie in personal contact with men who have seen action rather than in the classes themselves...

In this place and time, Buster found himself smack dab in the center of a brand-new chapter in U.S. military history.

Circuits of Victory

Here in Orlando, the Headquarters of the Army Air Forces School of Applied Tactics, "AAFSAT," gained traction as an advanced institution. In virtual secrecy, the school was established and rushed into operation. Only military insiders knew.

Buster, his Signal Corps officer contemporaries, and thousands of other men following orders lacked the broad view.

But then, come to find out, regular consumers of *The Orlando Sentinel* knew plenty.

Here's the scoop.

Three months earlier, in February, *The Sentinel* published a series of articles under the caption "This is the Army." They snapped back the magician's cape to expose tactical leadership at the school. Seasoned experts had been percolating for a lot longer than anyone, other than high ranking military and perhaps enemy operatives, really knew.

For example, on Friday, February 5, a spectacled Lt. Col. D.S. McChesney met the reader eye to eye on page five. In his capacity as Assistant to the Training Director, McChesney spelled out how the Army Air Force stretched its wings. AAFSAT did not teach specialized skills like "mechanics," "how to fly," "supply," or, in Buster's case, "radio." To be dispatched to Orlando, one had to be a *technical school graduate*. Here men with distinct skill sets *secretly assimilated* at an accelerated rate.

Saturday, February 6, the reader met Col. Morton H. McKinnon, the man in charge of the Air Support Department. Under the umbrella of air command, aviation units systemized: <u>Observation</u> from above; the eyes of the Army. <u>Light and dive bombardment</u>; the fangs and claws. <u>Troop carriers</u>; delivery of paratroops and air-borne infantry into action. Supplies followed.

The tactical lesson? Air Force personnel, united with ground troops, produced a compact, hard hitting, competent combat team.

Buster's wish for "personal contact with men who have seen action" came true.

In every other state in the nation, AAFSAT remained a military secret. Logically, the Greater Orlando Chamber of Commerce capitalized on good fortune. It became their business to place military families in homes.

Six Weeks for Boat Mail

In some combination of patriotic duty and smart marketing, real estate firms and property owners in Winter Park and Orlando assisted. Families eager to take up peace time pursuits after the war would find the Sunshine State a fine place to settle. His revelation, "Orlando is a lovely town..." was uncannily prescient.

For the benefit of *Sentinel* readers not at all interested in the business end of AAFSAT's tactical leadership, a write-up on "Action Overhead," scheduled for February 23, commanded their attention. It was no secret at all:

> Citizens from all over Central Florida, perhaps 12,000 to 15,000 strong, will attend the premiere showing at Greater Orlando Stadium of 'Action Overhead'...an army demonstration of a simulated air raid with exploding bombs, incendiaries and a vanishing model village that will go up in flames and smoke...one of the greatest educational demonstrations to come out of the present war...

News of "Action Overhead" first blew out of Washington over the International News Service (INS) in September 1942. That's when a mobile unit of the Chemical Warfare Service took to the road in a caravan of fourteen trucks. They played to overflow crowds in Massachusetts at the time Robin and Buster resided in Cambridge. When the convoy reached Orlando, by way of several southern states, nearly a million Americans had witnessed the precise and devastating effect of every type of air-borne missile. With maximum clarity, images of thermite and magnesium incendiary bombs burned into their brains. Simply put, the whole purpose of the breathtaking display was to educate citizens on the methods of attack used by the enemy, and to inform civilian defense officials and emergency responders how to meet such attacks.

In short, Buster knew all about the excitement of "Action Overhead" when he stepped off the train in Orlando, but nothing of the AAFSAT undertaking to which he would personally contribute. He was yet to fully comprehend this assignment.

His May 6 letter to Robin continued. On the evening of day three at AAFSAT, he had a date. It involved his rod and reel, feet planted on a grassy bank, casting into the unknown. In a small tacklebox he'd stowed everything an experienced Florida angler like him needed to be happy: hooks, leaders, swivels, lures, and monofilament line (a recent DuPont invention at the time).

...As I suspected, this lake in front of my barracks has bass in it...I caught a 1 ½ pounder last night...

The bass struck his red-headed plug. It surprised him. He expected the crippled frog jig to be the ticket. Though the fish was "good eating size," he took hold of its toothy lower lip, gently dislodged the lure, and set it free. The season didn't open until May 20, the day before his twenty-fifth birthday. It triggered this suggestion:

Let's not do anything about birthday presents for each other until I get back... If you will pick out a couple of cute summer dresses for yourself, I will get them for you about June 5th...Kiss Bobby for me...

While Robin awaited the postman's delivery of Buster's three letters, stuffed in one envelope, she wrote Nat and Ethel. I imagine she told them of his "safe arrival," then tickled them with baby Bobby's latest shenanigans.

Something in the tone of her correspondence led to this:

Western Union, NL=NK NEWARK NJ – May 6, 1943
Mrs. Nathaniel F. Bedford =
1557 North Broad Ave.
New Orleans (NRLNS) =

JUST RECD YOUR LETTER WE WOULD LIKE TO HAVE YOU COME HOME TO PELHAM UNTIL BUSTER COMES BACK OR MOTHER WILL COME DOWN TO BE WITH YOU IF YOU PREFER WIRE IMMEDIATELY NEWARK COLLECT WHAT YOU WANT TO DO LOVE:
= MOTHER AND DAD

 Six Weeks for Boat Mail

OH, no, no, NO.

Mother's Day, (May 9) 1943

My Beloved,

Your last letter arrived…I wish that you had arrived along with it. Next best thing was to hear your voice over the phone today.

It being Mother's Day (her <u>*first*</u>), he placed two calls early that morning, one to Robin and a second to Ethel. All Americans knew, due to the war, "Ma Bell" telephone lines were overloaded. Now, on the day *everyone* called mom, capacity was stretched even further.

The Bell System circulated "Tips on Telephoning," with information to demystify a gamut of long-distance call scenarios for boys who'd rarely, if ever, left home before now: station-to-station, person-to-person, collect. On the flip side of the tip sheet, a handy eight-and-a-half-by-eleven-inch Rand McNally map of the United States folded into a tidy four-and-a-half-by-three-inch manilla envelope, sized for a breast pocket.

GOOD LUCK!

"Here's a map of the United States to help you keep track of your travels. Also, there's information to assist you in making long distance calls.

Telephone wires are loaded with war calls—but we'll do our best to get **your** calls through. If there's a delay, it will help if you will remain nearby so we can tell you when your call is ready."

By instructing servicemen how to save time on calls, more calls could be connected. Buster knew to avoid the busiest hours. He'd also mastered the art of keeping it brief. It was enough to hear Robin's silken voice, then write her.

In his Mother's Day letter, she learned he and another 2nd lieutenant ventured off base to attend church. To get there, they caught the Orlando/

Winter Park "Dinky Line." So named by students at Rollins College a half-century before.

Rollins is Florida's oldest recognized college; a coeducational liberal-arts institution of higher learning founded by New England Congregationalists. It opened in the fall of 1885. Rail service on the Orlando-Winter Park commuter link to campus began three years later. The coeds found the locomotive unreliable and uncomfortable. Winding six miles north through a wilderness of pine trees and oaks, unstable cars were known to wiggle off the dinky tracks!

The two lieutenants stepped off onto campus at the Victorian-style Dinky Line depot.

...The Rollins Chapel is small but exceedingly lovely...the program was an interesting one—about mothers.

The Knowles Memorial Chapel, dedicated in 1932, was one he'd attended as a teen once before. His cousin Vicky, a Rollins '34 graduate, was a student at the time.

...things like that need time to mature to be really lovely. Ten years has done this one a world of good.

Ten years was, relatively speaking, a "long time" for a near twenty-five-year-old. Later deemed worthy of preservation, the chapel was entered into the *National Register of Historic Places* in 1997.

In the rear gallery, a great circular stained-glass window loomed over enormous organ pipes. During the service, majestic orchestral tones reverberated through the sanctuary. Hearts swelled in the music of God's Glory. On the way out, eyes lifted to read Ecclesiastes 9:16, the parting message etched into stained glass: "WISDOM IS BETTER THAN STRENGTH."

If only the evil triumvirate shared that sentiment. Many years later the Iron Lady of India, Prime Minister Indira Gandhi, laid it out from her perspective: "You cannot shake hands with a clenched fist."

...afterwards we stopped by the AWVS to ask about a good place to lunch.

The AWVS canteen was a swell spot for a Rollins' girl to fulfill her patriotic duty several hours a week while meeting eligible young men from all around the country. The American Women's Volunteer Service (AWVS), established in January 1940, was modeled on the British Women's Voluntary Service. Under the jumbo umbrella of this nonsectarian nonprofit, ladies of all ages donned distinctive uniforms according to the nature of their wide-ranging work on the home front. For example, those who knew how to drive filled the niche of heavy truck and ambulance operators. Especially popular among servicemen were the Button Brigadiers. These women manned a mobile sewing unit equipped to move between camps and bases around Florida, though I have no evidence Buster had the pleasure of meeting them.

It's fair to ask how the AWVS compared to the more widely known USO. That nonprofit, set up in February 1941, linked up with Hollywood stars to provide celebrity-boosted entertainment around the world. The "United Service Organization" brought together six religious and recreation enterprises for a "joint service" experiment in democracy. It included the YMCA, the National Catholic Community Service, the Salvation Army, the YWCA, the Jewish Welfare Board, and the National Travelers Aid Association.

With full bellies and happy hearts, Buster and his buddy pushed back from their Sunday lunch special and returned to the AWVS canteen where they played ping pong.

We worked up a lather at that, then decided we ought to go swimming to cool off.

To that end, the boyish lieutenants commandeered two pairs of swim trunks from a sympathetic Rollins professor. After a dip in Lake Virginia, (where, today, Dinky Dock Park commemorates the old depot site) they returned to their Orlando barracks.

Ironically, the *Orlando Evening Star* made this pitch in a newsclip three weeks later, May 24:

In answer to the appeal for swimming trunks for servicemen to enjoy the beaches provided for them on Lake

Virginia, some money has been left at AWVS to purchase some. Anyone wishing to give trunks or money, is assured of the appreciation of these men who come every day from the Orlando bases...

...Now we are going off to supper. Give Bobby a big kiss for me, little mother, and tell him to give you a big kiss for me. Be patient and I will be home before you know it...All my love, Buster

Three days later, news of AAFSAT broke around the country.

Under the "National News" banner of *The Tampa Bay Times*, Wednesday, May 12, United Press headlined this:

"Central Florida Area Converted Into Large Army Air Forces School"

...The School, which has been operating in virtual secrecy since March 2 attempts to provide its students with what one official described as 'the closest to actual air warfare we hope there ever will be in the United States.'

The vast AAFSAT training area laid out across the northern and central part of the Florida peninsula. Coast to coast, Atlantic to the Gulf of Mexico, it consumed about a *fifth* of the entire state. Training exercises flew well out over the shining sea, too. Headquarters in Orlando, where Buster attended ground school, was fixed in the southeastern corner of the "campus." Desert and jungle "classrooms" were scattered in places the likes of Leesburg.

Did this big reveal in the national news compromise military intelligence?

Absolutely not. The first edition of a "Code of Wartime Practices for the American Press," a voluntary censorship code, rolled out less than six weeks following the attack on Pearl Harbor. The premise was to nudge members of the press, broadcasters, and publishers, to do right by the nation; to balance wartime secrecy and the public's right to know. Stories were to be accurate, but not aid the enemy.

Six Weeks for Boat Mail

Brigadier General Hume Peabody, commander of the whole AAFSAT shebang, distilled it to sea, air, and ground coordination—of the over-air command.

Peabody, a veteran flyer and command pilot, reported directly to General Henry "Hap" Arnold, Commanding General of the Army Air Forces. Here, officers of all three branches of the military familiarized themselves with the capabilities and limitations of the other two.

On arrival, Buster took notes in hot, stuffy, but well-equipped classrooms. It wasn't all pencil and paper. Strategic minds stretched over engineered game boards. Given a set of battle conditions and complicated attacks, the men worked defensive problems and solutions. Then came the second half of the four-week training. Simulated combat operations, staged in make-shift swamp installations, replicated flying problems in other swampy places, like New Guinea.

The Tampa Bay Times described one reporter's escapade; "we were taken in A-20 fighter-bombers to attack an 'enemy' field at Leesburg, where we were 'intercepted' and technically 'shot down' by fighter planes assigned to protect the Leesburg field." Alas, the field was camouflaged amidst trees dripping with Spanish moss, and ringed by anti-aircraft batteries and searchlights. Radio, sound, and visual aircraft detection stations were manned around the clock. Planes on the ground were carefully dispersed, ready to defend the post. They'd done so brilliantly.

Proof that the nation-at-large quickly learned of AAFSAT's secret bag of tricks, a day later the New York *Daily News*, Thursday, May 13 reported this:

> To say that the Army Air Forces School of Applied Tactics (which everybody calls AAFSAT down here), is big, is putting it mildly. It is spread across some 15,000 square miles, includes a dozen impressive specialized sub schools, scores of flying fields, hundreds of planes and thousands of troops...It has grown to its present dumbfounding size within the past year, during which it operated behind

closed doors, until today the Army decided to take the cover off and reveal it to the public.

Ultimately, all the men dispatched to AAFSAT would be grateful for having learned, in four weeks, how to mesh areas of expertise in a practiced theater of war. Rank advancements were in the offing. In Buster's case, a 1st lieutenancy.

Newly formed combat groups learned they would soon deploy overseas. Buster couldn't sing a lick but, a kidder at heart, I imagine he pucker whistled well enough to infect everyone in his company with the chorus of this sticky, WWI-era earworm, "I Don't Know Where I'm Going but I'm On My Way."

I beg you, for an intoxicating two-minute lift me up, find the chipper tune by "Sheet Music Singer" on YouTube.

Tally-Ho
Chapter Eighteen

The delay between the date of Buster's letters and their postmark was due to the fact he batched them for dispatch in one envelope. Weight didn't matter; postage was FREE for servicemen. Excepting air mail. That required two three-cent stamps; Thomas Jefferson "prexie purples" cornered and canceled in the upper right.

Buster's letter of May 11 laid out "business." Proof that, no matter where a soldier landed, the constant of "housekeeping" followed; Robin carried out marching orders:

- Forward April's electric bill from Hobe Sound to Ray (their Hobe Sound housemate).
- Enter check #89 for $30 in the check book register. (No mention who it was made out to or what it was for.)
- Record his 2nd Lieutenant's paycheck; $245.40 and a $40 deposit from "Mother." He thoughtfully asked, "Can you get by for the rest of the month O.K.?"
- Had "Mother" sent a bill from Best & Co?

Best's, a New York department store, was known at the time for tastefully styled women's clothing and sturdy children's wear. Obviously, they'd charged something on the senior Bedford's house account. Buster speculated; perhaps she'd waive away the debt.

Why?

Tally-Ho

On the "NKP," the reporting mark for the New York, Chicago, and St. Louis Railroad Company, the common stock in his mother's portfolio "went way up again to 48." Trains were, after all, *vital* to the war effort. War posters captured the message; "TANKS DON'T FIGHT IN FACTORIES!... KEEP 'EM ROLLING...THE RAILROADS ARE THE FIRST LINE OF DEFENSE."

Then there was a baby gift to tend to. It took eight weeks for a birth announcement routed through Hobe Sound to surface. Buster and his best man, Ben Wood, started out together as PFCs at Fort Devens in 1941. Their respective aptitudes dispatched Buster to Signal Corps OCS at Fort Monmouth and Ben to the Army Air Force at Kelly Field in San Antonio. Ben's wife Barbara crashed through with their first-born son, Ramsey, on March 3; eight pounds, two ounces.

One more for the "war baby" score. Those born between 1939 and 1945, shoehorned between the "greatest generation" and "baby-boomers," came to be known as the "silent generation." Far from silent, they include a lengthy list of influentials, the likes of Joe Biden, Nancy Pelosi, John Kerry, Bob Woodward, and icons in the world of music and film, too.

Idolizing his bride, Buster, cast a wide net of salutations: "Robin Dearest;" "My Beloved;" and a novel "Squeaky." They made for more original reading when his batched letters arrived.

May 14, 1943

Squeaky Dearest,

Squeaky, her pet name. It derived from the familiar squeal she'd let loose as Buster advanced, splashing, in icy coastal waters of the Northeast. It excited them both in a physical feedback loop.

> *Spent three days this week studying about "tally-ho," so two weeks from Sunday night I shall bound forth from a taxi and shouting "tally-ho" at the top of my lungs. I shall break down the front door and dash into your arms...*

A Science Editor for the Associated Press explained the fox hunting phrase in *The Tampa Bay Tribune* of Sunday, May 16:

> The new game of tallyho's played on a small tabletop with high stakes: enemy bombers, the lives of American interceptor pilots, the safety of cities…The game is to chart, in red crayon on the glass top, the course of enemy planes over the map area, and in green crayon the course which interceptors must fly to meet the enemies before they reach an objective.

Picture two card tables covered with a map; the map anchored by a slab of glass. Players mind the locations of cities, towns, military installations, and assigned objectives. The scale: one inch is about ten miles. The advances: slow and strategic.

> Red moves perhaps a half inch a minute. Red's direction and speed change. Radio tells where red is in the sky, and the red player charts accordingly. Green moves about half an inch too. His moves depend on what red has done 10 seconds or more ago…Green fades, turns and shifts with red exactly like the defense in a football team…

Here, Buster's collegiate football experience paid off. So did his secret Camp Murphy radar training. And, like a yet-to-be-invented, multi-player, online simulation game, this training tool was fun!

> …The green course, on the table top, is sent, minute by minute, by radio, to the interceptor pilots in the air. In this game the crayons on the little table direct the battle, almost mile by mile.

The crayon of the green player determined whether interceptors hit the enemy at the right moment, altitude, and place.

In AAFSAT's training progression, the game graduated out of the classroom and into the field; players directed *real* planes flying over a large section of Florida. Variable speed, direction, altitude, and wind invited chaos along with tricks of "enemy pilots."

Tally-Ho

The game, then two years old, was considered new military science, credited in Britain's House of Commons as one of the saviors of England in the Blitz. Those trained in Tallyho eventually packed their skillset and a pocketful of odd-shaped chessmen whistling all over the world.

Buster found training to be fun, too. But he'd had it with mundane domestic chores. Literally busting buttons led him to this moment of misogyny.

...I am getting darned tired of sewing on my own buttons and washing my own sox and underwear. They don't have any laundry service on the post...I am getting washboard hands.

It's true. Underthings were laundered using a flat board set in a tin bucket. Up and down the ribbed metal surface he scrubbed with a cake of GI soap guaranteed to remove stains, as well as the skin on his fingers. In two sentences he pitifully, yet unwittingly, encapsulated the Greatest Generation's definition of "women's work."

Turning to more manly pursuits, he continued:

...Three times a week we exercise for two hours from three to five.

As a best practice laundry-saving measure, he and others went shirtless in the hot Florida sun.

...Today we took the obstacle course for the first time...About twice as long as the one at Camp Murphy...not quite so tough on the individual obstacles.

Conceived to separate the men from the boys in endurance, he felt fit and hardy. In a week they would take their Tallyho training into the field at Leesburg. After that? He would jubilantly tally-home to New Orleans.

...You are really a wonderful wife and I can hardly wait to get back and whisper it to you...

Four months passed with no news from Campamento Americano. Lelia, one who valued stability, couldn't keep up with the training transfers. While Buster advanced point to point, Bud dashed Kentucky-bound for more Armored Force training at Knox. Dorothy held the home fort in

Tacoma with Waynecito and, pronatalism being what it was, her second baby McLeod, "jig dancing in the pouch."

President Roosevelt was on the move again, too. The previous fall, in a trip made under conditions of extreme wartime secrecy, FDR visited nine of the nation's biggest war plants, two shipyards, seven naval stations, eight Army camps, and two Marine Corps training centers. He'd been to Detroit, then around the edge of the nation from the Northwest, down the Pacific Coast, into the Southwest, and back to Washington by way of the deep South. It worked out so well that he embarked on a springtime inspection. On this second tour, he traveled to military installations in twenty states, as far west as Colorado. They included twelve Army posts, a Marine training base, a naval air station, and four war plants. In Mexico, he met with President Avila Camancho.

The tour concluded at Bud's haunt, Fort Knox.

FDR arrived at Knox on Wednesday, April 28. The Field Artillery battalions offered up a customary 21-gun "presidential salute." The first section he inspected was the tank department. And the first tank to catch his eye was aptly named "Tojo's Misery," an M-4 Sherman, the likes of which made its debut at Fort Knox on Army Day one year ago.

A three-hour tour of the Armored Force School concluded when FDR was taken to Outpost Six. There he took a seat in a grandstand filled with officers. Because fashion was invariably newsworthy, *The Courier-Journal* of April 30 described how the Commander in Chief dressed for the occasion… "in a light gray, double-breasted suit, with soft gray hat. He sat on a big cape, which he pulled around his shoulders in the chill air. He smoked one cigarette after another in his long holder."

It wasn't just a cape he wore. His signature "naval boat cloak," made of a fine, heavy-weight wool with velvet collar and satin lining, fastened at chest level with an intricate corded barrel loop. A defining element of his image.

An impressive demonstration of mechanized warfare firepower unfolded. For almost an hour, tanks, guns, armored artillery, and armed infantrymen blazed away at the "enemy" while P-309 and P-40 planes from nearby Godman Field bombed and strafed.

Key to the demonstration was *air-ground coordination*.

Precisely the type of tally-ho tactics Buster perfected at AAFSAT.

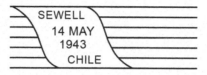

L.M. Skinner, Rancagua – Sewell, Chile S.A. – airmail

May 14, 1943
A Happy Birthday to Both Son and Daughter!!
Dearest Children:

We waited so long to know what your whereabouts would be after going up north...

Easter Sunday, April 25, had come and gone. The envelope of Robin's hand-picked Easter card divulged their Louisiana address.

We appreciated the thought of you remembering us...we made a journey to Santiago...

Per usual, they lodged at the Hotel Crillón on Augustinas Street while taking care of business. Lelia returned to a stack of tasks ahead of her.

The Vice Pres. of the Company from New York was here and staying in the Directors' House, for about 3 weeks. So I had to give more thought to that place...

But for once she didn't complain about it.

He was the dearest man—everyone was just crazy about him...

Four years older than Lelia, Carl Uhlrich rose through Kennecott's ranks in the New York office. Over thirty-plus years Uhlrich learned the company's inner workings. This empowered him to leapfrog up the corporate ladder from company cashier, to clerk, to vice-president.

Other than being a nice guy, how did Carl win her over? Before his return flight via Clipper to Miami, <u>three</u> boxes of Whitman's candy arrived at the Braden office in *her* name. T. Wayne phoned to tell her so.

Six Weeks for Boat Mail

Clever Carl. The Latin "rule of three," omne trium perfectum, points to the overarching principle that everything that comes in threes is perfect. His three-week stay in the directors' house was nothing less.

In 1942, Whitman candies celebrated one hundred years in the confection business, with their top-selling "sampler" introduced in 1912. The company built a solid reputation as the <u>one best</u> kind of candy; "a gift so fine it touches the heart with a special thrilling warmth," according to one advertisement.

Lelia evidently shared that sentiment.

Whitman's history reveals something even sweeter. Between 1942 and 1945, servicemen overseas were on the receiving end of *six million pounds* of chocolates packaged in one-pound tins marked "LAND SEA and AIR Chocolates." The winning image of a Boeing B-17 Flying Fortress flew across the lid. Radiant 1940s imagery rendered a 4,000-pound payload exploding below in a variegated burst of yellow to orange. Circling the tin's perimeter, a cityscape glowed hot enough to melt the contents. In an imaginary way.

But here's a fun fact. On the production line, women were melting hearts with handwritten notes tucked into packing boxes. Long-term friendships developed. Even a few post-war marriages ensued.

What else touched Lelia?

…Auntie Rhea and Mrs. Bedford have both written us how sweet and dear Bobby is. I expect he looks a lot different than his pictures you sent us. Babies all change so quickly…

A hint for new snapshots. Dorothy had recently sent adorable Kodacolor prints of Waynecito attired in his snow suit. But film, and the basic materials *in* film, were being used for war purposes. Officially declared a scarce commodity, it fell under the management and distribution of the War Production Board. Without it, Robin's 35-millimeter Contax remained in the dark of its stitched brown leather case.

What a roasting time you will have in New Orleans this summer with Bobby. I hope he can get by without any intestinal upsets through the hot weather…

Not a problem if Bobby still nursed. The greatest risk for cramping, bloating, and fussiness came from spoiled milk. Add to that the misery of itchy little red bumps. Prickly heat was common in the oppressive humidity of New Orleans. "Proper airing" was an oxymoron.

I wish Dorothy were going back to Missoula for "Susie Q." I worry so about her there alone with Waynecito, with Bud gone. It is the riskiest thing I ever heard of.

In a scenario familiar to young servicemen, Bud couldn't do anything about it. Were he to miss the birth of Wayne *and* Susie Q, too? So be it.

This go-round at Knox would be longer and tougher than his six-weeks training a year ago. Numbers of *technical* courses tracked for three months or more. With experience gained in a medium-tank company at Fort Lewis, Bud now ranked among the best qualified candidates selected from units across the country to attend the Armored School.

Armored divisions revamped to achieve peak efficiency. Nearly a complete army unto itself, each had its own artillery, mechanized infantry, signal corps units, tank and anti-tank units, and medical detachments. Supply units delivered ammunition, fuel, and food to fighting units by way of reliable armored force "truck trains." In a quiet but rapid change, the Armored Force, born at Fort Knox just three years before, was redesignated the "Armored Command," under the umbrella of Ground Forces.

She's counting Bud will be back home before the event, but babies have a way of not waiting on Dr. calculations sometimes. I just shiver for Waynecito if Dorothy would have to be rushed to a hospital, and only neighbors to lend a hand.

In a flap, Lelia muddled over her daughter's emergency obstetric scenarios. For Wayne, she feared severe emotional trauma. As if it were possible, she waved her pen like a wand to beam both out of Tacoma and home to Missoula.

What did she know?

On a nation-wide basis at the time, Montana boasted the lowest rate of deaths of mothers from childbirth; 1.6 per 1,000 live births.

I don't imagine McLeod's will hear to such a thing! They know the danger. They'll be going over and getting them.

Six Weeks for Boat Mail

As the happy birthday letter of May 14 continued, Lelia hinted at what in the world she knew; events she couldn't write about.

Hasn't the African news been wonderful?

Six months before, *Operation Torch* began with landings in French North Africa. It represented the first major U.S. effort against the Axis forces outside the Pacific theater.

What delighted Lelia?

In the seven-day blow of the "Tunisian Campaign," May 7 – 13, the last pocket of resistance among Axis forces in North Africa surrendered. The War Department reported the score out of Washington; in the six months and three days between the landings in French North Africa and the astonishing collapse of Axis resistance, Allied Air Forces destroyed approximately 2,000 enemy planes (losing 770). British sources estimated the whole North African campaign to have cost the Germans and Italians more than 600,000 men killed, wounded, or captured.

Now news came from every angle, faster than any optimist dreamed.

The Associated Press picked up and recorded a special communique soberly broadcast by Berlin Radio, the evening of May 13: "The heroic struggle of German and Italian Africa detachments today came to an honorable conclusion."

When, in fact, multiple news sources reported a complete, disastrous, and humiliating defeat.

The real dope, reported by the AP from Allied Headquarters in North Africa, was this: "Three of Germany's best and oldest armored divisions and every Italian armored division that ever existed are among the five Axis armies wiped out in the African campaign which ended in Tunisia. A total of thirty-six divisions [ten to fifteen thousand, each] have been annihilated."

Ned Russell, a United Press correspondent who ran with the British First Army, witnessed and reported the situation first-hand: "German and Italian truck drivers here have organized a shuttle service to deliver their own men to Allied prison pens…They come in loaded to capacity with shouting, waving Axis troops. The trucks dump the load of prisoners and go back for more. That is the measure of the debacle which has overtaken a once proud army...The First Army has so many prisoners it doesn't know what to do with them."

If this horrible war could only come to a quick end! But we fear the Jap angle of it is going to take considerable time...

In an agitated way, Lelia juxtaposed death and destruction with this score: a season of babies! Three boys and two girls were born into Campamento Americano that Chilean summer. Each one a reminder of the preciousness of life; the harbinger of a new generation. Her life choices stung. A home made with T. Wayne in a Chilean mining camp tainted her utopian dreams as a mother and now, a grandmother. She soldiered on... *Give Bobby a big hug and kiss for us—how we long to see the Grandchildren...Wish we could celebrate together...*

Buster would be sent to foreign soil soon. When he did, the "latch string" at House #71 would beckon.

Before sealing the envelope, she scribbled out and inserted a check for fifty dollars; twenty-five dollars apiece. Nearly four hundred in today's dollars. She suggested they each...*get something you long to have for your birthdays...*

Buster, too, picked up the birthday thread in his next letter from AAFSAT; *"they have started handing out assignments here now and I have been hopping."* He couldn't reveal the detail, so he didn't.

May 17, 1943

...Mother writes that she found a case for your Ray-Ban glasses...she sent it to me thinking it was for my glasses.

Written proof, Robin and Buster *both* glammed great optics of the dark-green lensed, wire-rimmed sunglasses. Developed by Bausch & Lomb for pilots to protect their eyes, the brand rapidly spread to outdoorsy types. High-performance anti-glare eyewear of Ray-Ban Aviators became the icon of men's glasses and a symbol of women's fashion, too.

...Mom sent me a beautiful little travelling alarm clock for my birthday.

Six Weeks for Boat Mail

Due to the increase in rotating defense job shiftwork, a problematic shortage of alarm clocks grew. Less expensive models flew off drug and department store shelves. Time-tested manufacturers suspended production and turned to war-time essentials, like small torpedo and timebomb mechanisms. There were no alarm clocks to be found.

A four-inch, square-fitted leather case with a solid snap closure secured the clock that shouted TIFFANY with lettering on the face and the lower eight-day dial. With a brass-bezel, thick glass face, a touch of Mother of Pearl on the hands, and innards of fifteen jewel Longines movement, Ethel bought the one gift he knew he needed—and asked for.

As long as this reliable timepiece held out, Buster would not fail when it came time to set up the radio-net at some ungodly hour.

She asked me if I knew what you wanted...I told her she had better ask you.

As his gift from Robin, he picked out a tropical worsted shirt. Trousers, too. An extra ensemble to lighten his laundry load.

...Honey, I am going to have to have $10.00 to get home. If you will number a check and enter it in the check book I will cash it here when you mail it to me...

Eagerly anticipating his return to Robin, Buster wrote note upon letter. Like a Whitman's sampler, she was never sure of the contents until she unwrapped and consumed them.

The semisweet, one-sided conversation went like this:

May 18, 1943...*When I leave for Leesburg I am going to mail some of my uniforms home. Will you please have them washed and ready for me when I get back...*

May 19, 1943...*Just had to drop you a little note to tell you how lovely the full moon is over the lake tonight...You take a good look at it and a week from Sunday night let's pretend it's still there. I'll give you a big kiss on it....*

May 22, 1943...*arrived safely at Leesburg yesterday...We are living in tents and sleeping on folding cots, but I love it...*

He'd packed an air mattress.

Tally-Ho

Trophy bass down around Leesburg

...Last night after supper I caught two 1½ lb. bass which we will have for supper tonight...A three pounder got away. The lake right next door to camp is just full of the darned things...my stay here will be a very pleasant one.

May 23, 1943...*Thanks for the check, dear. It will see me through safely... Rainy Sunday today, so no fishing. Just spent the day loafing around reading "One World."*

A new release by Simon and Schuster, *One World*, by Wendell Willkie, published just weeks before.

Willkie, a Republican businessman, faced off and lost to FDR in the 1940 presidential election. In an upworthy act of bipartisanship and global vision, the likes of which we could sure use today, he moved on to perform as Roosevelt's personal representative. *One World*, recounts Willkie's seven-week tour to meet with world leaders of allied nations. He wrote in favor of international peacekeeping after the war; a globally interdependent postwar piece that Buster deemed:

 Six Weeks for Boat Mail

...excellent, although sketchy due to the briefness of Willkie's trip.

May 25, 1943...*A birthday card and letter yesterday, and a box of brownies today—my, but you are wonderful!...How is the morale on the home front?...*

Semisweet? It depended. Had Buster's mother moved into the Broad Avenue house? It was one option unfolded in the May 6 telegram.

Are you and Bobby happy? I'll be right there to check on it in just five little old short skinny days, so keep those chins up, both of you.

Blue Notes
Chapter Nineteen

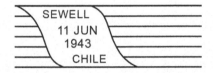

L.M. Skinner, Rancagua – Sewell, Chile S.A. – airmail

June 11, 1943

Dear Roberta, Buster and Bobby,

First of all "A Happy June 22!" and hopes that this will reach you by that date and that you can spend it together. It looks as if the McLeods would have to postpone their celebration until July 7th...

Bud was expected back from Fort Knox about then.

Was very happy to get your letter...

In which Robin convincingly described their living arrangement.

...It sounds really good, looks convenient and I trust it will prove as cool a one for the summer months as you think it may be. Wish I could get there to run around the historic old spots with you!

Metropolis of the south, Lelia knew New Orleans to be a melting pot with celebrated stories and traditions deeply embedded in a complex culture. Convenient in more ways than one, Robin lived within walking distance of the colonial-era French Quarter and within five miles of the deep Port of New Orleans. As one of the foremost harbors in America, along the Mississippi River, Lelia could get there by steamship!

Were it not for the bloody war.

Why was Buster sent to Louisiana?

He attached to a unit training at Camp Harahan, on the western outskirts of town. This authentic arena for water-borne maneuvers (and Cottonmouth vipers) stretched out along the shores and across the wide-open waters of Lake Pontchartrain.

Phony "surprise attacks" launched from one side of Pontchartrain. LCVP's (Landing Craft Vehicle and Personnel) shot across the water. At strategic points, troops piled out over the retractable bow ramps of "Higgins Boats." These "sea trials" simulated authentically splashy landings made by U.S. servicemen in war zones.

In the frenetic opening scene of Steven Spielberg's Oscar Winner, *Saving Private Ryan*, Higgins Boats backdropped Tom Hanks in choppy waters off Omaha Beach on D-Day. Front ramps drop down. A hailstorm of bullets pour in. Infantry men that make it into the water are greeted by more bullets and exploding shells.

Often referred to as "the boat that won the war" Higgins Industries designed and built the flat, shallow-bottomed boats at their New Orleans shipyard. The War Department contract of $40,000,000 enabled Andrew Higgins to employ 40,000 people, including young girls who graduated from the Higgins Welding School. With skill and determination, "Rosies" worked there. "Bertha the Burner" and "Wendy the Welder" did, too.

Do you and Buster count that he is getting near the time of being sent from U.S. soil? Dorothy wrote in her letter when Bud was sent east that they would at least have six weeks together after he returned...I tried to read between the lines...that might mean he expected to be moved on. It makes me shiver to think of the possibility!...

She shook off the sick gut feeling, then switched topics to one she better understood but still had no control over. America was considered the best-fed nation in a world at war, yet many men were rejected from the armed services because of malnutrition. Bad teeth and eyesight, too.

Now in the face of war-rations, government experts designed a National Wartime Nutrition Target. The idea was to promote something from each of the *seven* food groups each day, to hit "the bullseye of good health."

Lelia's anxiety fed off intrusive thoughts of starving, malnourished children in countries occupied by Axis enemies, so she took it seriously when Robin, in her last letter, described Bobby's "condition."

I can't think it was anything more than a beginning case of rickets.

Breast-fed infants rarely developed rickets. Lelia knew the disease, most common to bottle-fed babies, emerged between six and eighteen months. Bobby, now eight months, was constipated, restless, and sweating about the head. Robin wrote to tell her so.

You won't be able to keep giving him cod liver oil in that hot climate, will you?

Vitamin D—"the sunshine vitamin"—was naturally plentiful in the UVB rays of New Orleans' summer. Though, to her point, when combined with fish oil, it was possible to overdo it. Then she looked down her nose and asked this:

Can't they get his red blood cell count up to normal…?

Very nearly writing an intercontinental prescription for anemia, she recommended iron injections, as well as special food.

Iron deficiencies in infants were not unusual at the time, but flour, a leading cookery ingredient, was plentiful and *fortified*. Pillsbury's Best®, vitamin and iron enriched, cost $2.35 for a fifty-pound bag. Robin knew how to bake. In a form Bobby would enjoy, fairy-like molasses muffins contained extra B-vitamins, iron, and proteins of enriched flour.

However, in the dog days of a Louisiana summer without air conditioning, the conscious choice to twist the oven knob to 350 degrees was something else again.

…The war news cheers us up these days. Am so excited waiting for news of the invasion…

Flying under the mail censor's nose, she spoke in vague terms anticipating news over KGEI with an air of expectancy.

Lelia knew victory in Tunisia meant ports along the northern rim of the African continent became available to Allied forces. Newspaper maps pointed to the land of figs, almonds, olives, and ancient traditions—Sicily, the stepping-stone to the toe of Italy. From the "toe" to the mainland, it was a short, two-mile stretch across the Strait of Messina.

The invasion on July 10 would come to be known as "Operation Husky." General Eisenhower described it: "The first stage in the liberation of the European Continent." A long, brutal push began toward Mussolini's Rome, Nazi-held Paris, and, eventually, Berlin.

Well, my dears, have a celebration on this anniversary check and enjoy yourselves…get something for your comfort you can both have some service from. Too bad you haven't a permanent home, so you could get something lasting…

Hugs, kisses and loving thoughts, Mother and Dad

Without a "P.S." she added a note.

…I got a girl from Caletones, good as a cleaner but only fair as a cook.

Ten months had passed since Adela's dismissal. *Que sera sera.* In the mining camp, good help to meet Lelia's standards was nearly impossible to find. Then, cursed with a fact of life many people don't understand until their mid to late forties, she added this.

…I broke my glasses so have to spend my July vacation in Santiago. Don't want this prescription filled again.

Buster would sympathize. He couldn't function without his eyeglasses. In fact, when it came to the war effort, accurate vision was vital to victory. Mobile shops were a new development of mechanical war. Almost every type of repair service equipment was mounted on a truck or trailer. Truck-borne optical shops delivered speedy mobile service to soldiers in the field within rifle shot of the front line where eyeglasses were repaired or replaced. Same with footwear. And there was no better morale booster than "shower baths" on wheels. Wheeled laundries, too!

By virtue of age, education, call to duty, and experience, Buster and Bud landed amid what became the great American modern warfare experiment. The best chance to win against Germany and Japan came with the strongest and closest-knit combination of all arms. The Army's three-part reorganization was designed to that end: The Army Ground Forces, the Army Air Forces, and the Army Service Forces.

What could possibly make them stronger?

The AP out of Washington reported this:

> Washington, July 2 (AP) – The W.A.A.C. became the W.A.C. today as President Roosevelt signed legislation dropping the "A" for auxiliary and renaming the organization the Women's Army Corps.

Signed on July 1, 1943, the new law put the WACs under Army regulations and raised the membership age limit from 45 to 50 years. It gave women the rank, privileges, and benefits of their male counterparts. Recruitment posters with patriotic appeal read: "Are You a Girl with a Star-Spangled Heart?" Photographs of women with stylish uniform caps and right gloved hands raised, oathtaking to "solemnly swear," smattered newspapers across the country.

Married? No problem.

Except for this: Children afoot under fourteen were a deal breaker.

Dottie had every confidence in Bud's command over the timing of his return to Tacoma that July. Unlike Lelia, she rested assured that her man would be home to take her to the hospital, juggle Wayne off into someone else's hands, and wait for his moment to pass out cigars.

Number two son, Charles Herbert McLeod, kicked his way into the world on July 13.

"Herbie" was the namesake of Bud's grandfather, C.H. McLeod, a pioneer resident of Missoula. Out of familial obligation, Bud's mother arrived at Fort Lewis to assist. When Robin received the "look at what's new on our family tree" birth announcement, she responded with a lovely letter and specialized "welcome dear nephew" card in shades of pastel blue.

Six Weeks for Boat Mail

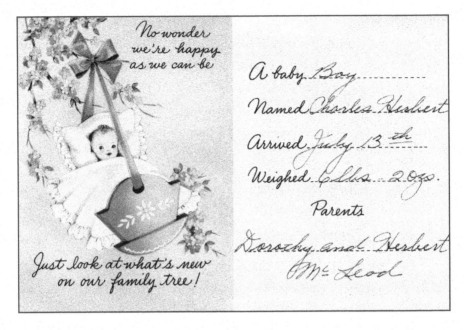

With two baby boys sixteen months apart, Dorothy made out to be happily adjusting to her "duty." As Herbie nursed, wet, slept, and cried, Waynecito's sweet-natured disposition lifted her spirits.

Or so she said.

At the end of August, with inspection-ready uniforms rolled into his properly stuffed duffle, Bud took off. His home-duty done, last licks at training awaited.

Three-hundred miles south, the first extended war games to be held in the northwest, the Oregon Maneuvers, commenced. Bud sheltered in a tent camp. Seventy-five thousand troops divided into the "Reds" on defense and "Blues" on offense. Ensconced in the Army's IV Corps, Bud solved "problems," just as Buster had, when he started as a PFC among 100,000 troops in the Adirondacks two years before.

Likewise in the New England and Carolina Maneuvers.

Citizens of the Beaver State were forewarned. During the months of September, October, and part of November, highways would be used extensively for hauling of supplies and troop movements, those including Highway 97, Redmond to La Pine; Highways 20 and 28 from Sisters to Redmond; Highway 395 and 31 from Bend to Burns. The maneuvers would test organization and technique, first with problems designed for high desert training; combat in sagebrush and dust through rolling desert terrain that stretched between Bend and Burns. Hot by day, cold (at 5,000' altitude) by night. In an active maneuver area of ten thousand square miles, weeks of combat rolled along the Deschutes River and near the town of Sisters.

Bud McLeod on Oregon Maneuvers. At the end of October, heavy snow fell in the mountains above 4,500'

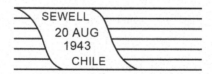

L.M. Skinner, Rancagua – Sewell, Chile S.A. – airmail

August 20, 1943
Dearest Roberta and Forrest,

Your birthday greeting reached me several days previous…The cards now days have such precious sentiment expressed…sometimes more personal than one could think up to express themselves…

For that very reason, a recent nation-wide survey conducted by expert psychologists revealed the importance of greeting cards. They unified people.

...You are exactly right in that I had been waiting to write—to know where you might be, in case Buster had been dispatched from New Orleans...Every week's extension is precious, isn't it?...

Yes. Then came this startling reveal:

I can imagine how Mother and Father Bedford suffered with the heat there...

Evidently when Robin refused to return to Pelham Manor last May, Nat and Ethel showed up to hover over the New Orleans' nest. It explains why Robin's morale dipped in the days before Buster tally-hoed home. As longtime Florida residents prior to Pelham, the heat didn't distress the senior Bedfords. Rather, Robin suffered under Ethel's overbearing nose.

Which is why many women agree on this point. Of all the relationships in family life, the mother-in-law and daughter-in-law connection is often the most tenuous.

Beset by many problems in and out of the mining camp, Lelia offered this practical medical breadcrumb:

Follow up that temperature he had, darling...Take his temp every day for a while and see whether he normally runs a degree or so. If his rickets weren't entirely held in check, he might run a degree...

Her concern multiplied by virtue of the Braden Copper family circle.

Two young children, one in Sewell and one in Coya, ran a daily temperature. They were discovered to have T.B.

...The parents...having to keep them in bed for over a year...or longer and that is an awful task.

Nearly half their small life! Let their mother's weary eye of hyper-vigilance never close.

I am going to send you Dorothy's letter telling all about her delivery and please send it right on to Auntie Rhea...I promised to send it to her....

In a birthday letter to Lelia, Dorothy recounted circumstances surrounding Herbie's birth:

"Mother McLeod couldn't stand the work and the loss of her rest in the P.M.'s and waking up in the night when Herbie awakened to nurse."

A fifty-three-year-old Mrs. McLeod couldn't get back to sleep once awakened so, in fact, she was no help at all. She returned to Missoula; Mr. McLeod sent his secretary to assist.

…Dorothy says she's a peach—a great big, husky foreigner, and a swell cook.

But she couldn't stay on forever.

…I don't know how Dorothy is going to manage with two babies with Waynecito still so young and not being able to get a speck of help. Nobody can imagine until they have a couple such dependent children just how dead tired one is from caring for them—doing the washing—preparing their food and doing the housework…

Sooner or later, it was enough to make a young mother go mad.

Of course if Bud should be sent overseas and she has to go back to Missoula and has an apt. of her own then Mrs. McLeod—Olive and Auntie Alta could take them for a couple hours to let Dorothy get away…

Her mother-in-law might not be up to it, but Bud's older sister, Olive, might pitch in. Little Mary Sharon, Olive's daughter with the "beautiful blue eyes," was just six weeks older than Wayne and a certain playdate match in a yet-to-be-invented babysitting co-op arrangement.

…Any mother owes that to herself. She can come back to babies with much more patience…I know from experience.

I know from experience, too.

The pictures you sent of Bobby were so cute. The colored one showed a swell coat of tan didn't it?

She asked for more recent photos, to get an idea of his size.

…Sounds as though he's going to walk sooner than Waynecito did—but <u>don't</u> hurry him…having had a tendency to rickets his legs might bow if he is heavy. Bow

Six Weeks for Boat Mail

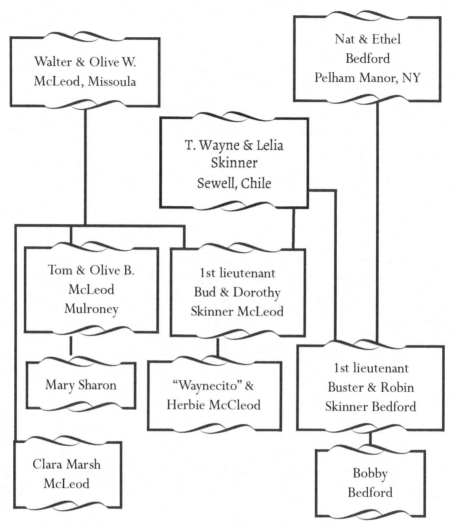

legs go with rickets you know...Don't try to make him walk before he naturally wants to...Once they start going by themselves you can't keep them off their feet—they patter around all their waking hours.

She didn't mention the fact that bulky cloth diapers adversely affect a baby's gait, because no one knew it at the time. One determined Frankenstein step in front of another, bobbing, weaving. Boop! Eighty years later, an NYU research study (Adolph, et al., 2012) quantified the way babies, twelve to nineteen months, muck about. The findings? Over six hours, the little darlings take 14,000 steps, pattering the distance of forty-six American football fields, toppling one hundred times.

...Russell is working in the electrical sub-station going to be an operator.

One would begin a skilled trade like that as an electrician's apprentice. An excellent choice for a person without a college degree back then, and still today. But the primary distribution voltage for a mine the size of El Teniente was enormous. Imagine Russell in the substation mixed up with the main transformer, a complex of switches, protection apparatus, and grounding devices. All had a function in safety. Regardless, dynamic power loads of a system subject to faults and overloads, or disturbances that caused abnormally high currents, made it shockingly (so to speak) dangerous; burned flesh, detached retinas, cardiac arrest. Lelia knew the electro-medical facts.

...He is so bored with Sewell—wants to get back to the U.S. but he has to go back on a Chilean passport.

Due to complications, the American Embassy was yet to produce his U.S. passport. Evidently at the time of his birth, T. Wayne and Lelia neglected to meet statutory requirements to establish Russell's U.S. Citizenship. As it often happens, small details fall through the cracks when it comes to the baby of the family.

...They said in a letter from the Embassy last week it probably wouldn't be long until he could get into the U.S. Army—but Dad won't let him go before he is 21.

Not necessarily. In truth, the moment Russell could enlist, his father would permit him to go straight away. In the Army or Navy his son's basic needs would be met: food, clothing, shelter. It's one reason, at age eighteen, T. Wayne and Lelia booted him out of House #71 to meet his military service requirements with the Chilean Cavalry. At the time Lelia described his "useless, idle, good-for-nothing existence." He needed discipline. Now, six months short of twenty-one, she complained Russell hadn't changed much. He understood little about the value of money and refused to save from his wages.

Dad doesn't want him just loafing around up there. If he would only go back up and get interested in his education—until he could get in the Navy or Army—but he just will not study.

On that sour note, Lelia rapid-fired a shortlist of life events that, thankfully, were other people's business. Each flapped in her face to reveal the tenor and tapestry of a "contemporary" time in the mining camp. For instance, health reasons forced one of T. Wayne's peers out of entering the mine any longer. He retired. About the same time, his wife's mother died. She vamoosed while he dutifully sold off their belongings and followed her back to the States.

With bad news, came happy. Nuptial blessings. A family friend had married his U.S. college educated Norwegian sweetheart in the Santiago Union Church. A celebration that followed the requisite "civil ceremony."

Lelia acknowledged each of these life events with vivid, thematic art and felicitous rhymes and meters, mercifully personalized with the precious sentiments of a gifted greeting card creative.

Light My Fire
Chapter Twenty

With Mardi Gras canceled for the second year in a row, the colors of Carnival; purple (for justice), gold (for power), and green (for faith) moved over for a red, white, and blue re-paint of the town. New Orleans adapted to uphold its famous reputation for wide-ranging amusements.

For example, on Canal Street, the evening of September 9, a simulated battle unleashed between military forces using tanks, anti-aircraft guns, land mines, and smoke screens. Far more impressive than "flambeaux" (the flaming torches that lit up the night sky during Mardi Gras), this evening kicked off with an entertainment program to hype the opening day of the Third War Loan drive.

I'd wager the staged shebang scared the bejesus out of babies like Bobby.

In her letter dated three weeks before, Lelia praised Buster's rank advancement.

"We are very happy over Buster's promotion to 1st Lieutenant…have a nice photo taken in his uniform. We want to put it on the piano—alongside of Bud's in his uniform."

Beyond the Oregon maneuvers, what did she know of Bud's status?

"…They expect him to be sent overseas within six or eight weeks after he gets home. I just can't bear to see him sent into the Pacific, to fight those yellow japs. We don't dare write about the war for fear our letters will be all cut up."

Six Weeks for Boat Mail

Lelia's foul language erupted over the sight of dead bodies on a beach. Her anger spit at those responsible. The September 20 issue of *LIFE* magazine shocked the consciousness of subscription holders, like Lelia, and their newsstand audience, too. A photo caption read, "Three dead Americans on the beach at Buna." The soldiers fell in December 1942. Deemed too graphic at the time, the full-page black and white image, snapped by photojournalist George Strock, was repressed. For nine months, the editors at *LIFE* argued for the work to be published. Finally, censors and FDR agreed. To jolt an American public, growing complacent, the photo would hammer home the reality of a war that was yet to be won. The accompanying editorial explained.

> The reason we print it now is that, last week, President Roosevelt…and the War Department decided that the American people ought to be able to see their own boys as they fall in battle; to come directly and without words into the presence of their own dead.

Indeed, the shutter clicks of *LIFE*'s heroic photojournalists went on to splash "never forget" still shots through "the forgotten war" in Korea and "the television war" in Vietnam. Naturally, they unfolded in two-page, centerspread fashion. Then came one of network television's greatest storytellers, the late CBS correspondent Morley Safer. From the Vietnam battlefield, he tried to explain the inexplicable to the likes of me by way of the evening news. Uncensored combat footage churned into a queasy compound of mud, blood, bombing, bodies, and burning villages, leading a whole generation left to ask, "what the shit is the reason for this?"

Buster's training, now complete, meant he would ship out before Bud. The question remained: where?

Smiling faces in uniform popped up in local papers across the nation batched under banners that read, "Fighters for Freedom" or "With the Armed Services." The news became everyone's business. "So and so spent a few days at home on furlough with family. His destination now is New York, from there unknown." Or "So-and-so spent a pleasant weekend with his wife, the former Miss So-and-so. He is leaving for the west coast this week and thence to an unknown destination."

In Buster's case, training at Harahan concluded with a lot of back-clapping and promises to write among the men. Over furlough, Robin and Buster packed their belongings out of the Broad Avenue bungalow. One last stop in the French Quarter placed them at their favorite haunt, the famed, century-old New Orleans restaurant, Antoines, for a last buttery lick of oysters Rockefeller. Rather than wait in line, Buster called ahead for the order. This was a ploy he'd learned from Nat. Upon arrival, the 1st lieutenant informed the maître d' their dinner was ready and asked to be seated.

The maître d', pleased to oblige, greeted the young family with a glorious smile and knowing laughter.

Naturally, Nat and Ethel paved the way to Pelham Manor. Robin's heart and spirit sank with news made palpably real when it appeared, permanently inked for posterity's sake, in the *Pelham Sun*: "Lieutenant Bedford's wife and son will stay with his parents for the duration."

Modern women must accept this 1940s fact. Most young wives of American servicemen lacked the means to get a place of their own. It explains why many returned to their parental home "for the duration." For example, when Robin's "pet" Dizzy deployed with the Army Air Forces to the ETO, her maid of honor, Gina, moved home with *her parents* in Manhattan. Ditto Prent's wife, Phyllis. Until he returned from the ETO, she lived with *her parents* in Boston.

What choice did Robin have? Lelia's "latch string" lay *five thousand* miles away.

They planned their last few days together, which included a family portrait. Each tried to be light-hearted and cheerful. I say with some certainty a night on the town included Rockefeller Center and the Rainbow Room. That's where, three years before, they'd dined, danced, and formally sealed the deal after Robin accepted Buster's proposal in a canoe on Princeton's Lake Carnegie. At the time, war seemed far away, on

Six Weeks for Boat Mail

Robin and Buster with Bobby in their 1943 keepsake service portrait.

the other side of the Atlantic. The London Blitz had just begun. They'd lived a lot of life together in three short years.

The final hour played like a gloriously cinematic scene that I can only imagine. On one point she was clear. Buster could do no less than be a leader in this war for freedom. In the privacy of the Pelham Manor guest bedroom, he held her closely and assured her of his return. For Bobby's sake, Robin smiled bravely. Tears, forced through her lashes, escaped down her cheeks. She swiped them away. He closed his officer's suitcase, oblivious to Robin's cleverly executed sleight of hand, and clicked two brass latches with a sense of finality. Later, he'd be pleasantly surprised by her gift of a silver Ronson lighter, stealthily tucked in with his stash of pipe tobacco, extra eyeglasses, and toiletries.

When the 1st lieutenant stepped into the front hall, Ethel smiled, held him tight, and whispered words of encouragement. As hard as it was for her to let him go, she'd raised a son she knew would give his all in this fight for peace and freedom. He'd say, as soldiers often did, "Don't worry about me." She'd bid him Godspeed.

One last squeeze for Robin and Bobby finished it. He silently prayed his wife and mother would get along under one roof.

Five smooth miles from the Bedford residence on Manor Circle, thousands of servicemen staged for overseas duty at Fort Slocum, conveniently located on David's Island, just off neighboring New Rochelle. Nat chauffeured. When Buster hopped from the car, his father parked it and stepped out. In some combination of a firm handshake and half hug, Nat kept it light with solidly southern advice, "Keep your saddle oiled and your gun greased."

Large movements of troops by train were expedited in secrecy toward unknown ports, which explains why I can only speculate on how Buster rolled. But one thing for certain, a troop train delivered him to the Pacific wartime gateway of the San Francisco Port of Embarkation. Camp Stoneman, located on the Sacramento River, was where almost all servicemen arrived via railroad. The trains whistled directly into the installation on spurs from both the Southern Pacific and Santa Fe mainlines. There he wrote his fist "chin up" letter to Robin, formally addressed (in keeping with etiquette) to:

> Mrs. N. Forrest Bedford
> 1283 Manor Circle
> Pelham Manor, New York

This was the hour for Robin to face the first unpleasant fact of life without him. Going forward, their personal correspondence would bow to the mail censor's ruling. She imagined a voyeuristic scissor-handed troll at the ready. One who would cut out the playful symbolic kiss "X" at the close of every letter. "Too much like code," they would say. She'd already rankled with heavily inked redactions, mutilated lines, and missing pages for nearly two years, in letters to and from Lelia. An officer and a gentleman, Buster remained steadfast, "its rules are for our protection."

He pledged this: *When the time comes that past happenings can be told, I will make my letters as long and interesting as possible. Meanwhile, think of our wonderful past together, and of our even more wonderful future. Have patience that we may realize all the good things in life which are yet to come; and if ever you worry over me or my absence, read over to yourself those ringing lines of Sir Richard Lovelace from "To Lucasta, On Going to the Wars"...*

Balladry he'd first imparted to her with his musings penned from the shade of a giant magnolia tree at Pinehurst, in October 1941:

"- I would not love thee, dear, so much,
Loved I not honour more."

Your own devoted husband, Buster

"Remember Me": Portrait of an only son of an only son.

Acknowledgements

My supreme gratitude goes to a trifecta of ambitious entrepreneurial women and then some. These are the people who made this second book in my trilogy possible.

- My editor and award-winning author friend, Stacy Dymalski, aka "The Memoir Midwife," a guiding light who patiently helped me carve out the exceptional elements of what would have become a too-long tale, born of the hundreds of letters upon which this trilogy is based.

- Katie Mullaly, another brilliant author, creator of the charming Land of… Children's Books® series, and owner of Surrogate Press®. From fonts to flourishes, credit of the design and layout of this book goes to her. It is by way of Katie's graphics that Robin's adventures are transformed into a geography lesson rooted in mid-century long-distance travel.

- To Michelle Rayner, Cosmic Design, cover artist extraordinaire for her deeply creative magic in the realm of book cover continuity. From *Brides of 1941* to *Six Weeks for Boat Mail*, she has pulled the soul of history straight through to the cover design.

I also acknowledge the usefulness of *Ancestry.com* and *Newspapers.com*, internet sites where, for my monthly subscription, I have researched people, places, and topics without leaving the safety of my standup desk for the duration of the COVID shutdown.

To my sister, Dorothy, and now late brother, Dr. Bob Bedford, thank you for your faith and thoughtful encouragement. You've allowed me, without pushback, to reveal what some would consider family skeletons. History in which we find humor. Robin and Buster would expect nothing less.

Most importantly, my books would not be possible without the support of my WWII aficionado husband, Pete. His collection of military memorabilia is an inspiration to my writing, and a great resource for Instagram posts @spikypigpress. As Boomers, we didn't necessarily accept the lectures of our Greatest Generation parents, but we now understand more than ever that freedom isn't free, evil world leaders still exist, and we cannot allow history to repeat.

About the Author

Life can only be understood backwards; but it must be lived forwards.
Soren Kierkegaard

When New Jersey born Bonnie Ann Bedford picked Park City, Utah, as a place to settle in the 1970s no one expected the old silver mining boomtown, turned ski town, would land on the world stage as host city to the likes of SUNDANCE Film Festival and the 2002 Winter Olympics. Fresh out of grad school, her first full-time job with the Park City Chamber of Commerce (then housed in the former Sheriff's office on Historic Main Street) placed her in a non-profit position to convince visiting travel agents and press writers "This is the Place!" It was a tough sell,

Six Weeks for Boat Mail

especially with Utah's weird liquor laws. But it's how she met her WWII history buff husband of forty years, Pete *Park*. Did his forebears own the city? No.

Fast forward. With two young sons underfoot, Bonnie took the reins of a startup recreation district born out of the family laundry room. With the good-hearted enthusiasm of character Leslie Knope (actress Amy Poehler) in NBC's seven-season sitcom *Parks and Rec*, she publicly faced off with NIMBYs (Not In My Back Yard), PITBYs (Put It In Their Back Yard), and DUDEs (Developers Under Delusions of Entitlement) to prevail in the development of community parks, non-motorized trails, recreation facilities, and the preservation of open space. Along that arduous path, Park City Rotary Club named her *Professional Citizen of the Year* (2003), Utah Parks and Recreation Association presented their "Lifetime Achievement Award" (2013), and the University of Utah Department of Parks, Recreation, and Tourism honored her with their "Outstanding Alumnus Award" (2019).

With age came new aspirations. As she began the painstaking process of transcribing family letters, hundreds of them, Bonnie exposed a WWII era story begging to be told. That's when life took a hairpin turn and came to a screeching halt. She became a caregiver. Not for her aging parents, Robin and Buster Bedford (they'd already passed), but for her firstborn son, then twenty-four years old. Along one of Utah's Scenic By-ways, out of cell range, he rode shotgun as a passenger in a Honda Civic head on into a pickup truck. By way of air ambulance, he landed on the helipad of a trauma one hospital. His survival proved to be nothing short of a miracle. In her Christmas letter that year, Bonnie wrote "the angels are among us." Conceivably those angels were the very family members who, like it or not, are cast as main characters in her books.

Before anyone looked to Internet memes and life coaches for empowerment, Robin and Buster fashioned Bonnie's future with words like this: *"You can do anything you put your mind to!"* Proving they were right, she helped her son help himself to get back on his feet and, with this WWII saga embedded in her head, kept writing.

About the Author

Bonnie is the published author of *Brides of 1941* (2018), and its sequel, *Six Weeks For Boat Mail* (2022). She is presently at work on a third book with more stories delivered in the context of momentous events in U.S. History. Set in the final two years of WWII, Lt. Buster gives his all in the liberation of the Philippines while Robin's feisty independent spirit shines through on America's Homefront.

This legacy project is derived from the heart and soul of industrious, church-going middle-class people who identified as Republican in a time when "civil discourse" in party politics sought to better our country, our democracy, and our national security.